Praise for Converting Witness

"Darrell Guder introduced me to the field of missiology in his own gracious, humble way. His work, especially on missional ecclesiology, has influenced my own thoughts and inspires my students. In addition, with all the warmth of his personality he helped me find my bearings in a discipline that was relatively new to me, and he introduced me to some brilliant students of his, both as colleagues and as PhD candidates. In short, as a brother and as a colleague, Darrell has been extremely important to me. This volume is a great tribute to the width of his theological scopus, his love for the church (and, of course, Karl Barth!), and his passion for Christian witness to a secularizing culture. I pray that God will bless it to carry Darrell 's missiological heritage further into this exciting century we are living in." —Stefan Paas, J. H. Bavinck Chair for Missiology and Intercultural Theology at Vrije Universiteit Amsterdam; professor of missiology, Theological University in Kampen

Converting Witness

Converting Witness

*The Future of Christian Mission
in the New Millennium*

Edited by John G. Flett
and David W. Congdon

LEXINGTON BOOKS/FORTRESS ACADEMIC
Lanham • Boulder • New York • London

Published by Lexington Books/Fortress Academic
Lexington Books is an imprint of The Rowman & Littlefield Publishing Group, Inc.
4501 Forbes Boulevard, Suite 200, Lanham, Maryland 20706
www.rowman.com

6 Tinworth Street, London SE11 5AL

British Library Cataloguing in Publication Information Available

Library of Congress Cataloging-in-Publication Data

ISBN 978-1-9787-0840-2 (cloth)
ISBN 978-1-9787-0841-9 (electronic)

For Darrell and Judy

Contents

Acknowledgments

We are grateful for the support of many who have made possible this volume, presented in honor of Darrell Guder. While the age of the Festschrift has long since passed, our editors Michael Gibson and Neil Elliott have fully supported this reflection upon and interrogation of Guder's ideas from the start. This book would not have been possible without them. It was our aim from the start to produce a volume that would not only celebrate Darrell's contributions to both church and academy but also contribute constructively to the missiological conversation. Our fellow contributors shared our vision and eagerly agreed to participate in the project. Thanks to Mike Lee for assisting with some translation from the original German of some submissions. Special thanks to Judy Guder for assisting us with biographical information about Darrell and her support more generally while we were students at Princeton Theological Seminary. Her hospitality is well-known to many in the Princeton Seminary community. Our thanks as well to President M. Craig Barnes for his support of the project, and to Pilgrim Theological College for its generous provision of sabbatical time for John.

John G. Flett and David W. Congdon

Abbreviations

AG *Ad Gentes Divinitus* (1965)

AL *Amoris Laetitia* (2016)

CD Barth, Karl. *Church Dogmatics*. 4 vols. in 13 parts. Edinburgh:
T&T Clark, 1956–1969, 1975.

DP *Dialogue and Proclamation* (1991)

EG *Evangelii Gaudium* (2013)

EN *Evangelii Nuntiandi* (1975)

ES *Ecclesiam Suam* (1964)

GS *Gaudium et Spes* (1965)

KD Barth, Karl. *Die kirchliche Dogmatik*. 4 vols. in 13 parts. Munich:
Chr. Kaiser, 1932, and Zürich: TVZ, 1938 1965.

IMC International Missionary Council

LG *Lumen Gentium* (1964)

LS *Laudato Si'* (2015)

NA *Nostra Aetate* (1965)

RM *Redemptoris Missio* (1990)

TCTC *The Cape Town Commitment* (2011)

TTL *Together towards Life* (2012)

WCC World Council of Churches

Chapter One

Darrell L. Guder

A Life of Continuing Conversion

David W. Congdon and John G. Flett

This book is in celebration of the life and work of Darrell Likens Guder. Given the range of Darrell's academic interests and constructive contribution, this work aims to address key issues in missiology, World Christianity, ecumenical relations, interreligious dialogue, and theological hermeneutics—all inspired by and in conversation with Darrell's legacy. In his 1985 work, *Be My Witnesses*, Darrell, drawing on Karl Barth, names his own approach "irregular dogmatics," that is, an approach to theology indebted to the person and his or her biography.[1] Given the importance of biography in understanding the direction, intent, and pastoral sensibilities of Darrell's own work, it is right to begin there.

THEOLOGY AS BIOGRAPHY

Born in Ventura, California, 1939, Darrell was raised in an evangelical Presbyterian family with his earliest formation at the renowned First Presbyterian Church of Hollywood. His academic life began at UCLA (1956–1959), but after embarking on what initially was to be a year-long visit to Germany, Darrell transferred his degree to the University of Hamburg. This encounter with Lutheran life and thought led Darrell to understand the Gospel in a new way and to "question parts of my own tradition as I discovered the evangel in other traditions."[2] He was exposed to a significant body of theological teachers, including serving as secretary and interpreter for Helmut Thielicke during his five-month tour through America (1963) and clerking for Hendrickus

1

Berkhof at the General Council of the World Alliance of Reformed Churches.

In 1965 Darrell completed his doctorate with a dissertation on the development and secularization of the curriculum at The College of New Jersey (now Princeton University). With PhD in hand, he was ordained in 1965 by the First Presbyterian Church of Hollywood to the position of Schülerpastor (an evangelistic minister to youth who had completed confirmation) for the Church of Schleswig-Holstein, Hamburg-Rissen. In 1967 he answered a call to serve as a minister of education at Hollywood Presbyterian Church, before returning again to Germany and becoming a lecturer in theology, pedagogy, and diaconic service at the Kirchliche Ausbildungsstätte für Diakonie und Religionspädagogik in Karlshöhe, Ludwigsburg (1971–1975).

In 1975 Darrell embarked on a two-year sabbatical with Fuller Theological Seminary to translate Otto Weber's *Foundation of Dogmatics*.[3] This was but the first of Darrell's significant contribution in the area of academic translation. Beginning in the mid-1970s, and continuing for the next few decades, he assumed key responsibilities for translation at the ecumenical gatherings of the Reformed churches. His later work includes assisting with the "Translation Fellows of the Center for Barth Studies" at Princeton Theological Seminary for work on translating volumes of Karl Barth's *Gesamtausgabe* (Collected Works). Further translations include Eberhard Jüngel's *God as the Mystery of the World* (1983) and Barth's *Theology of the Reformed Confessions* (2002).[4] In this service Darrell found an equal partner in Judy Guder, whom he married in 1979.

After his sabbatical, Darrell joined Young Life (1976–1985), initially to provide theological education for the staff, but eventually he came to serve as the director of the Institute of Youth Ministries. This was his first encounter with a parachurch organization. The experience with Young Life directed Darrell's attention to ecclesiology as a constructive exercise, one that needed to address issues of evangelization, formal and informal ministries, community development and pastoral formation, and the place of the sacraments with a mission that stretches beyond any single confessional tradition.

Leaving Young Life, Darrell took a position in academic administration as the vice president for Academic Affairs and dean of the faculty at Whitworth College (now Whitworth University) in Spokane, Washington (1985–1991). Darrell would also serve as dean of Academic Affairs at Princeton Theological Seminary (2005–2010). Such academic leadership reflects Darrell's commitment to shaping theological education to form people for ministry within the evolving contexts of Western societies, and more broadly in the context of reforming the church as a missionary body called and sent to witness to the Kingdom of God. Such commitments necessarily shape theological curricula and the educational policies and structures developed in support of that mission.

For the final stage of his career Darrell returned to the classroom, receiving calls as the William A. Benfield Jr. Professor of Evangelism and Mission at Louisville Presbyterian Theological Seminary, Louisville, Kentucky (1991–1997), the Peachtree Professor of Evangelism and Church Growth at Columbia Theological Seminary, Decatur, Georgia (1997–2001), and finally as the Henry Winters Luce Professor of Missional and Ecumenical Theology at Princeton Theological Seminary, Princeton, New Jersey (2002–2015). Through his teaching, Darrell modeled commitment to the academic task, to positive theological discourse in service to the church, gentleness and generosity of spirit, along with a deep and ongoing interest in his students and their work.

FRAMING HIS MISSIOLOGY

Darrell's acceptance of the call in 1991 to become a professor of "evangelism and mission" reflected a development in his own self-understanding; he began to view his own work as more properly situated within missiology. One might read the earliest stages of Darrell's career as a broadening of his perspective, from a more conservative Presbyterian horizon to one shaped by linguistic, cultural, and ecumenical diversity. This experience, in his own words, "awakened me to dimensions of the gospel I had not yet grasped."[5] This positive insight led to a critical awareness of the ways in which even faithful evangelical churches might themselves suffer from inappropriate forms of cultural accommodation. It also stimulated his interest in developing a theology and pedagogy that assisted the body of Christ in carrying out its "Christian commitments outside the congregation's organized life."[6] Darrell developed these insights in his 1985 work, *Be My Witnesses.*

Be My Witnesses introduced a number of themes that Darrell would develop throughout his career, the foremost being ecclesiology. Darrell's work is concerned primarily with the church—the church as a gathered community and so the church as a missionary community. However, this is not simply an interest in the church for its own sake, because it follows from an account of the God who acts in history. God acts in Jesus Christ to reveal Godself as creator of all things, and "an essential aspect" of the way in which this God acts is "through the human, the normal, the routine."[7] The church is the community called to serve and witness to this God. Its calling is not to the passive reception of "benefits" (the blessings of God, salvation), but to realize these as basic to mission, the "being sent" of God's people into history. To conceive mission simply as the enjoyment of these benefits is to promote a "reductionist" and so "distorted" gospel, one concerned only with "getting the individual saved."[8] Darrell, instead, locates the question of salvation within the cosmic scope of God's purposes for the whole of creation.

This leads to a second emphasis within Darrell's work: the incarnation.[9] Salvation is to be interpreted in terms of salvation history, and this history has the incarnation of Jesus Christ at its center. As a history, it is an ongoing and living event. On the one hand, this means that the "church is an essential part of the gospel, a necessary development within salvation history."[10] On the other hand, as the "Body of Christ, we are called and enabled to embody him as his ambassadors to the world."[11] The mission of the church is to be "incarnational."

There are, to be sure, better and worse ways of using "incarnational" to describe the ministry of the church. In Darrell's case the incarnation serves as a foundation stone upon which a wider scaffold is built. First, he defines mission in relation to the witness of the community. Because the community is called to embody the Gospel, mission is about discipleship and being formed as members of the body of Christ. This requires overcoming the problematic mission/worship divide. Darrell conceives of the church as an "equipping" community with a corresponding interest in developing "missional practices," and thus he declares evangelization and the external proclamation of the Gospel to be basic to the church.

Second, the incarnation allows him to understand mission as a "comprehensive" endeavor. The body of Christ is to be a creature of the Gospel—the whole Gospel. The church cannot retreat into its own private spiritual world but is necessarily a political entity. Reconciliation is therefore a key theme in Darrell's work.

Third, the incarnation supplies a critical category for navigating between the problem of cultural accommodation and the imperative of contextualization. Accommodation, or "cultural bondage," changes the Gospel by domesticating it, by forgetting that the "gospel is always before us."[12] A culturally accommodated Gospel lacks a prophetic edge and tends to reinforce existing and relative cultural values. By contrast, a church that understands itself as witnesses to and not dispensers of salvation is freed from a focus on itself and so liberated to follow its calling and undergo change in service to this calling.

Though these themes remain basic to Darrell's thinking, in later works he would extend them in a few critical ways. First, in his 2000 work, *The Continuing Conversion of the Church,* Darrell draws a tighter relationship between the idea of "reductionism" and cultural accommodation. The work of witnessing to the Gospel is also a work of translation. Translation includes both an expansion of meaning as it uncovers new readings of the Gospel message, and a reduction of meaning since not all the nuances of the message are capable of being expressed in a different language. One danger in this process of translation rests in treating our necessarily limited reading of the Gospel as normative, in which case the Gospel becomes identified with our culture. Instead of the church continually being converted through its witness to the Gospel, the process of evangelization expects others to be converted to this reduced message. Darrell explicitly addresses this concern to the churches within Western Christendom.

Second, Darrell expands his idea of the Kingdom of God and sets mission within the larger context of the *missio Dei*. For all the missionary direction expressed in *Be My Witnesses*, it would seem that his account of evangelization remained at some distance from the local congregation. In relation to his work within a parachurch organization, Darrell observed how evangelism often takes shape as a "program" and becomes understood "in terms of methods, effectiveness, and measurable results, and the gospel itself becomes a manageable 'product.'"[13] To understand mission in terms of the coming kingdom, by contrast, is to understand it in terms of God's own self-disclosure in history. This kingdom is not reducible to a simple formula, nor can it be harnessed to serve the purposes of a single community.

Third, as this position suggests, Darrell more firmly develops a missionary ecclesiology. It is God who acts in mission, and the community gathered by this acting God responds by participating in God's mission. The community proclaims the Gospel and does so through its witness to the "joyful message."[14] A number of implications follow from this single insight. It is no longer acceptable to approach the Bible in search of commands to mission; the whole of Scripture is to be read through a missional lens because the whole of Scripture points to this missionary God—a point to which we shall return below. Furthermore, there is no hierarchy of first and second in the relation between church and mission, nor is there an abstract set of church practices set over against this ministry of witness. The building up of the church is always and necessarily related to its sending into the world, because its being sent belongs to the nature of its gathering.

These three points all naturally feed into Darrell's involvement in the "Gospel and Our Culture Network" and the "missional church" discussion. The hugely significant 1998 book, *Missional Church*, edited by Darrell, examined what a missionary ecclesiology might look like in a post-Christendom North America.[15] Though "missional church" has since become an elastic term, encompassing everything from the study of church metrics to the development of often speculative cultural anthropologies, Darrell's contribution lies in constructing a coherent theology grounded in the missionary God and this God's missionary body.

His 2015 collection, titled *Called to Witness: Doing Missional Theology*, illustrates well the "integrative range" basic to his approach.[16] On the one hand, Darrell draws on the richness of the Christian tradition, moving between the historic creeds and confessions and the contemporary concern with World Christianity. On the other hand, he turns those resources to the immediate questions confronting God's people in the world today.

Take, for example, his essay "The Christological Formation of Missional Practice."[17] The essay begins with the expanding theological reflection on Christ as a consequence of his being confessed in a multitude of times, cultures, and tongues. Precisely as a positive development in the faith's catholicity, this expansion asks questions of established theological and ecclesial agendas. One such question is the dichotomy assumed between church and mission—which is itself a Christological problem. Revisiting how Jesus Christ appears in the Bible means paying attention to his own way of calling, forming, and sending his disciples. A sustained critique then follows concerning how the Western theological tradition inserted a distinction between the person and work of Jesus Christ and how this distinction became institutionally embodied in the separation of church from mission. As more and more cultures read the Jesus of scripture, so they expose the problems of Western missions during the colonial era and the ecclesiology that promoted this missionary form. Darrell then turns to the biblical text to develop an account of Jesus's own life that includes the calling, equipping, and sending of his disciples as integral to that life. The biblical text must be read, he argues, with a missional hermeneutic because of who Jesus Christ is.

In other words, in this single essay Darrell combines key insights from World Christianity and the ecumenical missionary movement, fundamental Christological themes within the Western tradition, and a close reading of scripture to produce a constructive and critical solution: "To do a Christology that does not attend to the missional formation of the witnessing community by the encounter with Jesus in his earthly ministry, that does not engage the dynamic movement from discipleship to apostolate, is to maintain those dichotomies in theology that are so problematic a part of our theological legacy."[18] Darrell calls on us to acknowledge those dichotomies in our own thinking and provides ample resources to move beyond them in constructive ways.

KARL BARTH AS A MISSIONAL THEOLOGIAN

As to Darrell's own theological ancestors, he found great resources in the Reformed tradition and the ecumenical movement, including the work of John Mackay and Lesslie Newbigin, and he was significantly impacted by Gerhard Lohfink's text *Jesus and Community: The Social Dimensions of the Christian Faith*.[19] Karl Barth, however, remains Darrell's most enduring and profound interlocutor.

In his inaugural lecture at Princeton Theological Seminary in December 2002, Darrell observed that "the relationship between theology and mission was mainly seen as a matter of theory and practice," with theology establishing the content of the faith and mission serving as one among many ministry

activities applying the faith practically.[20] Darrell proposed "missional theology" as the solution to the problematic bifurcation between theoretical theology and practical mission, and he did so by drawing extensively on the work
of Karl Barth. As he points out in his inaugural lecture, "the theological
revolution ignited by Karl Barth . . . would eventually substantially reshape
the theology of mission."[21] Darrell did so not by drawing on the more obvious resource—Barth's 1932 address to the Brandenburg Mission Conference, "Theology and Mission in the Present Situation," which is erroneously
referenced in the missiological literature as the origin of the theology of
missio Dei—but rather by looking to Barth's mature ecclesiology in the
Church Dogmatics.[22]

As indicated by the title of his lecture, Barth, in 1932, still separated
theology from mission. He affirmed both as necessary activities of the church
of Jesus Christ, but he viewed mission—in common with many of his day—
as gospel proclamation to unbelievers, whereas theology was the enterprise
that critically reflected on the task of proclamation. Barth was still operating
with a theory/practice distinction, which was likewise reflected in his dogmatics at the time. Darrell's concern was to do away with the "and" separat-
ing theology and mission, and to achieve this he turned instead to Barth's
mature theology in the later volumes of his *Church Dogmatics*. As Darrell
points out, one can "trace an intensification of the linkage between mission
and theology in Barth's own process as he moved through the project of the
Church Dogmatics."[23] To be sure, like everything else in Barth's theology,
this intensification is not consistent. Near the very end of *Church Dogmatics*
IV/3, in which he presents the twelve ministries of the church, Barth begins
by describing the ministries related to the proclamation of the Gospel *within*
the community of the church (praise, preaching, and teaching) before turning
to those activities that are "for the most part directed outwards to the world"
and thus "characteristically apostolic."[24] He distinguishes between evangelization, which is directed, he says, to nominal Christians and those who
belong to "non-Christian Christendom,"[25] and mission, which he defines, in
its "true and original sense," as the church's "sending out to the nations to
attest the Gospel."[26] While Barth makes some adjustments to the old coloni-
alist paradigm—stressing that the task belongs to the whole church and not a
special group, and that the task is not conversion but witness—he nevertheless views mission as "foreign missions." Moreover, the next ministry in his
list of twelve is theology, defined once again as the critical analysis of the
church's proclamation and witness.[27] So even here, in the heart of his mature
ecclesiology, Barth still separates theology and mission and defines each in
problematically narrow ways.

Darrell thus turns not to the places where Barth explicitly refers to mission but rather to his account of ecclesiology proper, in which he develops an
implicitly missional ontology of the church. Darrell highlights the way Barth,

in the fourth volume of the *Church Dogmatics*, defines the Gospel as justification, sanctification, *and vocation*, and then defines the church according to each aspect of the Gospel under the rubric of its gathering (justification), upbuilding (sanctification), and sending (vocation).[28] He points, in particular, to Barth's small-print observation in *Church Dogmatics* IV/1 (§62) that "[the church's] sending is not a secondary factor alongside its being, but rather the church *is* insofar as it is *sent* and is *active* in its sending."[29] Darrell calls this a "succinct definition" of what he has in mind in speaking about the "missional church."[30] Nor is this an isolated statement. Later, in his discussion of the church's sending in *Church Dogmatics* IV/3, Barth says that "the true community of Jesus Christ is *the community sent by God into the world* in and with its foundation. As such it is the community for the world."[31] Statements like these preclude any straightforward separation between theology and mission, between being and act, or between theory and practice. The well-known actualism of Barth's dogmatic theology—represented especially by the way he defines God's being as always a being-in-act, in which this action is the history of Jesus's mission of reconciliation—is already implicitly missional insofar as it overcomes the hierarchical bifurcation between theory and practice by which mission was subordinated to theology and excluded from the understanding of God, church, and the task of theology itself.

In §55.3 of *Church Dogmatics* III/4, Barth develops his account of human action ("the active life") that corresponds to divine action, and because the obedient human action is to participate in the community of faith, this section serves as a minor ecclesiology.[32] Barth defines the Christian community here as the people constituted and commissioned by Christ and his coming reign, and for this reason he repeatedly says the church's existence is "not an end-in-itself."[33] The task of the church cannot be to "satisfy itself"; instead, its proper edification consists in building itself up for the sake of its "external service" of proclaiming the reign of its Lord.[34] This external service is the church's "*cosmic* commission to the overwhelming majority of people who are *not* Christians."[35] The Christian community gathers together in order to live as witnesses of God's coming reign, to declare God's Yes to the world. Anticipating a key insight of later missional theology, Barth argues that the church's institutional forms exist for the sake of this commission: "What the Christian community has to do must not be determined by its institutions, but rather these institutions must always be newly determined by what the community has to do."[36] The church, according to Barth, is missionary by its very nature, to borrow the words of Vatican II's *Ad Gentes*.[37] For these and other reasons, Darrell argues that we can describe Barth's theology as missional theology, even if this language was conceptually foreign to him.

By interpreting Barth as a missional theologian, Darrell provided the field of missiology with the dogmatic resource to combat the misconception that mission was merely of practical and not also of distinctively theoretical interest. If Barth's theology is itself missional theology, then it confirms that theology does not *become* missional only when it talks explicitly about the topics usually assigned to missiology, such as evangelism and cross-cultural communication. Instead, theology is itself already missional simply by speaking of the Gospel of the God who, by the power of the Spirit, sent Jesus Christ for our salvation and now sends the church as Christ's witness. Theology is therefore "missional" insofar as it speaks of the God who sends and the humans who are sent for the purpose of witness.

In addition to dogmatically enriching and expanding the subject of mission, Darrell's work on Barth was also an intervention in the field of Barth studies. Much of the research on Barth in both Europe and North America focused on prolegomenous issues in epistemology and biblical interpretation or on the doctrine of God, including Trinity and election. There was comparatively little research on Barth's ecclesiology, and what work had been done largely interpreted Barth from the perspective of Anglo-American mainline Protestant assumptions and was frequently critical of Barth's anti-sacramentalism. The idea of seeing Barth's ecclesiology—along with the rest of his theology—in terms of mission was one of Darrell's contributions to the anglophone field of Barth scholarship, which was mostly unfamiliar with prior Dutch and German work on this topic. This culminated in the 2010 Karl Barth Conference at Princeton Theological Seminary, organized by Darrell, on the theme: "The Church Is as Such a Missionary Church: Barth as a 'Missional Theologian.'" The conference featured Eberhard Busch as the keynote speaker and included a number of younger Barth scholars who had been influenced by Darrell's pioneering work on Barth and mission. Moreover, for several years Darrell also developed and applied this reading of Barth for Master of Divinity students at Princeton Seminary in a popular course titled "Missional Theology and Practice," which he co-taught with Christian Andrews.

MISSIONAL HERMENEUTICS

As important as it was to identify mission as integral to the doctrines of God and the church—and to systematic theology as a whole—it was not enough to bring mission into the subject matter of theology; a fully missional theology needed to integrate mission into theological prolegomena, into the very method of how theologians interpret scripture and construct Christian doctrine. The name for this project, in which Darrell has played a decisive role, is missional hermeneutics.

The term "missional hermeneutics" originated with the 1998 publication of James V. Brownson's *Speaking the Truth in Love: New Testament Re-*

sources for a Missional Hermeneutic, which began as a 1994 article in the *International Review of Mission*.[38] The publication of this proposal came at the same time that biblical scholars and theologians in the postliberal tradition were developing what is now called "theological interpretation of scripture" (TIS).[39] The scholarship associated with TIS developed out of the earlier work in narrative theology and canonical interpretation pioneered by Hans Frei and Brevard Childs. In addition to being a rejection of overconfidence in the tools of historical criticism, TIS argued that genuinely Christian interpretation of scripture ought to read the biblical texts in accordance with the "rule of faith," defined especially by the ancient ecumenical creeds. But as R. R. Reno observes, the rule of faith according to TIS is ultimately "the animating culture of the church in its intellectual aspect."[40] In other words, most of the work in TIS understands the church to have its own culture—defined by doctrines, ritual practices, images, moral norms, and the like—and then reads the text according to these purportedly Christian cultural presuppositions. Brownson's proposal for a missional hermeneutic accepted the importance of a common tradition or rule, but it was more sensitive to the multiple cultural contexts in which the Bible is read and understood and did not conflate the Gospel with a particular culture, such as Western Christendom. His hermeneutic triangulates interpretation by exegeting the biblical text in view of the message of the Gospel, the historical context, and the Christian tradition.[41] Whereas TIS all too often seems to assume that the church is a single, uniform entity, missional hermeneutics takes the intercultural complexity of Christianity as its starting point.

In 2002, a group of scholars began to meet over breakfast at the annual meetings of the Society of Biblical Literature and American Academy of Religion to discuss missional hermeneutics, guided in subsequent years by presentations by Brownson (2002), Michael Barram (2003), and Grant Le-Marquand (2004). Starting in 2005, the gathering received the sponsorship of the Gospel and Our Culture Network and established an additional meeting with a call for papers. Over the next several years participants at these sessions presented papers expanding and nuancing the idea of a missional hermeneutics, often expressing sharply different views about what this means. In 2008, George R. Hunsberger "mapped" the emerging conversation and identified "four differing streams of emphasis" regarding the "orienting vision" of this hermeneutic, connecting each stream to the work of one or more scholars.[42] Reordered thematically and chronologically, we can summarize Hunsberger's typology as follows:

1. *The missional matrix of scripture* (James Brownson). According to Brownson's position, the text should be read as part of the Gospel's critical enterprise of ongoing cross-cultural engagement. This hermeneutic is missional in the way it embraces and navigates cultural and

historical diversity. Mission here refers to the formal matrix in which the Bible is read.[43]

2. *The missional framework of scripture* (Christopher Wright and Michael Goheen). Wright's *The Mission of God* and Goheen's *A Light to the Nations* understand mission to refer to the actual content of scripture, and thus a missional hermeneutic in their view requires that we read the text as a single overarching narrative about the mission of God.[44]

3. *The missional location of scripture* (Michael Barram). Barram's work situates the interpretation of the text in light of the "social location" of the community sent in mission. A missional hermeneutic, according to Barram, interrogates how the text functions in the local congregation.[45]

4. *The missional purpose of scripture* (Darrell Guder). Similar to Barram, Darrell's understanding of missional hermeneutics reads the text for the purpose of equipping the community in its missional vocation, but whereas Barram focuses on the present-day congregation, Darrell places more emphasis on the original intention of the apostles who wrote to equip and build up the early Christian community.[46]

Hunsberger admits that these four emphases are by no means mutually exclusive; most imply at least one or more of the others. For our purposes here, we will focus on Darrell's proposal.

Darrell presented his account of missional hermeneutics in his keynote lectures for the Shenk Mission Lectureship at Anabaptist Mennonite Biblical Seminary on November 30, 2007. In contrast to those approaches that view mission in terms of the form or content of theology, Darrell's approach, as indicated by Hunsberger's category, is eminently practical and focuses on the *purpose* of scripture. The meaning of scripture, as Wittgenstein might say, is found in its use. The "basic hermeneutical question," according to Darrell, is: "How did this particular text continue the formation of witnessing communities then, and how does it do that today?"[47] Darrell sees the early Christians engaged in an "apostolic strategy" of writing texts for the purpose of forming witnessing communities. The authorial intention, so to speak, of the biblical text is to form and equip communities "to continue the witness that had brought them into being."[48] We read scripture in continuity with the apostles when we interpret the text for the purpose of providing a specific congregation "the formation it needs to be able to live out both its gathered life and its scattered life faithfully."[49] The authority of scripture is therefore not found in scripture's capacity to infallibly convey propositional truths about history or God. Instead, scripture is authoritative "in its wonderful and releasing power to bring about the increase of faith in practice," which occurs as God's Spirit, by means of the biblical witness, "calls together the church and equips each

community to be a part of the universal movement of God's people."[50]
Darrell thus agrees with TIS in understanding scripture as being *for the church*, but he defines this in a specifically missional way. Scripture exists for the church's missional vocation, and any exegesis that ignores this vocation, or makes mission merely one practical end among others, fails to understand mission as the beating heart of the church and scripture as God's instrument for equipping the church for its divine commission.

ADVENT

We write this during Advent. A great deal more can and must be written concerning Darrell's contribution to the body of Christ, both locally in the North American context, and internationally through his writings, lectures, and ecumenical partnerships. Darrell's work, though of the highest academic quality, looked always to translate that work into the life of the church. More than a simple theoretical interest, this occurred through his sustained pastoral interest in his students and colleagues. If "irregular dogmatics" is a theological approach indebted to the person and his or her biography, then Darrell's theology is an ongoing story being told through the lives, ministry, and writing of all those he informed by his theology and witness. The significant portion of his contribution lies in the beginnings he himself has created and nurtured. Advent is the hope of all things new. It is the eschatological opening of the world to the Kingdom of God. And though the present work is offered in celebration of a life lived, this life points us to the incarnation and to our calling as children of the new creation, to the missionary nature of our being in Christ. Here we all find our beginning.

NOTES

1. Darrell L. Guder, *Be My Witnesses: The Church's Mission, Message, and Messengers* (Grand Rapids, MI: Eerdmans, 1985), vii.

2. Guder, ix.

3. Otto Weber, *Foundations of Dogmatics*, trans. by Darrell L. Guder, 2 vols., (Grand Rapids, MI: Eerdmans, 1983).

4. Eberhard Jüngel, *God as the Mystery of the World: On the Foundation of the Theology of the Crucified One in the Dispute between Theism and Atheism*, trans. Darrell L. Guder (Grand Rapids, MI: Eerdmans, 1983); Karl Barth, *Theology of the Reformed Confessions*, trans. Darrell L. Guder and Judith Guder (Louisville, KY: Westminster John Knox Press, 2002).

5. Guder, *Be My Witnesses*, viii.

6. Guder, xi.

7. Guder, 7.

8. Guder, 11.

9. For a summary statement, see Darrell L. Guder, *The Incarnation and the Church's Witness* (Harrisburg, PA: Trinity Press International, 1999).

10. Guder, *Be My Witnesses*, 16.

11. Guder, 31.

12. Guder, 202.

13. Darrell L. Guder, *The Continuing Conversion of the Church* (Grand Rapids, MI: Eerdmans, 2000), ix.

14. Guder, 53.

15. Darrell L. Guder, ed., *Missional Church: A Vision for the Sending of the Church in North America* (Grand Rapids, MI: Eerdmans, 1998).

16. Darrell L. Guder, *Called to Witness: Doing Missional Theology* (Grand Rapids, MI: Eerdmans, 2015).

17. Guder, "The Christological Formation of Missional Practice," in *Called to Witness*, 44–62.

18. Guder, 61.

19. Gerhard Lohfink, *Jesus and Community: The Social Dimension of the Christian Faith*, trans. John P. Galvin (Philadelphia, PA: Fortress Press, 1984).

20. Guder, *Called to Witness*, 4.

21. Guder, 7.

22. See Karl Barth, "Die Theologie und die Mission in der Gegenwart [1932]," in *Vorträge und kleinere Arbeiten 1930–1933*, ed. Michael Beintker, Michael Hüttenhoff, and Peter Zocher, Gesamtausgabe 3.49 (Zürich: TVZ, 2013), 156–208.

23. Guder, *Called to Witness*, 11.

24. *CD* IV/3, 872; *KD* IV/3, 999.

25. *CD* IV/3, 872–73; *KD* IV/3, 1000–1.

26. *CD* IV/3, 874; *KD* IV/3, 1002.

27. *CD* IV/3, 879; *KD* IV/3, 1007.

28. Guder, *Called to Witness*, 100.

29. *CD* IV/1, 725; *KD* IV/1, 809. Translation mine.

30. Guder, *Called to Witness*, 11.

31. *CD* IV/3, 878; *KD* IV/3, 768. Translation mine.

32. *CD* III/4, 493; *KD* III/4, 565.

33. *CD* III/4, 489; *KD* III/4, 560.

34. *CD* III/4, 497; *KD* III/4, 569.

35. *CD* III/4, 502; *KD* III/4, 575.

36. *CD* III/4, 489; *KD* III/4, 560.

37. *Ad Gentes* §2.

38. See James V. Brownson, *Speaking the Truth in Love: New Testament Resources for a Missional Hermeneutic* (Harrisburg, PA: Trinity Press, 1998); James V. Brownson, "Speaking the Truth in Love: Elements of a Missional Hermeneutic," *International Review of Mission* 83, no. 330 (1994): 479–504.

39. Key early works in this movement include Stephen E. Fowl and L. Gregory Jones, *Reading in Communion: Scripture and Ethics in Christian Life* (Grand Rapids, MI: Eerdmans, 1991); Francis Watson, *Text, Church and World: Biblical Interpretation in Theological Perspective* (Edinburgh: T&T Clark, 1994); Stephen E. Fowl, *Engaging Scripture: A Model for Theological Interpretation* (Malden, MA: Blackwell, 1998).

40. R. R. Reno, "Series Preface," in Jaroslav Pelikan, *Acts*, Brazos Theological Commentary on the Bible (Grand Rapids, MI: Brazos, 2005), 14.

41. Brownson, *Speaking the Truth in Love*, 42.

42. George R. Hunsberger, "Proposals for a Missional Hermeneutic: Mapping the Conversation," *The Gospel and Our Culture Network*, https://gocn.org/library/proposals-for-a-missional-hermeneutic-mapping-the-conversation/. Originally presented at the 2008 AAR (Nov. 1) and SBL (Nov. 22) annual meetings under the title, "Starting Points, Trajectories, and Outcomes in Proposals for a Missional Hermeneutic: Mapping the Conversation." Barram and Brownson responded to Hunsberger at AAR and SBL, respectively. See Michael Barram, "A Response at AAR to Hunsberger's 'Proposals . . .' Essay" (paper presented at the Annual Meeting of the AAR, Chicago, IL, November 1, 2008): https://gocn.org/library/a-response-at-aar-to-hunsbergers-proposals-essay; James V. Brownson, "A Response at SBL to Hunsberger's 'Proposals . . .' Essay" (paper presented at the Annual Meeting of the SBL, Boston, MA, November 22, 2008): https://gocn.org/library/a-response-at-sbl-to-hunsbergers-proposals-essay.

43. See Brownson, *Speaking the Truth in Love.*
44. See Christopher J. H. Wright, *The Mission of God: Unlocking the Bible's Grand Narrative* (Downers Grove, IL: IVP Academic, 2006); Michael W. Goheen, "Continuing Steps towards a Missional Hermeneutic," *Fideles* 3 (2008): 49–99; Michael W. Goheen, *A Light to the Nations: The Missional Church and the Biblical Story* (Grand Rapids, MI: Baker Academic, 2011).
45. See Michael Barram, "'Located' Questions for a Missional Hermeneutic" (paper presented at the Annual Meeting of the AAR/SBL, Washington, DC, November 1, 2006), https://gocn.org/library/95/; Michael Barram, "The Bible, Mission, and Social Location: Toward a Missional Hermeneutic," *Interpretation: A Journal of Bible & Theology* 61, no. 1 (2007): 42–58. For an earlier essay highlighting the missiological emphasis on the cultural location of the reader, see Tim Bulkeley, "Where Do You Read?," in *Mission without Christendom: Exploring the Site*, ed. Martin Sutherland (Auckland, NZ: Carey Baptist College, 2000), 13–22.
46. See Darrell L. Guder, "Missional Hermeneutics: The Missional Authority of Scripture—Interpreting Scripture as Missional Formation," *Mission Focus: Annual Review* 15 (2007): 106–24; Darrell L. Guder, "Missional Hermeneutics: The Missional Vocation of the Congregation—and How Scripture Shapes That Calling," *Mission Focus: Annual Review* 15 (2007): 125–46. Both essays are reprinted as "The Missional Authority of Scripture" and "The Scriptural Formation of the Missional Community," respectively, in Guder, *Called to Witness*, 90–120.
47. Guder, *Called to Witness*, 92.
48. Guder, 90.
49. Guder, 116.
50. Guder, 103.

BIBLIOGRAPHY

Barram, Michael. "The Bible, Mission, and Social Location: Toward a Missional Hermeneutic." *Interpretation: A Journal of Bible and Theology* 61, no. 1 (2007): 42–58.
———. "'Located' Questions for a Missional Hermeneutic." Paper presented at Annual Meeting of the AAR/SBL. Washington, DC, November 1, 2006.
———. "A Response at AAR to Hunsberger's 'Proposals . . .' Essay." Paper presented at Annual Meeting of the AAR. Chicago, IL, November 1, 2008. https://gocn.org/library/a-response-at-aar-to-hunsbergers-proposals-essay.
Barth, Karl. "Die Theologie und die Mission in der Gegenwart [1932]." In *Vorträge und kleinere Arbeiten 1930–1933*, ed. Michael Beintker, Michael Hüttenhoff, and Peter Zocher, 156–208. Gesamtausgabe 3.49. Zürich: TVZ, 2013.
———. *Theology of the Reformed Confessions*. Translated by Darrell L. Guder and Judith Guder. Louisville, KY: Westminster John Knox Press, 2002.
Brownson, James V. "A Response at SBL to Hunsberger's 'Proposals . . .' Essay." Paper presented at Annual Meeting of the SBL. Boston, MA, November 22, 2008. https://gocn.org/library/a-response-at-sbl-to-hunsbergers-proposals-essay.
———. "Speaking the Truth in Love: Elements of a Missional Hermeneutic." *International Review of Mission* 83, no. 330 (1994): 479–504.
———. *Speaking the Truth in Love: New Testament Resources for a Missional Hermeneutic.* Harrisburg, PA: Trinity Press, 1998.
Bulkeley, Tim. "Where Do You Read?" In *Mission without Christendom: Exploring the Site*, edited by Martin Sutherland, 13–22. Auckland, NZ: Carey Baptist College, 2000.
Fowl, Stephen E. *Engaging Scripture: A Model for Theological Interpretation*. Malden, MA: Blackwell, 1998.
Fowl, Stephen E. and L. Gregory Jones. *Reading in Communion: Scripture and Ethics in Christian Life*. Grand Rapids, MI: Eerdmans, 1991.
Goheen, Michael W. "Continuing Steps towards a Missional Hermeneutic." *Fideles* 3 (2008): 49–99.

———. *A Light to the Nations: The Missional Church and the Biblical Story*. Grand Rapids, MI: Baker Academic, 2011.

Guder, Darrell L. *Be My Witnesses: The Church's Mission, Message, and Messengers*. Grand Rapids, MI: Eerdmans, 1985.

———. *Called to Witness: Doing Missional Theology*. Grand Rapids, MI: Eerdmans, 2015.

———. *The Continuing Conversion of the Church*. Grand Rapids, MI: Eerdmans, 2000.

———. *The Incarnation and the Church's Witness*. Harrisburg, PA: Trinity Press International, 1999.

———, ed. *Missional Church: A Vision for the Sending of the Church in North America*. Grand Rapids, MI: Eerdmans, 1998.

———. "Missional Hermeneutics: The Missional Authority of Scripture—Interpreting Scripture as Missional Formation." *Mission Focus: Annual Review* 15 (2007): 106–24.

———. "Missional Hermeneutics: The Missional Vocation of the Congregation—and How Scripture Shapes That Calling." *Mission Focus: Annual Review* 15 (2007): 125–46.

Hunsberger, George R. "Proposals for a Missional Hermeneutic: Mapping the Conversation." *The Gospel and Our Culture Network*. https://gocn.org/library/proposals-for-a-missional-hermeneutic-mapping-the-conversation/.

Jüngel, Eberhard. *God as the Mystery of the World: On the Foundation of the Theology of the Crucified One in the Dispute between Theism and Atheism*. Translated by Darrell L. Guder. Grand Rapids, MI: Eerdmans, 1983.

Lohfink, Gerhard. *Jesus and Community: The Social Dimension of the Christian Faith*. Translated by John P. Galvin. Philadelphia, PA: Fortress Press, 1984.

Pelikan, Jaroslav. *Acts*. Brazos Theological Commentary on the Bible. Grand Rapids, MI: Brazos, 2005.

Watson, Francis. *Text, Church and World: Biblical Interpretation in Theological Perspective*. Edinburgh: T&T Clark, 1994.

Weber, Otto. *Foundations of Dogmatics*. Translated by Darrell L. Guder. 2 vols. Grand Rapids, MI: Eerdmans, 1983.

Wright, Christopher J. H. *The Mission of God: Unlocking the Bible's Grand Narrative*. Downers Grove, IL: IVP Academic, 2006.

Chapter Two

Catholicity

A Missional Mark of the Church

Stephen Bevans, SVD

Perhaps the most important thing that I have learned from Darrell Guder is his interpretation of the four classic "marks" of the church described in the Nicene Creed. The marks should be understood as dynamic and missional rather than as static and descriptive. Guder builds upon Charles van Engen's interpretation of the church's "four distinctives." These should not be understood "as adjectives which modify a thing we know as the Church, but adverbs [verbs?] which describe the missionary action of the Church's essential life in the world."[1] In this way we would speak about the church's unifying, sanctifying, reconciling, and proclaiming missional ministry.[2]

Guder (along with the authors of *Missional Church*), however, suggests something further. "In order to capture the fundamental character of the church's missional vocation, the Nicene marks should be also read and understood in reverse order. The church is called and sent to be apostolic, catholic, holy, and one—or, with van Engen, to be proclaiming, reconciling, sanctifying, and unifying."[3]

From this perspective, apostolicity becomes the "fundamental and definitive" mark or characteristic of the church,[4] the one that sets the tone for the other three. "The apostolicity of the church is translated into human experience through its catholicity, and its multicultural and simultaneously centered diversity. Its holiness follows as the Holy Spirit equips missional communities in all their diversity to present to the watching world the witness of unity."[5]

In this way, Guder has taken a significant step in developing a more coherent theology of the church that recognizes that it is "missionary by its very nature," rooted in the very mission of the Triune God.[6] The marks of the church set out in the Nicene Creed are not simply grace-given characteristics of any true community of God's People. They are at the same time mission-ary tasks, to be accomplished both *ad intra* and *ad extra*. Every true church, in other words, *is* already apostolic, catholic, holy, and one; and yet its task is to conform itself more to its identity as God's partner in mission by becom-ing a more credible witness to apostolicity, catholicity, holiness, and unity "to the watching world." Its task as well is to join in God's work of making the world more catholic, holy, and unified, by sharing and continuing the mission of Jesus in apostolic fidelity.

Darrell Guder's student, John Flett, has written extensively and powerful-ly about the first of the church's "missional marks," that of apostolicity. "Apostolicity," he writes, "is the church following the living Word, its being sent into and for the world."[7] In a much more modest way, I propose to explore in this chapter the mark of catholicity—the mark that defines aposto-licity and which is defined by it in turn.[8] I will carry out this exploration in three parts. A first part will survey the various meanings of catholicity in the history of theology. A second part will reflect on more contemporary under-standings of catholicity as the radical inclusivity of the local and particular within the universal and normative reality of the church. A third and final part will reflect on the missional nature of catholicity as a witness to the Gospel's vitality as it is developed within the church (mission *ad intra*) and as a task of the church as it engages in prophetic dialogue with the world (mission *ad extra*). While my intention in this chapter is to be as inclusive and ecumenical as possible, I write from my particular perspective as a Roman Catholic theologian.

CATHOLICITY IN THE HISTORY OF THEOLOGY: EXTENSION, ORTHODOXY, INCLUSION, UNIFORMITY

The understanding of catholicity has been quite diverse in the history of theology, as the following brief treatment will demonstrate.

Patristic and Medieval Understandings

Catholicity (based on the adjective *katholikos*, derived from the Greek *kath'holou*), is not a biblical word, although in an adverbial form (*katholou*) it appears in Acts 4:18—the Jewish leaders ordered the apostles "not to speak or teach *at all* in the name of Jesus." Yves Congar looks to the secular meaning it had in Greek literature as a possible hint to its theological mean-ing, but, as Avery Dulles comments, this turns out not to be very helpful. The word "has a wide range of meanings such as general, total, complete, and perfect."[9] Such meanings hint at what catholicity will come to mean in

Christian usage, but the Christian usage is much richer and more nuanced—if not entirely clear.

Catholicity's first appearance in Christian literature is in Ignatius of Antioch's letter to the Smyrnaeans (8, 2): "wherever there is the bishop, there is the community; just as wherever Jesus Christ is, there is the *catholic* church." Interpretations of what this means differ. Does Ignatius mean the *universal* church presided over by Christ in distinction to the local church presided over by the bishop? Or does the term refer to the completeness and fullness of the truth—to authenticity? What one finds in its earliest usages is that both meanings are understood. In the account of the martyrdom of Polycarp about forty years later, for example, it is first used to signify the *true* church as opposed to other groups, but later in the account it means the *whole* or *universal* church.[10]

By the mid-fourth century, these two ideas come together. The catholic church is basically understood as "the great Church in opposition to dissident Christian groups."[11] This was Augustine's argument against the Donatists. The true and authentic church was the one spread throughout the world, in contrast to the Donatists who were localized only in Africa.[12]

Dulles notes that Cyril of Jerusalem in his *Catechetical Lectures* offers "the fullest discussion of the term in Christian antiquity,"[13] moving the understanding away from simply extension or orthodoxy to include a qualitative dimension:

> The Church is called Catholic because it is spread throughout the world, from end to end of the earth; also because it teaches universally and completely all the doctrines which [women and men] should know concerning things visible and invisible, heavenly and earthly; and also because it subjects to right worship all [humankind], rulers and ruled, lettered and unlettered; further because it treats and heals universally every sort of sin committed by soul and body, and it possesses in itself every conceivable virtue, whether in deeds, words or in spiritual gifts of every kind.[14]

Many images of the church in the patristic literature testify to this rich understanding of catholicity. Among them are the image of Joseph's coat of many colors, Peter's vision on the roof at Joppa of a large cloth containing every sort of animal, and the miracle of the many languages but one understanding at Pentecost.[15] In these images we see the connection between extension and particularity that will mark the more contemporary discussion.

Dulles points out that the great scholastics like Bonaventure, Albert the Great, and Thomas Aquinas follow along the same line. Aquinas, in particular, understood "catholicity as freedom from all the limitations of particularity. Because it possesses this property, the church, he says, is able to transcend the frontiers of place and time and to include people of every kind and condition."[16] Such transcendence and inclusion, however, was operative in the church because the church participated in the life of Christ. Aquinas's understanding of catholicity, says Congar, was rooted not so much in ecclesiology as such as it was in Christology.[17]

Catholicity in Modernity

This would change with the development of an apologetic stance on both sides at the time of the Reformation in Europe. For the Reformers, catholicity was unswerving faithfulness to Scripture and ancient tradition, without the doctrinal and liturgical innovations that had developed in the Catholic Church over the centuries.[18] Catholicity, in other words, was about orthodoxy, fidelity, authenticity—quite close to an earlier understanding.

For Catholics, what Congar named as a more *qualitative* catholicity gave way to a more *quantitative* understanding. Catholic apologists also drew on the earliest understandings of catholicity to argue that the church of Rome was indeed the true church of Christ. The proof, however, was in the geographical extension of the Catholic Church to the ends of the earth as missionaries made the church present in the newly-"discovered" lands of North and South America and Asia.[19] Along with this emphasis on geographical extension, Robert Schreiter points to an understanding of catholicity in the Roman Church that focused on the uniformity of Catholic doctrine and practice in the context of the centralization that took place in the aftermath of the Council of Trent.

In the nineteenth century, with the challenges from republicanism and nationalism, catholicity was understood by Catholics as the church's immutability in the face of pressures to change. Thus catholicity was about the church spreading throughout the world with the same doctrines and practices that could never and would never change.[20] It was commonplace to speak of catholicity as the same as universality.

The Liberal Protestant answer (e.g., of Adolf van Harnack) to this was to reject catholicity completely. As Dulles describes it, for Liberal Protestants, "Catholicity was . . . a kind of original fall from grace which overtook the Church in the course of its history. The Reformation was seen as a protest against this defection and as a call to evangelical renewal."[21] Robert Schreiter, however, suggests that alongside this rejection of catholicity appears a Protestant appropriation of the Orthodox view of catholicity—an understanding of the fullness of the church that would only be revealed as an eschatological reality. The church on earth is broken and imperfect, fragmented and sinful, but it is moving to a wholeness that only will be accomplished at the end of the ages.[22]

Catholicity Today: Communicating in Unity-in-Diversity

In the first years of the twentieth century, in the wake of the renewal in both ecclesiology and Christology, the more medieval qualitative understanding of catholicity began to reemerge in Roman Catholicism. As Congar explains it, the emphasis was less on an apologetic demonstration to others of orthodoxy or extension, as it was a deeper appreciation of the internal dynamics of the church itself. "From something purely exterior and sociological, the idea of catholicity once more became something interior and Christological." This more qualitative understanding focused on relationships among the churches and the reality of the church's unity-in-diversity.[23]

This new perspective on catholicity had been hinted at in past understandings (in the patristic images mentioned above, in Aquinas's inclusive description, even in Ignatius's disputed phrase). In the changing world of the twentieth century, however, catholicity as unity-in-diversity began to make more and more sense. The early years of the century saw the emergence of the social sciences, and, especially in the new fields of anthropology and ethnology, a new understanding of culture was being articulated. Rather than a "classical" notion of culture that was normative and universalizing, and so would commend uniformity of expression, anthropologists and ethnologists were proposing an "empiricist" approach to culture that recognized it as a set of meanings that shaped a people's approach to life.[24] From one standard of validity, the perspective had shifted to many ways of seeing truth and goodness that were rooted in particular contexts.

This new realization came just at the time when the foundations of European colonialism were being undermined by the very European education to which the colonized had been exposed. Such education had often been given by Catholic and Protestant missionaries, who either explicitly or unwittingly contributed to the subversion of the colonial system. The outcome was the demand for local autonomy and independence, on the one hand, and an emerging nationalism and appreciation of local cultures, on the other.

By mid-century, with the convocation of the century's most significant religious event—the Second Vatican Council (1962–1965)—German Catholic theologian Karl Rahner could speak of the reality of a truly "world church," one in which the church's full catholicity was being experienced for the first time in history.[25] Rahner's essay referred specifically only to the Catholic Church, but its validity went beyond to include Protestants and Orthodox as well. Toward the end of the century and into our own, scholars began to speak about the reality of "World Christianity."[26]

It is in this context that Vatican II's brief treatment of catholicity can be best understood. As Dulles notes, the council's treatment is "securely rooted in the tradition," but "is attuned" as well "to the new situation that became evident after World War II."[27] Its treatment appears in the second chapter of its document on the church, in the context of which the council speaks about the church as the People of God. To this People, it says, all peoples are called. While it begins with a reference to geographical extension and inclusivity in terms of membership and temporality, it soon moves to the dynamic of unity-in-diversity. While the People of God and the unity it anticipates in the Reign of God are one, this unity is not a worldly uniformity. It is different. Because it is "not of this world," it "takes nothing away from the temporal welfare of any people by promoting that kingdom." Rather, the church takes into itself, "in so far as they are good, the talents, resources, and customs of each people." In this process, it "purifies, strengthens, and elevates them." It goes on to say that "in virtue of this catholicity each individual part contributes through its special gifts to the good of the other parts of the whole Church. Through the common sharing of gifts . . . the whole and each of the parts receives increase." The passage talks about the catholicity of the structure of the church, and then of the particular churches that make up the entire church communion. Catholicity "protects legitimate differences, while at the same time assuring that such differences do not hinder unity but contribute toward it." The passage hints at a kind of "ecumenical catholicity" as it moves on to talk about how other churches, other faiths, and indeed sincere people of no faith are in some sense related to the Catholic communion.[28]

The document on the church was approved by the council in 1964. In 1968, the Uppsala Assembly of the World Council of Churches issued a document entitled "The Holy Spirit and the Catholicity of the Church." In ways that echo Vatican II's treatment, Uppsala teaches that "the purpose of Christ is to bring people of all times, of all races, of all places, of all conditions, into an organic and living unity in Christ by the Holy Spirit under the fatherhood of God. This unity is not solely external; it has a deeper, internal dimension, which is also expressed by the term 'catholicity.' Catholicity reaches its completion when what God has already begun in history is finally disclosed and fulfilled."[29] Through the church's catholicity, the Spirit leads the church to a unity that embraces a rich diversity of doctrinal truth, celebration, and church order. In this way, "the Spirit leads us forward on the way to a fully catholic mission and ministry."[30]

While it is important to recognize the danger of falling into the subtle initiation into a "culture" that imitates past colonial and ecclesial practices that John Flett so powerfully exposes in his work on apostolicity,[31] the vision outlined by Vatican II and Uppsala is a noble and challenging one. Indeed, it is a major task of a missionary church, a church of missionary disciples. We will treat of this missionary dimension—the point of this chapter, in fact—in the next section. What needs to be mentioned here, however, precisely in an attempt to avoid the cultural and colonial imperialism that Flett warns against in his work, is to focus on the dimension of catholicity in terms of a commitment to open and honest communication.

What Vatican II and the Uppsala Assembly sketch in their treatment of catholicity is a portrait of the church growing and thriving as the result of a dynamic and creative tension of unity and diversity. Avery Dulles, as summarized by Robert Schreiter, characterizes catholicity as "the ability to hold things together in tension with one another."[32] Schreiter cites German theologian Siegfried Wiedenhofer's definition of catholicity as "wholeness and fullness through exchange and communication."[33] Wholeness, says Schreiter, refers to the classic understanding of worldwide extension, while fullness refers to the classic understanding of orthodoxy and authenticity of faith. These dimensions are still important. The newer aspect of catholicity, however, is expressed in the commitment to exchange and communication in the context of the many faceted, multicultural reality of World Christianity. It is in the constant openness of one church, with its varied cultural and contextual gifts, to each other and all the others, that makes catholicity not just a quality that the church possesses, but an activity in which the church engages—despite the inevitable tensions that will undoubtedly surface in such engagement.

It is this active, dynamic, and creative communication that is the basis for an understanding of the missionary nature of catholicity. The church *is* catholic because it participates through baptism in the missionary life of the Trinity as it communicates unity in difference to the whole of creation. Catholicity is a missionary *gift*. Such participation in Trinitarian life is a call to make such unity-in-diversity a living reality in the church and among the churches. Catholicity is a *task*, a *mission ad intra*. Catholicity is finally a task and mission *for the world*, or a *mission ad extra*. The church's mission expressed in its catholicity is to work with the Triune God in bringing about the unity-in-diversity among all peoples in God's creation.

CATHOLICITY AS A MISSIONARY MARK OF THE CHURCH: TRINITARIAN LIFE, MISSION *AD INTRA*, MISSION *AD EXTRA*

The 1968 study document of the World Council of Churches, "The Holy Spirit and the Catholicity of the Church," puts it beautifully: "Catholicity is a gift of the Spirit, but it is also a task, a call and an engagement."[34] This section will explore this statement from a missionary perspective.

Catholicity: Participating in the Missionary Life of the Trinity

"In the remotest beginning," Leonardo Boff has written, "communion prevails."[35] God does not exist as a transcendent monad but as a community of persons, in an act of eternal giving and receiving, communicating and being

understood. God's Mystery is perhaps better expressed by imagining or im-
aging God as a *verb* (an embrace, a flow) rather than a *noun*. The one God
exists in perfect unity, but it is a unity that is alive with relation, a unity that
pulses with love and born of true encounter. Catholicity begins here.[36] Theologians speak of this interpenetrating of communion, communication, and
love as *perichoresis* (from *perichoreo*, to circle around). In addition, many
theologians today have played with the word—so similar to the word *peri-
chorein*—of *perichoreuein*, which means to dance.[37]

The love and communication of love that is God spills over and pours out
in the act of creation. God, in the words of the medieval theologian Bonaventure, is love diffusive of itself, or, in the engaging words of contemporary
missiologist Anthony Gittins, "love hitting the cosmic fan."[38] Creation, however, was not accomplished all at once or within a short time span as a
fundamentalist reading of the two Genesis accounts in the Bible might lead
one to believe. Its mystery is much more powerfully captured by the "New
Creation Story" that is told by astrophysicists, and by the marvel of the
theory of evolution that is sketched out by evolutionary biologists.[39] This
creation is marked with the image of God in all its dazzling variety, on the
one hand, and its basic unity-in-relation, on the other. Reality itself, as a
sacrament of its creator, exists in catholicity. It is one, but in a unity of the
relatedness of all things. Even further, creation bears the image of God in the
way that God creates. As Elizabeth Johnson puts it stunningly, God creates
not with the hand of a monarch but the hand of a lover.[40] God creates in
partnership with what God is creating, endowing it with freedom, present by
coaxing, persuading, letting be, inspiring.[41] Understood in this way, creation
is the first act of God's mission, and one in which God is still involved today.
The act of catholicity that is God is working for the completion of a world
that is itself catholic, where God will eventually be "all in all" (see 1 Cor.
15:28).

Christians have come to know this because of God's revelation of God's
self in God's Spirit and in Jesus of Nazareth. As Karl Rahner has written
famously, we know who God is by what God has done. Edward Hahnenberg
notes that since we can see that God is always working in mission for communion, that is indeed what God is in God's deepest self.[42] God's Spirit has
been present and active in the universe since the first nanosecond of the "Big
Bang." There never was a time when the missionary God was not present and
working in the overflow of God's catholicity that is the created universe. It
was the Spirit's presence that women and men grasped, even though partially
perhaps, as they recognized in themselves a drive toward life's transcendent
dimension. It was the Spirit's presence that was experienced in Israel and
expressed in the elusive images of wind (Gen. 1:2), breath (Gen. 2:7), water
(Ezek. 47:1–12; Joel 3:1), fire (Ex. 13:21–22), or oil (Isa. 61:1).[43] It was the
Spirit, finally, that anointed Jesus of Nazareth to mission: to bring good news

to the poor, announce freedom to captives, give sight to the blind, wholeness to the lame, and a new chance of recognizing God's love (see Luke 4:18–19). Jesus's mission was articulated in parables, sacramentalized in healings and exorcisms, personified in his personal freedom and inclusiveness, and summarized in his image of the Kingdom, Reign, or "Kin-dom" of God. His was a vision of catholicity, of a fullness and unity that took care to respect the identity and freedom of every created thing.

God's mission of catholicity, of course, met with opposition. The Spirit-inspired message of Jesus was not accepted by his people and he was done away with. Soon after his death, however, his followers experienced him as alive, raised from the dead. But more than that. They experienced the fact that the same Spirit that had been given to Jesus had now been given to them. Although the community struggled to understand itself as a new reality beyond Judaism, the Holy Spirit "has led Christians from the very beginning to preach the gospel to all nations. All cultures are potentially receptive to the gospel, and all cultures have gifts to offer for the enrichment of the gospel."[44] The Pentecost experience and the continued prodding of the Spirit in the early chapters of Acts are images of the catholic unity-in-diversity that the Spirit brings.

The community of disciples recognized more and more clearly that the baptism that celebrated and marked their faith in the risen Christ had plunged them into his identity as God's people, Christ's body, the Spirit's temple. Baptism had clothed them with Christ's identity, conformed them to Christ's self, given them the mind of Christ, given them participation in God's very missionary and catholic nature, and so charged them to "become the gospel" in their world.[45] Paul's image for all of this was the missionary image of the church as the body of Christ. The church, sharing in Christ's very life through baptism, continued his mission of embodying, witnessing to, and proclaiming the Reign of God.

The missionary community to which they belonged was itself a sign of the catholic fullness that baptism had committed it to witness to and work for. Paul, in particular, wrote of this in his letters to the Corinthian, Roman, and Ephesian churches. While "there are different kinds of spiritual gifts," there is still "the same Spirit." While "there are different forms of service," there is "the same Lord." While there are "different workings but the same God who produces all of them in everyone." This is because, like a body, the church has "many parts." "For in one Spirit we were all baptized into one body, whether Jews or Greeks, slaves or free persons, and we were all given to drink of one Spirit" (see 1 Cor. 12:1–30). The church is rich in "gifts that differ" (see Rom. 12:1–8). Some are apostles, others are prophets, others evangelists, pastors and teachers, but all work together to equip the church for ministry, "for building up the body of Christ, until we all attain the unity of faith and knowledge of the Son of God, to mature manhood, to the extent of the full stature of Christ" (see Eph. 4:1–16).

The catholicity that is the full and open relationship and communion of the Triune God, working for the completion of creation through history, has been lavished upon Christians through their baptism. Because of this, catholicity is a gift that the church can never lose.[46] It is an ineradicable dimension of the church's missionary nature.

Catholicity *Ad Intra*: Witnessing to the Possibility of the Reign of God

Catholicity may be a gift that the church can never lose, but it is also a task in which it needs constantly to engage. Yves Congar puts it well:

> The church is catholic and is not yet catholic: the principle of "now and not yet" is here retrieved, signifying its wholly pilgrim nature. It is already in virtue of its institution, in its formal principles as *Eclessia congregans*; it is not there yet and must become constantly in its historical nature, as *Ecclesia congregate*. . . . Catholicity is therefore a property both actual and virtual, a dynamic property, given and to be realized (*Gabe* and *Aufgabe*).[47]

An essential part of the church's missionary nature is to work to be what it is—a sign and sacrament of the catholic fullness that is the Reign of God. Unfortunately, however, as is all too evident, the church has failed in history and continues to fail in the present to do and to be this. Engaging in the mission *ad intra*, therefore, to *become* catholic, is a major task. Becoming catholic and maintaining catholicity, however, is not easy. As Richard Gaillardetz expresses it, catholicity "lies in the tension between the universal and particular"; or, in Avery Dulles's description, it "consists in a dynamic interplay of mutually opposed but complementary principles."[48] Some of these tensions and seemingly opposed realities in the church are its openness to ambiguity, its recognition of the integrity of the local church, its inclusion of all cultures, and its valuing of every form of discipleship. As the church works at cultivating the "fullness and wholeness" in a dynamic process of "exchange and communication," of catholicity, it can become a witness to the world of how living a life of gospel fidelity and relationship to Jesus the Christ can offer women and men and all creation a way of abundant life. Striving for catholicity demonstrates that the Kingdom, the Reign, the Kindom of God is actually possible.

Openness to Ambiguity

The genius of Pope Francis has been to call the Catholic Church to a renewed openness and inclusion that has been a clear witness to the church's catholicity. While Francis's two predecessors, John Paul II and Benedict XVI, emphasized the importance of new efforts of evangelization in terms of clarity of doctrine and a new "ardor" and boldness in preaching (the "New Evangelization"), Francis has emphasized the importance of making the church more welcoming, more tolerant of ambiguity, and in this way more credible in its witness.[49] In a widely-published interview with Antonio Spadaro soon after he was elected pope, Francis spoke of the church as a "field hospital after battle." The important thing is to heal people's wounds, he said—"then we can talk about everything else." Francis went on to say: "I dream of a church that is a mother and shepherdess. The church's ministers must be merciful, take responsibility for the people, and accompany them like the good Samaritan, who washes, cleans, and raises up his neighbor. This is pure gospel. God is greater than sin."[50]

Several months later, in the Apostolic Exhortation *Evangelii Gaudium* (EG), Francis offered several other metaphors of the kind of church he envisioned.[51] The church should be "A Mother with an Open Heart" (see EG §§46–49), or "the house of the Father, with the doors always open" (EG §47). "The Church is not a tollhouse," he insists. "It is the house of the Father, where there is a place for everyone, with all their problems" (EG §47). Francis speaks of a more open attitude to baptizing children of couples who are not married in the church or who are not active Catholics, and he insists that the Eucharist, "is not a prize for the perfect but a powerful medicine and nourishment for the weak" (EG §47).

Regarding the Eucharist, there has been a vigorous and somewhat divisive discussion in the Catholic Church about the possibility of divorced and remarried Catholics being able to receive communion under certain circumstances. This would be a clear reversal of Catholic teaching and practice up until now. Francis alludes to this and perhaps other gestures of openness in the church in his 2016 Apostolic Exhortation *Amoris Laetitia* (AL) or "The Joy of Love."[52] He is quite clear. "It is important that the divorced who have entered a new union should be made to feel part of the Church. 'They are not excommunicated' and they should not be treated as such, since they remain a part of the ecclesial community" (AL §243). It is in chapter 8 of the document, however, entitled "Accompanying, Discerning and Integrating Weakness," where Francis cautiously and yet strongly points to the church's catholicity of all-inclusiveness despite ambiguity. Among many passages that can be quoted, one perhaps stands out: "The Church's pastors, in proposing to the faithful the full idea of the Gospel and the Church's teaching, must also help them to treat the weak with compassion, avoiding aggravation or unduly harsh or hasty judgments. Jesus 'expects us . . . to enter into the reality of other peoples' lives and to know the power of tenderness. Whenever we do, our lives become wonderfully complicated'" (AL §308).

It is this kind of inclusivity demanded by catholicity that becomes a witness to the Gospel, the real presence of God's love and mercy, a living sign of God's new "Kin-dom." This is what the church ceaselessly needs to work at becoming.

The Integrity of the Local Church

Although perhaps there have been different emphases in Roman Catholic and Protestant contexts, the last several decades have insisted on the importance of the local, particular churches within the context of the wider, universal church. As Richard Gaillardetz puts it strongly, "only an affirmation of the simultaneity of the local and universal church can provide an adequate foundation for considering the full catholicity of the church."[53] It is this tension between the local and the universal that the church needs to cultivate, witnessing to the appreciation that it has for local customs, expressions, and forms of governance and leadership. This dynamic conversation becomes a sign of the Kingdom toward which the church journeys.

In the Catholic Church, a major break from "not seeing catholicity except as the extension of unity"[54] was accomplished at the Second Vatican Council. In *Lumen Gentium* (LG) and the context of its teaching on episcopal collegiality in the Roman church, the council explains that "in and from" the local churches "comes into being the one and only Catholic Church" (LG §23). As pastors of these "particular" (the council's preferred term) or local churches, the individual bishops are "vicars and ambassadors of Christ." They are not "to be regarded as vicars of the Roman Pontiff," but have a certain independence from him while remaining loyal and in communion with him (LG §27).

In LG, in the context of its treatment of catholicity as such, the text affirms that "within the Church particular Churches hold a rightful place. These Churches have their own traditions without any way lessening the Chair of Peter. This Chair presides over the whole assembly of charity and protects legitimate differences, while at the same time it sees that such differences do not hinder unity but rather contribute toward it." This passage is referenced in the council's decree on mission, in the chapter that deals with "Particular Churches" (AG §§19–22). What the mission document makes clear is that even though Christian communities may not be fully established in terms of institutions, local leadership, and financial independence, they are nevertheless fully "churches." In other words, it is the *community* that makes the church, not any kind of institutional shape that might merely reflect Western structures. These "young Churches," in communion with Rome, are "adorned with their own traditions" and "will have their own place in the ecclesiastical communion" (AG §22).

Pope Francis has made efforts to develop this conversation of catholicity in a good number of places. In his interview with Antonio Spadaro, for example, he encourages a new conversation about collegiality and the importance of local churches. He insists that "we must walk together: the people, the bishops, and the pope. Synodality should be lived at various levels."[55] In EG, Francis comments that papal pronouncements should not "be expected to offer a definitive or complete word on every question," and that "it is not advisable for the Pope to take the place of local Bishops in the discernment of every issue which arises in their territory." He wants "to promote a sound 'decentralization'" (EG §16). At the beginning of AL, he says something similar: "Each country or region . . . can seek solutions better suited to its culture and sensitive to its traditions and local needs" (AL §3).

Francis is talking at the level of pope and bishops, but much more is at stake here. If his more catholic understanding of authority can become more and more operative in the church it will involve a commitment to dialogue in every sector of the church, something that Paul VI saw clearly in his great 1964 encyclical *Ecclesiam Suam*, in which he linked dialogue to "the very heart of the church's nature and mission."[56] Catholicity in terms of the integrity of the local church means a real, concrete appropriation of the spirit of collegiality that had been worked out at the council, however hesitatingly (see LG §§22–24). It entails a commitment to dialogue at every level of the church, between bishops and the parishes in their dioceses, between pastors and their people, and leaders and their communities of vowed religious.[57]

From a different perspective, of course, Protestants have also wrestled with the issue of the integrity of the local church over the last century. Already at the time of the 1910 Edinburgh Conference, a Scottish delegate insisted that "China, Japan, India must bring their own traditions and their own passion of patriotism into a Church of Christ, truly become also the Church of China, Japan, India."[58] The issue of the integrity of the local churches was an issue at the International Missionary Council's (IMC) Jerusalem Conference in 1928, and, in the aftermath of World War II, with the demise of colonialism, at Whitby, Canada, in 1947. In fact, it has been an issue in almost every conference since the IMC merged with the World Council of Churches (WCC) in 1961, together with the issue of the Gospel and culture, which we will take up in the next section.[59] The WCC's latest mission statement, *Together towards Life* (TTL), has a substantial section on the local church as well. It calls on the church to "honour the ways in which each local congregation is led by the Spirit to respond to its own contextual realities," insisting that "today's changed world calls for local congregations to take on new initiatives."[60]

In the tension of the local church and the universal church we see the creative tension involved in the process of catholicity that is maintained by "communication and exchange." It is not something done once and for all, but something always in process, always in motion. The danger is, on the one hand, too much interference from the center, with the result of the continuing "colonization" of the particular churches—a danger only too real if the missionary nature of the church is neglected or subordinated, or if becoming Christian means the enculturation into a new Christian culture. [61] On the other hand, there is the real danger of the local church cutting itself off from the wider communion. Only a catholic church that continually makes efforts at "communication and exchange" can succeed at being a witness to the world what the Reign of God is, and what the world can be.

Dialogue with Cultures

Writing in the context of Paul VI's call for a truly African Christianity, Richard Gaillardetz comments that, for Paul, catholicity virtually *demands* "a spirit of dialogue with local cultures." [62] Pope Paul was building on strong statements on the importance of culture in the process of evangelizing and in doing theology that were made by the Second Vatican Council. Catholicity, according to LG §13, is about the fostering and appropriation of "the ability, resources, and customs of each people," purifying them and ennobling them and in that way strengthening them. AG, the council's decree on mission, is full of passages that call for a deep respect for cultures. AG §11 calls for a "sincere and patient dialogue" that will disclose "what treasures a bountiful God has distributed among the nations of the earth." Paul VI called for a deep respect for culture in his Apostolic Exhortation *Evangelii Nuntiandi*, and John Paul II made the call for such dialogue one of the hallmarks of his pontificate. [63] John Paul II's successor, Benedict XVI, was less sanguine about a dialogue with culture, but, again, Pope Francis has insisted on cultural relevance as a major task of the church. "We would not do justice to the logic of the incarnation if we thought of Christianity as monocultural and monotonous," he wrote in EG §117. Indeed, "whenever a community receives the message of salvation, the Holy Spirit enriches its culture with the transforming power of the Gospel" (EG §116).

The WCC has also distinguished itself with a commitment to and openness toward the world's cultures, most recently in its 2013 document TTL. In a section entitled "Evangelism and Cultures," TTL strongly insists that "the enforcement of uniformity discredits the uniqueness of each individual created in the image and likeness of God" (TTL §99). [64] Although its approach to culture was hesitant in the Lausanne Covenant, the Lausanne Committee on World Mission and Evangelism's 2010 *The Cape Town Commitment* is much stronger. Its first part is a confession of faith that is divided into ten statements about what Christians love. The seventh of these loves is "We love God's world," which includes loving "the world of nations and cultures." While cultures also reveal "the fingerprints of Satan and sin," the document looks forward "to the wealth, glory and splendour of all cultures being brought into the city of God—redeemed and purged of all sin, enriching the new creation."[65]

"At the level of official discourse," Robert Schreiter has noted, the Roman Catholic Church has been encouraging of efforts of inculturation and contextual theologizing, thus offering the conditions of the possibility of a catholicity that can witness to the validity of "every nation, race, people, and tongue" (Rev. 7:9), and to the possibility of a world completely ruled by God's grace. This is certainly true as well of both Conciliar and at least many Evangelical churches. Equally true, however, is that there is a general sense "that very little actual inculturation was being permitted, and so the rhetoric of inculturation was beginning to sound more and more hollow."[66] In order to make the possibilities of the Kingdom witness of catholicity a reality, therefore, Schreiter presses for the churches "to take a far more generous attitude toward efforts at inculturation than has been the case up to now."[67]

What this means for the church is that it needs to commit itself to the missionary practice of intercultural communication and intercultural living, a practice that, according to Anthony Gittins, can only be accomplished by openness to grace. And it is hard work. It "demands graciousness, diplomacy, compromise, mutual respect, serious dialogue, and the development of a common and sustaining vision."[68] Intercultural living, communication, and theologizing demands as well a commitment in trust to the Spirit, who moves within peoples and cultures in ways that challenges and disorients dogmatic formulae and certainties. It demands as well a recognition of what Schreiter calls a certain "indeterminacy," meaning "that the message can be communicated via a variety of codes and signifiers"—in dance, perhaps, or in proverbs, or through narratives, poetry, or local symbolism.[69] This practice of catholicity demands the courage both of "letting go" on the part of those from the West who have heretofore led the church, and of "speaking out" on the part of local and contextual subjects.[70] Courage will involve even the risk of syncretism—a term, Schreiter says, "is often too quickly invoked without a careful reading of what is going on."[71] Much more dangerous than a creative effort that pushes boundaries, says Pope Francis, is to "hold fast to a formulation while failing to convey its substance" (EG §41).

Hard work indeed. And yet the effort of a continuing "communication and exchange" among cultures will be a powerful witness to the world of the possibilities of a life in Christ that, like him, empties itself (Phil. 2:9) to receive the unimagined fullness of God's Reign.

Valuing Discipleship

In its treatment of catholicity in LG §13, Vatican II devotes a short section to the church's "inner structure" that "is composed of various ranks." The language of "rank" may sound a bit hierarchical, but it needs to be understood within the context of chapter 2 of the document on the church, the chapter entitled "The People of God." The placement of this chapter in the document is important. Originally the treatment of "The People of God" was *after* the chapter on the hierarchical structure of the church and was coupled with the treatment of the Laity. During the debate on the document, however, it was suggested that the chapter be split, with "The People of God" placed *before* the one on hierarchy. This would indicate that *before* there were any differences of states or roles in the church, it was first and foremost a community of fundamental equality because of baptism.[72] In §32, we read that members "share a common dignity from their rebirth in Christ. They have the same filial grace and the same vocation to perfection. . . . If therefore everyone in the Church does not proceed by the same path, nevertheless all . . . have received an equal privilege of faith through the justice of God (cf. Col. 3:11)." As the council turns to the specific structure of the church, it speaks about how "Christ the Lord instituted in His Church a variety of ministries, which work for the good of the whole body." In this way, "all who are of the People of God, and therefore enjoy a true Christian dignity, can work toward a common goal freely and in an orderly way, and arrive at salvation" (LG §18). Here we see a real catholicity of structure in the church. Baptism is the all-inclusive sacrament, but it is lived out in the concrete form of a variety of ministries. There is a symphony, or a dance, of unity and diversity, calling every person in the church to a particular participation in God's mission, which is shared and concretized by the entire church.

This dynamic of unity and diversity of mission in the church has been captured in a particular way by the use of the word "discipleship" in contemporary ecclesiology and theology of ministry. Kathleen Cahalan, in particular, has developed the notion of discipleship—a very ancient and very biblical word to describe a follower of Jesus of Nazareth—in a particularly fresh way. For Cahalan, "Discipleship is the shared communal calling to a life of service for the sake of God's world. Through the waters of baptism, Christians together heed God's call and promise to embrace a common way of life—a life of discipleship in communion for mission."[73] Discipleship is the basic identity of every Christian, but it is an identity marked with variety, for every disciple has a particular vocation, one inspired by the Holy Spirit for some kind of service in the world. That service, within the church, might be made more public through a vocation to a particular ministry in the church, but discipleship, for Cahalan, as one moves into maturity and adulthood, is always a participation in mission. There are no passive Christians.

The image of discipleship as the fundamental Christian way of being has also been taken up by Pope Francis. Drawing on the central image of the Latin American bishops in their 2007 meeting in Aparecida, Brazil, Francis images the church as "a community of missionary disciples" (EN §24). For

Francis, the two words belong together. One cannot simply be a disciple any more than one can be just a missionary (EN §120). Each implies the other, and the source of each is baptism. Francis does not emphasize the variety of gifts with which Christians are endowed in his treatment of discipleship as such. However, he does recognize this unity in diversity among God's People. "We are all in the same boat heading to the same port," he writes, and therefore we need to "rejoice in the gifts of each, which belong to all" (EN §99). Altogether, with the various gifts of each, Francis implies, there is a certain "connaturality with divine realities" (EN §119) with which God's People are endowed, and which leads them to the truth. As the church engages at dialogue on every level, using and respecting every member's gifts—but only then—the church is assisted by the Holy Spirit.[74]

One has to recognize, however, that such catholicity of consultation and dialogue, rooted in the rich variety of disciples' gifts, is not always practiced in the church. Indeed, difference is often interpreted as "greater or lesser" rather than simply "different." Rather than the more Pauline and more biblical image of the inclusive circle where various gifts can interact with each other creatively, the church works with the imaginary of a pyramid or ladder of higher or lower, privileged and ordinary, holy and secular. The conversation demanded by the catholicity of "inner structure" is a task in which the church needs to engage if it is to be the church that it is in its deepest identity. Should the church take this catholicity seriously, it could be a model and a credible witness to the world of what the world itself could be and is called to by the Gospel—a place of real equality and equity, of justice, of Kin-dom.

Doing the hard work of building a community that reflects God's Reign, like the hard and risky work of being open to ambiguity, cherishing the dynamics of the local church, and mutually profiting from a dialogue with the world's cultures and contexts, is therefore a genuine missionary task. Lesslie Newbigin famously spoke of the Christian community as the "hermeneutic of the gospel," or, as the saying goes, "the only gospel that many people ever read."[75] Engaging in the difficult yet rewarding conversation of catholicity can present this gospel in a powerful, credible way to the world.

CATHOLICITY *AD EXTRA*: WITNESSING TO, SERVING AND PREACHING GOD'S REIGN IN THE WORLD

The catholicity that is the Triune God has been lavished upon the world in God's act of creation, and shared with the church as it "joins in with the Spirit"[76] in bringing creation to completion. Not only, therefore, is catholicity a task for the church to work toward within itself—*ad intra*. It is also a task for the church to work for in the world—*ad extra*—through its service to God's entire created world, through its cooperation with all peoples of faith,

and through its witnessing to, working for, and preaching a clear and sometimes challenging message of justice and reconciliation. The task of God's
mission is to work for the catholicity of the world. The church "joins in"
God's mission through its "ministry of catholicity": witnessing to, serving
and preaching what God is doing always and everywhere.

The Service of All Creation

Soon after his election, Pope Francis traveled to the island of Lampedusa,
often the first landfall of the thousands of migrants and refugees that have
come to Europe over the Mediterranean Sea in boats that, instead of "vehicles of hope," had become "vehicles of death."[77] In his stirring homily on
that day, Francis used for the first time a phrase that has become a hallmark
of his pontificate: the "globalization of indifference." Such indifference is, of
course, the opposite of catholicity. A truly catholic church is one that reaches
out to everyone and everything, but especially to the poor, the marginalized,
the "leftovers" (EG §53) of this world. Such a catholic outreach in mission
has been a major concern and theme from the beginning of Francis's papal
ministry. Francis calls for the full inclusion of the world's poor within human
society, and calls on the church to be an agent in that inclusion. Quoting the
words of John XXIII's *Mater et Magistra*, Francis calls the church to work
for the poor's "'general temporal welfare and prosperity.' This means education, access to health care, and above all employment, for it is through free,
creative, participatory and mutually supportive labor that human beings express and enhance the dignity of their lives. A just wage enables them to have
adequate access to all the other goods which are destined for our common
use" (EG §192).

Pope Francis goes further, however. A truly catholic church is called to
"be poor and for the poor." "We need to let ourselves be evangelized by
them" (EG §198). It is this same "turn" that the WCC's TTL advocates when
it speaks on "mission from the margins" (see §§36–42). TTL insists that the
direction of mission needs to be changed. Rather than an affluent center
serving the poor margins, a truly missionary church is profoundly catholic. It
recognizes the power and wisdom of those systematically excluded from
agency. "A major common concern of people from the margins is the failure
of societies, cultures, civilizations, nations, and even churches to honor the
dignity and worth of *all* persons. Injustice is at the roots of the inequalities
that give rise to marginalization and oppression" (TTL §42). Catholicity in
mission is about the engagement of the whole church in the agency of service. It not only works *for* all peoples, but *among* them and *with* them,
recognizing their own work *of* mission.[78]

In EG, Pope Francis includes the entire creation—animals, plants, soil,
the seas, the stars—within the category of "weak and defenseless beings"

(EG §215), and so charges the church, as part of its mission, "to watch over and protect the fragile world in which we live, and all its peoples" (EG §216). The church's catholicity is thus expressed and exercised in a missionary outreach beyond the human in the service of the animal and physical world. Francis's charge is only made more urgent in his 2015 encyclical *Laudato Si'*, which calls the church to work with peoples of all faiths and of no faith in the protection and service of "our common home." Catholicity demands a commitment to dialogue and action on the international level, the local level, in the area of economics, and with the scientific community.[79]

One of the freshest aspects of TTL is its extension of mission to the entire creation. It calls the church "to move beyond a narrowly human-centered approach and to embrace forms of mission which express our reconciled relationship with all created life" (TTL §19). The document goes on to challenge the church to think of this mission less as "something done by humanity *to* others" and more as working to establish communion *with* the whole of creation. Practicing catholicity in this sense is recognizing that creation is also in mission to us, offering us refreshment and healing when we are in harmony with it.

The task of mission includes the service of all creation and letting creation serve us, so that all creation might reflect the catholicity that is God's vision of the future when God's gentle and freedom granting rule will permeate all things.

Cooperating with All Peoples of Faith or No Faith

German theologian Hans Küng has famously written that there will be no peace among the world's peoples if there is no peace among the religions. He further writes that there will be no peace among religions if there is not dialogue among these religions.[80] The commitment to interreligious dialogue is not something extraneous or peripheral to the catholicity that is lived out in mission. It is constitutive of catholicity and therefore of mission itself.

The Second Vatican Council pointed to the catholicity that fuels the need for interreligious dialogue in its document on non-Christian religions, *Nostra Aetate*. In §2 the council notes that while it must always proclaim the truth in Jesus Christ, it must nevertheless look "with sincere respect upon those ways of conduct and of life, those rules and teaching which . . . reflect a ray of that Truth which enlightens all women and men."[81] Vatican II's Pastoral Constitution on the Church and the Modern World, in a famous passage, speaks of how "the Holy Spirit in a manner known only to God offers to every person the possibility of being associated with [the] paschal mystery."[82] In a similar way, TTL admits that the Spirit "works in mysterious ways and we do not fully understand the workings of the Spirit in other faith traditions" (TTL §93).

Documents from the churches and the writings of theologians recognize four types of interreligious dialogue, all of which might be ways that Christians engage in the ministry of catholicity.[83] The first type of dialogue is spoken of as the dialogue of life, the simple yet intentional practice of people of different faiths, no faith, or Christian faith living with one another, becoming friends, getting to know each other as persons. Such a practice can go a long way to the establishment of a real catholicity among the world's peoples. The unity born of such catholicity comes from an acceptance and enjoyment of others' diversity, as people engage in an informal "communication and exchange" in their daily lives. A second type of dialogue—that of shared action—is particularly important for our discussion here. People of various faiths or Christian commitment join together to work for a particular issue—more just immigration laws, for example, or anti-racist practices, or working together for better infrastructures in areas of poverty. Working together, people of every kind of religious or secular commitment can bring about a better world where equality, dignity, and mutual sharing can be better practiced and experienced as real fruits of catholicity. A third type of dialogue is that of theological exchange, and perhaps most often carried out among professional theologians or philosophers. While the effect of such exchanges might seem limited, they can contribute to a real understanding among women and men who might have a wider influence on society. The "communication and exchange" in which they engage can help toward a deeper understanding of the other, even though full agreement is not always possible. Finally, there is the dialogue of spirituality, as people of faith and no faith exchange their deepest convictions, and, where possible, even pray together. This kind of dialogue has been beautifully exemplified in several meetings of religious leaders at Assisi, under the leadership of Popes John Paul II, Benedict XVI, and Francis. At every level, dialogue is catholicity in action, striving to create a real unity-in-diversity—not of beliefs or practices, but of hearts, honest seeking, and basic attitudes.

Early on in his pontificate, Pope Francis ruffled some conservative feathers when he suggested that even atheists could be saved if they are sincere and do good in this world.[84] Francis was, however, very much in line with the teaching of Vatican II on atheism, which said basically the same thing (see LG §16 and GS §21). *Gaudium et Spes* (GS) notes that "believers themselves frequently bear some responsibility" for atheism, "to the extent that they neglect their own training in the faith, or teach erroneous doctrine, or are deficient in their religious, moral, or social life" (GS §21). It is on this basis that Christians need to hear the voices of nonbelievers, enter into dialogue with them, work with them, seek to understand them better. Often, unbelievers are not enemies of people of faith, but can be allies with them in building a world of real equality and of the unity in diversity that catholicity calls for.

Working for Justice and Reconciliation

In a world torn apart by extreme violence, the exploitation of peoples, and all sorts of injustice, the role of the Christian church needs to be that of a witness to and worker for justice, peace, and reconciliation. As Robert Schreiter insists, the "new catholicity" that he advocates needs to recognize "the asymmetries of power, the experience of loss through forced migration, the sense of risk and contingency in a world threatened ecologically and other ways."[85] Catholicity means that the church "must be present at the boundaries between those who profit and enjoy the fruits of the globalization process and those who are excluded and oppressed by it."[86] The church engages in this way in the ministry of catholicity, working toward a world in which women and men can recognize each other's basic dignity as created in the image of the triune God.

The church is to be, first of all, a voice for justice in the world. Such a voice might be that of individual Christians who by personal witness, letters or phone calls to legislators or political leaders, editorials in newspapers or contributions to blogs are committed to standing up for people's rights and dignity. That voice might also be raised institutionally, with official church statements and positions on issues such as opposition to the death penalty, support the rights of the unborn, or the care of creation. Even more importantly, perhaps, would be Christians' efforts to develop and highlight the voices of oppressed and marginalized peoples themselves.[87] As policies are drawn up and laws enacted through such commitment to communication and exchange, the church works for ways that the voices of all peoples can be heard and respected in all their diversity.

Working for reconciliation of people with one another is another important aspect of the church's exercise of catholicity *ad extra*. Whether that reconciliation is the personal reconciliation between spouses or among families or between victims and perpetrators, the cultural reconciliation of indigenous peoples throughout the world, or the reconciliation needed within the church itself, Christians are called by their catholicity to proclaim the possibility of reconciliation, witness to it in their own lives, or engage in the painstaking process of helping to bring it about.

It is noteworthy that Charles van Engen speaks of catholicity as the *reconciling* ministry of the church.[88] Catholicity is bringing difference and tension into fruitful, reconciling dialogue. Such a ministry might serve to bring together destructive differences among cultures, or among religions. It might be working to bring about new relationships among victims and perpetrators, or among peoples estranged from one another. It might be the ministry of reconciling traditional enemies or cultures torn apart by years of racial injustice. Whatever it might be, the dynamics of a missional church will move the church to work for such greater catholicity in the world.[89]

CONCLUSION

The church *is* catholic, and can never cease to *be* catholic. This is because its origin and continuing source of its being is in the catholicity of God as such, a God whose being is expressed in loving, freeing, healing, and reconciling mission in God's world. This is why the church must exercise its catholicity in mission. It must constantly become what it is, so that it can be a credible witness to what God is always doing in God's creation. This is its mission *ad intra*. But it must always be an agent, as God's partner, of catholicity in the world—including all peoples, all creation, all religions and value commit-ments; working and struggling for dignity and justice. Through the dynamic exercise of its catholicity, the church makes concrete its missional nature: sent as a community of apostolic disciples to continue God's mission of sanctifying and unifying the world.

NOTES

1. Charles E. van Engen, *God's Missionary People: Rethinking the Purpose of the Local Church* (Grand Rapids, MI: Baker Academic, 1991), 68. As indicated by the brackets in the text, I wonder if these distinctives might not better be called *verbs* (participles) rather than adverbs. They describe what the church does, and not just how it does it.

2. "Missional Connectedness: The Community of Communities in Mission," in *Missional Church: A Vision for the Sending of the Church in North America*, ed. Darrell L. Guder (Grand Rapids, MI: Eerdmans, 1998), 255. In *Missional Church*, the chapters are deliberately not designated by author, since the entire group of scholars that contributed to the book had such an active role in writing the book. However, on p. vii, Darrell Guder is mentioned as the drafter of this particular chapter. In a later lecture, Guder related that the idea goes back to a remark by George Hunsberger at a meeting of the *Missional Church* group in 1996. See Darrell L. Guder, "The Nicene Marks in a Post-Christendom Church," in *Called to Witness: Doing Missional Theology* (Grand Rapids, MI: Eerdmans, 2015), 78–89.

3. "Missional Connectedness," 255.

4. Darrell L. Guder, "A Multicultural and Translational Approach," in *The Mission of the Church: Five Views in Conversation*, ed. Craig Ott (Grand Rapids, MI: Baker Academic, 2016), 24.

5. Guder, "A Multicultural and Translational Approach," 33.

6. "Decree on the Mission Nature of the Church, *Ad Gentes Divinitus* (AG)," in *Vatican Council II: The Conciliar and Post Conciliar Documents*, ed. Austin Flannery (Northport, NY: Costello, 1996), §2.

7. John G. Flett, *Apostolicity: The Ecumenical Question in World Christian Perspective* (Downers Grove, IL: IVP Academic, 2016), 336.

8. Guder, "A Multicultural and Translational Approach," 25.

9. See Yves Congar, "La Chiesa é cattolica," in *Mysterium salutis Volume 7: L'evento salvifico nella comunità di Gesù Cristo (parte I)*, ed. Johannes Feiner, and Magnus Löhrer (Brescia: Queriniana, 1975), 577–78, and Avery R. Dulles, *The Catholicity of the Church* (Oxford: Clarendon Press, 1985), 14. I am following these classic texts in what follows.

10. See Congar, "La Chiesa," 579. The references are to chapters XVI, 2 and XIX, 2.

11. Dulles, *The Catholicity of the Church*, 14.

12. Congar, "La Chiesa," 581.

13. Dulles, *The Catholicity of the Church*, 14.

14. Dulles, Appendix I, 181. *Catechetical Lectures*, XVIII.

15. Congar, "La Chiesa," 583. Congar provides copious patristic references.

16. Dulles, *The Catholicity of the Church*, 15. In Appendix I, 181, Dulles cites Aquinas's "In Symbolum Apostolorum."

17. Congar, "La Chiesa," 586.

18. Dulles, *The Catholicity of the Church*, 16.

19. Congar, "La Chiesa," 586.

20. Robert J. Schreiter, *The New Catholicity: Theology between the Global and the Local* (Maryknoll, NY: Orbis Books, 1997), 121.

21. Dulles, *The Catholicity of the Church,* 17.

22. Schreiter, *The New Catholicity*, 121.

23. Congar, "La Chiesa," 587.

24. See Bernard J. F. Lonergan, *Method in Theology* (London: Dartman, Longman and Todd, 1972), xi.

25. Karl Rahner, "Toward a Fundamental Theological Interpretation of Vatican II," *Theological Studies* 40, no. 4 (1979): 716–27. For the claim that the Second Vatican Council is the most important religious event of the twentieth century, see, for example, Robert J. Schreiter, "The Impact of Vatican II," in Gregory Baum, ed., *The Twentieth Century: A Theological Overview* (Maryknoll, NY: Orbis Books, 1999), 158–72.

26. Scholars such as Lamin Sanneh, Andrew Walls, and Dale Irvin and Scott Sunquist argue that there has always been a World Christianity and that Christian history needs to be written from a "World Christian Perspective." See especially Irvin and Sunquist's several volumes published since 2000 by Orbis Books. See also Jonathan Y. Tan and Ahn Tran, *World Christianity: Perspectives and Insights* (Maryknoll, NY: Orbis Books, 2016).

27. Dulles, *The Catholicity of the Church*, 24.

28. See "Dogmatic Constitution on the Church, *Lumen Gentium* (LG)," in *Vatican Council II: The Conciliar and Post Conciliar Documents*, ed. Austin Flannery (Northport, NY: Costello, 1996), §§13–16.

29. "The Holy Spirit and the Catholicity of the Church," §6, in *The Uppsala Report*, ed. Norman Goodall (Geneva: WCC, 1968), 13.

30. "The Holy Spirit and the Catholicity of the Church," §12 (p. 15).

31. See Flett, *Apostolicity*, in particular chapters 3 and 4, 102–85.

32. See Schrieter, *The New Catholicity*, 128.

33. Schrieter, 128, quoting Siegfried Wiedenhofer, *Das katholische Kirchenverständnis* (Graz: Verlag Styria, 1992), 279.

34. "The Holy Spirit and the Catholicity of the Church," §7 (p. 13).

35. Leonardo Boff, "Trinity," in *Mysterium Liberationis*, ed. Ignacio Ellacuría and Jon Sobrino (Maryknoll, NY: Orbis Books, 1993), 389.

36. Dulles speaks of Trinitarian life as "divine catholicity." See *The Catholicity of the Church*, 32.

37. See, for example, Elizabeth A. Johnson, *She Who Is: The Mystery of God in Feminist Theological Discourse* (New York: Crossroad, 1992), 220–21.

38. Bonaventure, *De Trinitate*, 3, 16. The quotation from Gittins is not, as far as I know, in print. I heard Tony use this expression at a symposium of which I was a part in the 1990s.

39. See, for example, Brian Swimme and Thomas Berry, *The Universe Story: From the Primordial Flaring Forth to the Ecozoic Era—A Celebration of the Unfolding of the Cosmos* (Cambridge: International Society for Science and Religion, 2007); Denis Edwards, *Breath of Life: A Theology of Creator Spirit* (Maryknoll, NY: Orbis Books, 2004); Ilia Delio, *The Emergent Christ: Exploring the Meaning of Catholic in an Evolutionary Universe* (Maryknoll, NY: Orbis Books, 2011); Elizabeth A. Johnson, *Ask the Beasts: Darwin and the God of Love* (London: Bloomsbury, 2014).

40. Johnson, *Ask the Beasts,* 159.

41. See Johnson, 159.

42. Karl Rahner, *The Trinity* (New York: Crossroad, 1997); Edward P. Hahnenberg, *Ministries: A Relational Approach* (New York: Crossroad, 2003), 85.

43. See Christopher J. H. Wright, *Knowing the Holy Spirit through the Old Testament* (Downers Grove, IL: IVP Academic, 2006).

44. Richard R. Gaillardetz, *Ecclesiology for a Global Church: A People Called and Sent* (Maryknoll, NY: Orbis Books, 2008), 36.

45. See Michael J. Gorman, *Becoming the Gospel: Paul, Participation, and Mission* (Grand Rapids, MI: Eerdmans, 2015).

46. Joint Theological Commission, "Catholicity and Apostolicity," *One in Christ* 6 (1970): 452–83. See Dulles, *The Catholicity of the Church*, 25.

47. Congar, "La Chiesa," 595–96.

48. Gaillardetz, *Ecclesiology for a Global Church*, 39; Dulles, *The Catholicity of the Church*, 121.

49. See Stephen Bevans, SVD, "Beyond the New Evangelization: Toward a Missionary Ecclesiology for the Twentieth Century," in *A Church with Open Doors: Catholic Ecclesiology for the Third Millennium*, ed. Richard R. Gaillardetz and Edward P. Hahnenberg, (Collegeville, MN: The Liturgical Press. A Michael Glazier Book, 2015), 3–22.

50. Antonio Spadaro, *A Big Heart Open to God: A Conversation with Pope Francis* (New York: HarperOne, 2013). Quotes are from the section "The Church as Field Hospital," 30–35.

51. Francis, Apostolic Exhortation *Evangelii Gaudium* (EG) (Vatican City: Vatican Press, 2013).

52. Francis, Apostolic Exhortation *Amoris Laetitia* (AL) (Vatican City: Vatican Press, 2016).

53. Gaillardetz, *Ecclesiology for a Global Church*, 119. Gaillardetz is speaking in the context of the debate between Joseph Ratzinger and Walter Kasper, both cardinals, on the relationship of the local to the universal church. The debate took place in an exchange of articles in late 1990s and the opening years of this century. The result of the debate was a basic agreement on the "simultaneity" of both the universal and local church.

54. Congar, "La Chiesa," 587.

55. Spadaro, *A Big Heart Open to God*, "The Roman Curia, Collegiality and Ecumenism," 38–40.

56. Paul VI, Encyclical Letter *Ecclesiam Suam* (ES) (Glen Rock, NJ: Paulist Press, 1965); Gaillardetz, *Ecclesiology for a Global Church*, 57.

57. See William A. Clark, *A Voice of Their Own: The Authority of the Local Parish* (Collegeville, MN: The Liturgical Press, 2005; Bradford Hinze, *Practices of Dialogue in the Roman Catholic Church: Aims and Obstacles, Lessons and Laments* (New York: Continuum, 2006).

58. *Life and Work: The Church of Scotland Magazine and Mission Record* 32, no. 8 (August, 1910): 244, quoted in Brian Stanley, *The World Missionary Conference, Edinburgh 1910* (Grand Rapids, MI: Eerdmans, 2009), 258.

59. See Daesung Lee and Stephen Bevans, "Culture," in *Ecumenical Missiology: Changing Landscapes and New Conceptions of Mission*, ed. Kenneth R. Ross, Jooseop Keum, Kyriaki Avtzi, and Roderick R. Hewitt (Oxford: Regnum and Geneva: WCC, 2016), 201–17.

60. Commission on World Mission and Evangelism of the World Council of Churches, *Together towards Life: Mission and Evangelism in Changing Landscapes* (TTL) (Geneva: WCC, 2013), §72.

61. John Flett points out this danger in his *Apostolicity*. See, in particular, chapters 2 and 3.

62. Gaillardetz, *Ecclesiology for a Global Church*, 57.

63. Paul VI, Apostolic Exhortation *Evangelii Nuntiandi* (EN) (Washington, DC: United States Catholic Conference, 1999), see especially §20. See also, for example, John Paul II, Encyclical Letter *Redemptoris Missio* (RM) (Washington, DC: United States Catholic Conference, 1999), §§52–54. On culture in the writings of John Paul II up to 1992, see Stephen B. Bevans, *Models of Contextual Theology* (Maryknoll, NY: Orbis Books, 2002), 49–53. See also Lee and Bevans, "Culture."

64. For a fuller development of the WCC's openness to culture with its roots in the Edinburgh 1910 Conference, see Lee and Bevans, "Culture."

65. The Third Lausanne Congress, *The Cape Town Commitment: A Confession of Faith and a Call to Action* (TCTC) (Peabody, MA: Hendrikson Publishers, 2011), I, 7, B.

66. Schreiter, *The New Catholicity*, 116.

67. Schreiter, *The New Catholicity*, 129.

68. Anthony J. Gittins, *Living Mission Interculturally: Faith, Culture, and the Renewal of Praxis* (Collegeville, MN: The Liturgical Press, 2015), 5.

69. Schreiter, *The New Catholicity*, 131.

70. See Stephen B. Bevans and Roger P. Schroeder, "Letting Go and Speaking Out: Prophetic Dialogue and the Spirituality of Inculturation," in Stephen B. Bevans and Roger P. Schroeder, *Prophetic Dialogue: Reflections on Christian Mission Today* (Maryknoll, NY: Orbis Books, 2011), 88–100.

71. Schrieter, *The New Catholicity*, 131. See also Mika Vahahängis and Patrik Fridlund, eds., *Theological and Philosophical Responses to Syncretism* (Leiden: Brill, 2016).

72. See Gaillardetz, *Ecclesiology for a Global Church*, 187.

73. Kathleen A. Cahalan, *Introducing the Practice of Ministry* (Collegeville, MN: The Liturgical Press, 2010), 27.

74. See Spadaro, *A Big Heart Open to God*, "Thinking with the Church," 25–28. See also Richard R. Gaillardetz, "The Francis Moment: A New Kairos for Catholic Ecclesiology," *Proceedings of the Catholic Theological Society of America* 69 (2014): 63–80, here 72. Interestingly, the image of discipleship has also been chosen as the theme for the 2018 World Mission Conference sponsored by the WCC and CWME in Arusha, Tanzania, in March, 2018. See the Conference Concept Paper of October, 2016.

75. Lesslie Newbigin, *The Gospel in a Pluralist Society* (Grand Rapids, MI: Eerdmans, 1989), 222–33; see also, for example, http://www.icatholic.ie/reflection-2016-ot-3-sunday/.

76. Rowan Williams, cited in Kirsteen Kim, *Joining in with the Spirit: Connecting World Church and Local Mission* (London: Epworth Press, 2010), 1.

77. Pope Francis, Homily at Lampedusa, available online at: https://w2.vatican.va/content /francesco/en/homilies/2013/documents/papa-francesco_20130708_omelia-lampedusa.html (accessed, 1 January 2019).

78. See Stephen Bevans, "Mission *among* Migrants, Mission *of* Migrants: Mission of the Church," in ed. Daniel G. Groody and Gioacchino Campese, *A Promised Land, A Perilous Journey* (Notre Dame, IN: University of Notre Dame Press, 2008), 89–106.

79. Francis, Encyclical Letter *Laudato Si'* (LS) (Washington, DC: United States Conference of Catholic Bishops, 2015), 163–201.

80. Hans Küng, *Christianity: Essence, History, Future* (New York: Continuum, 1995). 783.

81. "Declaration on the Relationship of the Church to Non-Christian Religions, *Nostra Aetate* (NA)," in *Vatican Council II: The Conciliar and Post Conciliar Documents*, ed. Austin Flannery (Northport, NY: Costello, 1996), §2.

82. "Pastoral Constitution on the Church in the Modern World, *Gaudium et Spes* (GS)," in *Vatican Council II: The Conciliar and Post Conciliar Documents*, ed. Austin Flannery (Northport, NY: Costello, 1996), §22.

83. See, for example, the 1991 document jointly published by the Pontifical Council of Inter-religious Dialogue and the Congregation for the Evangelization of Peoples, *Dialogue and Proclamation* (DP), available online at: http://www.vatican.va/roman_curia/pontifical_councils/interelg/documents/rc_pc_interelg_doc_19051991_dialogue-and-proclamatio_en .html, §§42–46 (accessed, 1 January 2019); World Council of Churches, *Ecumenical Considerations for Dialogue and Religions with People of Other Religions* (Geneva: WCC, 2003), §§31–33; Stephen B. Bevans and Roger P. Schroeder, *Constants in Context: A Theology of Mission for Today* (Maryknoll, NY: Orbis Books, 2004), 383–84.

84. See, for example, "Pope Francis Says that Atheists Can Do Good and Go to Heaven Too," http://www.catholic.org/news/hf/faith/story.php?id=51077 (accessed, 1 January 2019).

85. Schreiter, *The New Catholicity*, 129.

86. Schreiter, 130.

87. See David J. Bosch, *Transforming Mission: Paradigm Shifts in Theology of Mission* (Maryknoll, NY: Orbis Books, 1991), 400–8; Bevans and Schroeder, *Constants in Context*, 369–78.

88. See van Engen, *God's Missionary People*, 68.

89. On reconciliation and mission, see, for example, Robert Schreiter and Knud Jørgensen, eds., *Mission as Ministry of Reconciliation* (Oxford: Regnum Books, 2013); see also Robert J.

Schreiter, R. Scott Appleby, and Gerard F. Powers, ed., *Peacebuilding: Catholic Theology, Ethics, and Praxis* (Maryknoll, NY: Orbis Books, 2010).

BIBLIOGRAPHY

Bevans, Stephen B. "Beyond the New Evangelization: Toward a Missionary Ecclesiology for the Twentieth Century," in *A Church with Open Doors: Catholic Ecclesiology for the Third Millennium*, edited by Richard R. Gaillardetz and Edward P. Hahnenberg, 3–22. Collegeville, MN: The Liturgical Press, 2015.

———. "Mission among Migrants, Mission of Migrants: Mission of the Church," in *A Promised Land, a Perilous Journey: Theological Perspectives on Migration*, edited by Daniel G. Groody, G. Campese, and Ó. A. R. Maradiaga, 89–106. Notre Dame: University of Notre Dame Press, 2008.

———. *Models of Contextual Theology*. Maryknoll, NY: Orbis Books, 2002.

Bevans, Stephen B., and Roger P. Schroeder. *Constants in Context: A Theology of Mission for Today*. Maryknoll, NY: Orbis Books, 2004.

———. "Letting Go and Speaking Out: Prophetic Dialogue and the Spirituality of Inculturation," in *Prophetic Dialogue: Reflections on Christian Mission Today*, edited by Stephen B. Bevans and Roger P. Schroeder, 88–100. Maryknoll, NY: Orbis Books, 2011.

Boff, Leonardo. "Trinity," in *Mysterium Liberationis: Fundamental Concepts of Liberation Theology*, edited by Ignacio Ellacuría and Jon Sobrino, 389–404. Maryknoll, NY: Orbis Books, 1993.

Bosch, David J. *Transforming Mission: Paradigm Shifts in Theology of Mission*. Maryknoll, NY: Orbis Books, 1991.

Cahalan, Kathleen A. *Introducing the Practice of Ministry*. Collegeville, MN: The Liturgical Press, 2010.

Clark, William A. *A Voice of Their Own: The Authority of the Local Parish*. Collegeville, MN: The Liturgical Press, 2005.

Commission on World Mission and Evangelism of the World Council of Churches. *Together towards Life: Mission and Evangelism in Changing Landscapes*. Geneva: WCC, 2013.

Congar, Yves. "La Chiesa É Cattolica," in *Mysterium salutis Volume 7: L'evento salvifico nella comunità di Gesù Cristo (parte I)*, edited by Johannes Feiner and Magnus Löhrer, 577–78. Brescia: Queriniana, 1975.

"Declaration on the Relationship of the Church to Non-Christian Religions, *Nostra Aetate*," in *Vatican Council II: The Conciliar and Post Conciliar Documents*, edited by Austin Flannery, 569–74. Northport, NY: Costello, 1996.

"Decree on the Mission Nature of the Church, *Ad Gentes Divinitus*," in *Vatican Council II: The Conciliar and Post Conciliar Documents*, edited by Austin Flannery, 813–62. Northport, NY: Costello, 1996.

"Dogmatic Constitution on the Church, *Lumen Gentium*," in *Vatican Council II: The Conciliar and Post Conciliar Documents*, edited by Austin Flannery, 350–426. Northport, NY: Costello, 1996.

Dulles, Avery R. *The Catholicity of the Church*. Oxford: Clarendon Press, 1985.

Edwards, Denis. *Breath of Life: A Theology of the Creator Spirit*. Maryknoll, NY: Orbis Books, 2004.

Flett, John G. *Apostolicity: The Ecumenical Question in World Christian Perspective*. Downers Grove, IL: IVP Academic, 2016.

Francis, *Amoris Laetitia*. Vatican City: Vatican Press, 2016.

———, *Evangelii Gaudium*. Vatican City: Vatican Press, 2013.

———, *Laudato Si'*. Washington, DC: United States Conference of Catholic Bishops, 2015.

Gaillardetz, Richard R. *Ecclesiology for a Global Church: A People Called and Sent*. Maryknoll, NY: Orbis Books, 2008.

———. "The Francis Moment: A New Kairos for Catholic Ecclesiology." *Proceedings of the Catholic Theological Society of America* 69 (2014): 63–80.

Gittins, Anthony J. *Living Mission Interculturally: Faith, Culture, and the Renewal of Praxis.* Collegeville, MN: The Liturgical Press, 2015.

Gorman, Michael J. *Becoming the Gospel: Paul, Participation, and Mission.* Grand Rapids, MI: Eerdmans, 2015.

Guder, Darrell L. "A Multicultural and Translational Approach," in *The Mission of the Church: Five Views in Conversation,* edited by Craig Ott, 21–40. Grand Rapids, MI: Baker Academic, 2016.

———. "The Nicene Marks in a Post-Christendom Church," in *Called to Witness: Doing Missional Theology,* 78–89. Grand Rapids, MI: Eerdmans, 2015.

Hahnenberg, Edward P. *Ministries: A Relational Approach.* New York: Crossroad, 2003.

Hinze, Bradford. *Practices of Dialogue in the Roman Catholic Church: Aims and Obstacles, Lessons and Laments.* New York: Continuum, 2006.

"The Holy Spirit and the Catholicity of the Church," in *The Uppsala Report 1968: Official Report of the Fourth Assembly of the World Council of Churches Uppsala July 4–20, 1968,* edited by Norman Goodall, 7–20. Geneva: WCC, 1968.

Johnson, Elizabeth A. *Ask the Beasts: Darwin and the God of Love.* London: Bloomsbury, 2014.

———. *She Who Is: The Mystery of God in Feminist Theological Discourse.* New York: Crossroad, 1992.

Joint Theological Commission. "Catholicity and Apostolicity." *One in Christ* 4, no. 3 (1970): 425–83.

Kim, Kirsteen. *Joining in with the Spirit: Connecting World Church and Local Mission.* London: Epworth Press, 2010.

Küng, Hans. *Christianity: Essence, History, Future.* New York: Continuum, 1995.

Lee, Daesung, and Stephen Bevans. "Culture," in *Ecumenical Missiology: Changing Landscapes and New Conceptions of Mission,* edited by Kenneth R. Ross, Jooseop Keum, Kyriaki Avtzi and Roderick R. Hewitt, 201–17. Geneva: WCC, 2016.

Lonergan, Bernard J. F. *Method in Theology.* London: Dartman, Longman and Todd, 1972.

"Missional Connectedness: The Community of Communities in Mission," in *Missional Church: A Vision for the Sending of the Church in North America,* edited by Darrell L. Guder, 248–68. Grand Rapids, MI: Eerdmans, 1998.

Newbigin, Lesslie. *The Gospel in a Pluralist Society.* Grand Rapids, MI: Eerdmans, 1989.

"Pastoral Constitution on the Church in the Modern World, *Gaudium et Spes,*" in *Vatican Council II: The Conciliar and Post Conciliar Documents,* edited by Austin Flannery, 163–282. Northport, NY: Costello, 1996.

Paul II, John. *Redemptoris Missio.* Washington, DC: United States Catholic Conference, 1999.

Paul VI. *Ecclesiam Suam.* Glen Rock, NJ: Paulist Press, 1965.

———. *Evangelii Nuntiandi.* Washington, DC: United States Catholic Conference, 1999.

Rahner, Karl. "Toward a Fundamental Theological Interpretation of Vatican II." *Theological Studies* 40, no. 4 (1979): 716–27.

———. *The Trinity.* Translated by Joseph Donceel. New York: Crossroad, 1997.

Schreiter, Robert J. "The Impact of Vatican II," in *The Twentieth Century: A Theological Overview,* edited by Gregory Baum, 158–72. Maryknoll, NY: Orbis Books, 1999.

———. *The New Catholicity: Theology between the Global and the Local.* Maryknoll, NY: Orbis Books, 1997.

Schreiter, Robert J., Scott Appleby, and Gerard Powers, eds. *Peacebuilding: Catholic Theology, Ethics, and Praxis.* Maryknoll, NY: Orbis Books, 2010.

Spadaro, Antonio. *A Big Heart Open to God: A Conversation with Pope Francis.* New York: HarperOne, 2013.

Stanley, Brian. *The World Missionary Conference, Edinburgh 1910.* Grand Rapids, MI: Eerdmans, 2009.

Swimme, Brian, and Thomas Berry. *The Universe Story: From the Primordial Flaring Forth to the Ecozoic Era—A Celebration of the Unfolding of the Cosmos.* Cambridge: International Society for Science and Religion, 2007.

Tan, Jonathan Y., and Anh Q. Tran, eds. *World Christianity: Perspectives and Insights.* Maryknoll, NY: Orbis Books, 2016.

Third Lausanne Congress. *The Cape Town Commitment: A Confession of Faith and a Call to Action*. Peabody, MA: Hendrikson Publishers, 2011.

Vahahängis, Mika, and Patrik Fridlund, eds. *Theological and Philosophical Responses to Syncretism*. Leiden: Brill, 2016.

van Engen, Charles E. *God's Missionary People: Rethinking the Purpose of the Local Church*. Grand Rapids, MI: Baker Academic, 1991.

World Council of Churches. *Ecumenical Considerations for Dialogue and Religions with People of Other Religions*. Geneva: WCC, 2003.

Wright, Christopher J. H. *Knowing the Holy Spirit through the Old Testament*. Downers Grove, IL: IVP Academic, 2006.

Chapter Three

The Sending of the Whole Christian Church

Reflections after Karl Barth

Eberhard Busch

"A church that is not 'the church in mission' is no church at all" (Lesslie Newbigin). Darrell Guder has interpreted this sentence in an exemplary and ground-breaking way. In doing so, he often referred to Karl Barth and made clear that the theme of the church's sending is much more central to Barth's work than was commonly perceived. His insight will, with appreciation, be taken up and reflected upon here.

THE ONE SENT BY GOD

In the year 1914, Jewish theologian Franz Rosenzweig wrote an essay with the title "Atheistic Theology." He argued that any theology based on the denominator "religion" was atheistic and directed this critique toward both Jewish and Protestant theology. In terms of Jewish theology, Israel is abstracted into a national entity, disregarding its God and God's election. In terms of Protestant theology, Christ is reduced to a mere human being in contrast to the confession of the "true God and true human," and through this abandonment Christianity undoes itself. In both cases, the mere human subject is deified. "The distinction between God and [the hu]man, which was a stumbling block for all new and old paganism, appears to be abolished; the offensive notion of revelation as the pouring forth of a superior content into an unworthy vessel is silenced."[1] The "struggle between a superhuman revelation and human unwillingness" is replaced by a "polarity within the human itself."[2] Rosenzweig concludes as follows: "theology may be as scientific as it will and can, yet it cannot do without the notion of revelation."[3] This applies to both Judaism and Christianity. The difference is that Judaism has *to watch over* that knowledge of the difference between God and the human which keeps it from paganism. Christianity has the task of *mission* among the pagan nations of proclaiming the God who is unknown to them, and which contrasts with their religiously pupated atheism. But this means, first and foremost, that it is necessary for Christians to convert the pagan *in themselves*. The existence of the Jews reminds us of this fact.

In 1920, Karl Barth came into contact with Rosenzweig and was probably inspired by him when emphasizing the difference between God and the human in the second edition of his commentary on Romans. Like Rosenzweig, Barth also treats religion as unbelief in his *Church Dogmatics*. This notion does not indicate contempt for other non-Christian religions. Rather, the fundamental point is that religion, understood as a path from the human to God, never reaches its own goal. This is because God takes a different way, and in so doing proves that God is God and not a creation of the human. Talking of God can therefore not be connected with such religion. God goes God's own way to us in his Son. According to the Gospel of John, Jesus is "*sent*: as the Son of God, he is sent by his Father into the world, sent to the earth and among human beings, and come as his sent one."[4]

Everything hinges upon this one crucial act of sending. As a consequence, Barth dares the following sharp theses: "(1) The world would be lost without Jesus Christ, without His work and Word. (2) The *world* would not necessarily be lost if there were no church. (3) The *church* would be lost if she did not have her counterpart in the world."[5] This means that church is not the salvation of the world, that is, God could direct people to find their salvation without her. This means that people are not lost if the church fails. Does this not mean, however, that it is a matter of life and death for the church that she turns to the "world," to the people and to the surrounding creatures?

In *CD* IV/4 one finds that it is above all *God in Godself* who missionizes. This is also a central insight for Darrell Guder; God's mission is simply foundational.[6] The world is absolutely dependent on *God,* but not necessarily on the *church*. The church is not redundant, but she is only herself if she follows God's own model of being with the people. The significance of this idea—that God missionizes—Barth demonstrates through a bold new interpretation of Matthew 28 and a new version of the teaching of the Trinity.

> The mention of Father, Son and Holy Spirit is . . . the enumeration of the *dimensions* of the one name of God, i.e., God's own deed and word, God's act of salvation and revelation, by which one may believe, love, obey, serve, and by which pagans may be turned into disciples, and called to repentance and therefore to baptism, and led to enter and pursue the way of Jesus Christ. The

words "Father," "Son," "Holy Spirit" . . . together indicate the *expansion* of the one name, deed and word of God. This is why they occur here in the context of the missionary command. Mission is objectively: the *expansion* of the reality and truth of Jesus Christ.[7]

These sentences make clear what the church is good for: that she follows this One into the world. The then Lutheran bishop of Bavaria, Hans Meiser, once remarked that "one cannot build the church with Karl Barth."[8] By contrast, the South African David Bosch understood why Barth thought differently from the regional bishop: since, according to Barth, God, and not the church, is the *ground* for mission, the church is not the *goal* of mission.[9] Bosch continues by saying that "church people" think about how one can bring people into the church, whereas "Kingdom of God people" think about how the church can be brought into the world. Barth asks whether (but considers it an impossible presumption) the work "of this divine messenger and ambassador actually ceased in the dead end of the church as an institution of salvation for those who belong to her?"[10] More pointedly, he says that the church "does not exist *before* her commission and later acquire it. Nor does she exist *apart* from it, so that there can be no question whether or not she might have to execute it. She exists for the world. Her task . . . forms the center and the horizon of her existence."[11] This leads to the categorical conclusion: "That the community of Jesus Christ is for the world means that it is for all, for each and every human being. . . . She exists ecstatically, eccentrically: also within the world to which she belongs she does not exist with reference to herself, but wholly with reference to them, to the world around. She saves and maintains her own life as she uses it and surrenders it for all other human creatures."[12] And again in *CD* IV/4 we find the sentence: "She is the church of Jesus Christ as this church sent into the world, as this missionary church, or she is not the church at all."[13]

THE SENDING OF THE
WHOLE CHRISTIAN COMMUNITY

Is the community not there prior to her commission? Certainly, without her being gathered she could not be sent. Without this, she would not know who sent her, why and for what purpose she was being sent, how her sending is justified, and the nature of the task she is sent to do. In being gathering she gathers around this One sent of God. This is the Christian interpretation of the thought that Christianity is dependent on the ministry of Israel, it is so that she herself does not become pagan in her being sent into the "Gentile world." In so becoming pagan, she would forget her commission. Moreover, according to Barth, the church is "the assembly of those who, according to the Vulgate rendering of Mk. 3: 34, *in circuitu eius sedebant*, continuing in a circle around Jesus, are engaged in doing the will of God as His people."[14] Drawing a similar conclusion to Barth, Lesslie Newbigin states that "[i]t is surely a fact of inexhaustible significance that what our Lord left behind Him was not a book, nor a creed, nor a system of thought, nor a rule of life, but a visible community. He committed the entire work of salvation to that community."[15]

However, inasmuch as the one she gathers around is the sent One, her gathering around him is inseparable from her sending. Just as everyone gathers around him, so everyone in her is also sent. The Second Vatican Council confirms this basic premise—every baptized Christian participates in the threefold ministry of Christ: as prophet, king, and priest. This affirms, in a way similar to Barth, that the laity are *full* members of the people of God and are more suitable than the priests in carrying out these three functions in their secular everyday lives.[16]

This position, taken both by Barth and the Catholic council, differs from that taken by the *Evangelische Kirche in Deutschland* as developed in a 2006 position paper.[17] Here the laity are unsuitable for missionary service in the profane world. Pastors accomplish such service by administering those rites which follow the life cycle: infant baptism, consecration during adolescence, marriage, and burial. Is this mission? This chain is more reminiscent of pagan rites of the natural life-cycle. And here not all members of the church are sent, but only the clerics to the laypeople within their church. According to Luther, *baptism* and the *Lord's Supper* are sacramental actions which have to do with the foundation and the preservation of the *Christian* life. With regards to baptism, Luther writes that it can only be received appropriately in *faith*.[18] If faith were lacking, then "baptism cannot help at all." Calvin agrees: "For what is a sacrament received apart from faith but the most certain ruin of the church?"[19]

For Barth, Matthew 28:19 goes further—baptism stands in relation to the Great Commission, the goal of which is not just preaching to others but making them *disciples*.[20] In *CD* IV/4 one finds the astonishing sentence, which Barth added to the galley proofs during the Israel War in 1967—as the very last sentence of his *Dogmatics*: "a person becomes in baptism an active member of the holy people of Israel, which according to Isaiah 42:6 is set as a 'mediator among the nations.'"[21] Baptism, by this definition, is also an act of *sending*.[22] This leads Barth to conclude that baptism is "a 'consecration' or 'ordination' for participation in the sending entrusted to the whole church."[23] Beside this ordination, a second to an ecclesiastical office is seen to be "superfluous" and even "forbidden."[24] If special ministries do exist, the holders of these offices do not stand above the laity. Along with the laity, they are *together* members of the people of God. The task of all the church members in such a sending is not to be understood as the realization of an egocentric urge for expansion and, with this, domination over their neighbors. In this task, all Christians are only servants of the One of whom Barth says: he himself is "the Lord as Servant."[25] This constitutes what Guder describes as "the Christological formation of missional practice."[26]

This determines the *how* but not the *that* of the missional task of all Christians in their worldly environment. It is important to again stress that they carry out this task not in caprice, but in listening to God's word. They have to realize that the church must always exist in that double movement that Rosenzweig understands as applying to both Jews and Christians. She acts in the service of God by having been entrusted with the missionary *task* and having been *called* to it. In this respect the following applies: "Being *called out* of the world, the community will be and is actually called *into it*."[27] The first two parts of book four in the *Church Dogmatics* talk respectively about the gathering and upbuilding of the Christian community that is called out of the world. Part 3 talks about the sending of the community into the world. At this point it appears that this sending is the purpose and goal of both her being gathered and upbuilt. Both of these movements position the members of the community in relation to her sending. It is *for this* that they live in discipleship to Jesus Christ and are called into his service. In this One, God is there for the world, and it is this One that the believers are to follow. For Barth, the word of Jesus is decisive: "You are the salt of the earth."[28] The word connects the two sides of this movement: on the one hand, salt becomes useless if it loses its saltiness; on the other hand, salt is useless if it only exists for itself. In Barth's words, the call "out of the world" resists the secularization of the community and the call "into the world" stands against her sacralization.[29] That the community exists ec-centrically means that the center around which she moves is not the world as such, "but the world for which God is." As she lives "*for* God," so she lives "for the *world*."[30] She does not live in conformity to the regulations of the world. Christians must know that they are to live in the world as "aliens and exiles" (1 Pet. 2:11).[31] As Christians they live only as they are bound to the directive of their one master. But so bound to him, they do not live in isolation from the contemporary world. It needs to be taken with upmost seriousness that the community's "most inward being has an irresistible impulse towards that which is without, [her] proper being towards that which is alien . . . [she] exists as [she] is pledged to the one Jesus Christ and therefore basically and without reservation to the *world*."[32]

So the community continuously needs her gathering in order to be strengthened through the power of the Gospel and its directive. This is why worship is essential for a community as a pause for breath in her being sent. But the world is already unmistakably present in her worship, especially in the intercession and offering. In this regard, the benediction at the conclusion of worship should not be understood as a *dismissal* of a now completed holy activity, but as a word of *sending* to the whole church as ambassadors of

Christ to their daily environment. For the church is such a "missional community."[33] In her being sent, the priority of God as seen in Jesus Christ's own
existence before the world determines the kind of existence the Christian
community is to have for the world. It is the way of *solidarity*, and so neither
domination nor conformity.[34] Solidarity works in such a way that Christians
always look first to those at the very underside of society—as suggested by
the title of Gilbert Cesbron's book: *Les saints vont en enfer* [*Saints go to
Hell*].[35]

For what purpose will different Christians be used when they are sent out
as missionaries from Sunday worship under the blessing of the Lord? The
Second Vatican Council dealt also with this question and answered that there
were two categories of offices: on the one hand, there is the ecclesiastical
hierarchy; on the other, there are those who, according to Paul, have been
given one of the several charisms. Barth rejected this doctrine because, according to Romans 12 and 1 Corinthians 12, there are *only* different *charisms*
in the community.[36] The ecclesiastical offices in the churches are themselves
charisms of the one body of Christ lest they fail their calling. For Barth,
special offices do indeed exist *in* the community, but none which stand *above*
her. While there are different tasks in the community these are not to be
carried out by one person alone, nor according to Paul, are they to be gov-
erned by one person alone.

THE SITUATION OF THE CHURCHES IN
THEIR ENVIRONMENT IN CENTRAL EUROPE

The situation in which Christians are being sent out is always a particular one
and is different in different times and places. In terms of the message's
orientation, it is necessary to take into account *to whom* it is addressed so that
it does not talk past her or him, but also so that it does not lead to incorrect or
excessive adaptations. Precisely as "salt," which according to Matthew 15:3
is what the followers of Jesus must be, it must not become "stupid," that is,
fail to speak in an intelligible way, but it must also not lose its saltiness in
this process.[37]

The following comments are addressed to the context of central Europe.
To a noticeable degree one can no longer take for granted that people belong
to a church. In recent years, church membership has declined in a considerable way and especially so in the cities. But it is also true that churches in
rural areas are being closed and manses sold. Theological faculties today
assume that the focus of their work is no longer the equipping of future
pastors and so have turned to the study of religion. Despite this decline in
membership, however, representatives of the church leadership still talk of
leading the *Volkskirche*—a word that conveys the impression that the people

as a whole belong to this institution. This process—reminiscent of the play "Happy Days" where a woman progressively sinks into the ground while asking her audience "isn't today a happy day?"[38]—Karl Barth examined in his 1935 essay "Das Evangelium in der Gegenwart."[39] It makes no difference whether one understands the traditional conjunction of the Christian faith with the powers of the old age as a fiction that is dangerous for both sides or as a divine sign of blessing: in either case, this time is doomed to pass. The time is now for Christianity to stand on its own feet over against the rest of the world, not being indifferent toward the problems of this world, but not being submissively dependent upon it either. This would also mean that Christianity would have to part with all kinds of privileges in order to be a light in the world in a new way.

But in which direction would a society emancipated from all churchdom move? Dietrich Bonhoeffer assumed in his prison letters that "[w]e are approaching a completely religionless age; people as they are now simply cannot be religious anymore."[40] Was he wrong? People in their daily activities, in truth, do not behave religiously. And yet, it appears that today a new religious wave has washed over the breadth of humanity. We encounter a multifaceted religious interest that can use Christian words but can easily do without any Christian knowledge. One learns in the media two times more about Far Eastern religions than about the Gospel of Jesus. In 1872, David Friedrich Strauß observed, in telling fashion, that though we are not Christian, we are still religious.[41] Some people today say that what one believes is a matter that one decides for oneself. Furthermore, one expects church officials to confirm this approach to believing.

Was this also Karl Barth's point when he described the human as being religious by nature, and noted that even as a modern human being one is unable to free oneself from religion? Even Christianity as it exists is not free from this! In 1963, Barth stated that it would be evil should one claim that people do not *need* to be freed from this at all. "The worst sin of (Christian) theology happened . . . when it began to understand itself as 'the science of religion.'"[42] That the human *must* be freed and *can* be freed is something which he or she realizes first only when *being* freed from it. This happens because God, for God's part, turns to the human. For we have to deal with God alone, where God approaches the human. This is something to which the Holy Scriptures of both testaments testify: "In distinction, yes in contrast to all religions" it is not about "the human's movement towards God but about God's movement towards the human."[43]

And what shall the church do in light of the declining numbers of church members? This question occupies much church leadership and, to this end, one encounters astonishing suggestions. A single individual congregation should include at least one thousand seven hundred members lest it be fused together with as many other congregations as necessary to reach this limit. A regional synod should have at least one million registered members lest they be fused with other synods until this number is attained. In this way one counts oneself to still be a "people's church" after all. This, in turn, sets the name of the game for the church: a church must be willing to grow. Does mission therefore mean that "the church," meaning here the pastorate, gives to the people what they wish because the ministers are, after all, being paid by them? In fact, one can hear the following thesis forwarded: "The church" should assume the form of a rich department store in competition with similar sized companies, one in which people get all that their heart desires. In that way the church would be in demand again. And what the people (really) want is an offer of liturgies for special occasions, and, where possible, ones which follow the individual's own line of interpretation.[44]

It should be assumed, however, that this calculation will not work because you are doing the math without the host. When it says in John 6 that many disciples turned away from Jesus, what did Jesus say to the remaining twelve? Probably not what one might expect a manager of the church to say: "At least you have remained! We will set up an advertising agency." Instead the savior of all humanity asks: "Do you not want to go away as well?" This freedom of Jesus, the freedom from numbers, is unheard of! In reply to Jesus's question, Peter says what is self-evident to all the others: "You have words of eternal life." The oppressed Huguenots of seventeenth-century France, who could only gather together in a forest hideaway for worship, carried as their identifying mark a coin with the message from Luke 12:32: "Fear not, little flock."

In his final lecture Barth noted that how difficult it is for Christians to be in the minority because God in Christ reconciles the *world* to Godself. But now a Christian lives as a "lonely bird on the housetop," one "constantly exposed to the danger of being shot down by the first comer"—to use the imagery of Psalm 102:8.[45] Barth even thought that under these circumstances the Christian community could live outside "baptized and confirmed humanity."[46] The community as well as the work of theology "will not be ashamed of the solitude in which the community of the last days finds itself placed by the execution of its missionary charge."[47] She should not escape this solitude by chasing after popularity nor by becoming desperate, bitter, or skeptical.[48] Barth concludes that the community has "to endure and bear her loneliness with dignity and cheerfulness."[49]

CHURCH IN RENEWAL

The possible end of the so-called "Christian West" will not be the end of the Christian church. Karl Barth after the World Council of Churches' Assembly in Amsterdam referred to the image first developed by Martin Luther: "that a general cessation of the 'driving downpour' of the word of God here in Europe would now only mean that for a while it had moved somewhere else."[50] Our spreading would then be dependent on the missionizing activity from there, outside of Europe. Our churches would then be different, but they would not be gone from here. This is not a sentence of historical probability, nor a sentence that follows from earlier cultural and otherwise spiritual achievements of the church. Such an approach would mean that the church could provide for her own preservation. This is a sentence rightfully spoken in the faith in him who promised his own that "I am with you always, even to the end of the age" (Matt. 28: 20).

This does not lead the church to laziness. She has something to do. In the first place she has always ever anew *to listen* to her Lord. Karl Barth understood the word *aggionamento*, as coined by Pope Johannes XXIII, in this sense: not primarily as a new adaptation to a new time, but as a new listening to the voice of her Lord in the testimony of the Holy Scriptures.[51] He understood the old formula of *ecclesia reformata semper reformanda* [the church reformed, always reforming] in the same way. Christianity has to learn anew on a case-by-case basis first to listen anew to the Holy Scriptures. She will then learn on a case-by-case basis that it is first the living *God* who renews the church through God's Spirit.

The one who listens right will act right. The renewing acting of God also calls us to action. And there is much to do. *CD* IV/3 notes twelve "ministries of the church."[52] In the first place, perhaps astonishingly for many people, Barth sets the praise of God sung together by the congregation. This would have pleased Calvin. Next comes the sermon, through which the church reminds herself of the witness entrusted to her and is once again equipped for ministry in the world. Among the activities of the community, again perhaps surprisingly for many, Barth names prayer as the basic element of the whole activity of the whole community.[53] This was the central idea of his planned ethics of reconciliation: *Ora et labora* [prayer and work] belong inseparably together. Of the further ministries, Barth refers to diaconal service, the wider social offering of physical and psychological help to suffering people. He also mentions here concern for the coexistence of people in view of the interaction of races, from close and afar, which is an ever-increasing need today. In these tasks he distinguishes between evangelism and mission. Mission is addressed to nonbelievers and evangelization to members of the church who are passive, sleeping members who are especially to be addressed because they think of themselves as Christians. This distinction is important because such passive members are to be built up for their service to the nonbeliever.

Of the different tasks to be considered, when dealing with people in mission, Christians must continuously learn how to make themselves *comprehensible* to others. Barth understood this early on when he trained workers and socialists estranged from the church in *solidarity* in his church. According to Friedrich Wilhelm Marquardt, Barth brought the word solidarity from the socialist movement and introduced it to theological discourse.[54] In my own witness to the Gospel I certainly cannot force others to listen to it—nor should I intend this, knowing the problems involved in my own speaking and acting, and knowing that others in their non-Christian state could show me a new light. Either way, in witnessing to the Gospel I have to adapt myself to others on a case-by-case basis. There is no temptation to a positivism of revelation, as Dietrich Bonhoeffer feared with Barth.[55] The Gospel is to be translated into the life context of others.

Barth says this in his 1947 lecture in the ruins of the University of Bonn: the Christian message

> must be fundamentally translatable into the speech of Mr. Everyman, the man and woman in the street, into the language of those who are not accustomed to reading Scripture and singing hymns, but who possess a quite different vocabulary and quite different spheres of interest. . . . The Christian Confession in its original Church form will always be exposed to the misunderstanding that the Christian regards the Creed as a matter of heart and conscience, but that here on earth and in the world other truths hold good. The world lives in this misunderstanding; it regards the whole of Christianity as a friendly "magic," connected with the "realm of religion," which is respected and which ought to be left untampered with; and so we get rid of the matter. But this misunderstanding might even come from within; a Christian might quite well wish to have this realm for himself and to guard faith like a sensitive plant. . . . By the very nature of the Christian Church there is only one task, to make the Confession heard in the sphere of the world as well. Not now repeated in the language of Canaan, but in the quite sober, quite unedifying language which is spoken "out there." . . . If a man cannot, let him consider whether he really knows how to speak edifyingly even in the Church.[56]

In this dealing with the other, Karl Barth warns that there are always two dangers to avoid in mission. And one should watch out: *Incidit in Scyllam, qui vult vitare Charybdim* (One falls into Scylla in trying to escape Charybdis)! *On the one hand*, one has to learn anew that the others are already in God's hand, even when *they* and even when *we* ourselves do not notice this. But we *should* notice it. In the midst of the world, Christianity hopefully *listens* to this Lord. However, certainly not only Christianity *belongs* to God but "[e]ven the world without, which seems to be and is so very different, belongs to [God]."[57] That the world outside of the Christian community already belongs to Christ, even if she does not know it, removes the *fear* of humanity from Christians, and, at the same, removes the desire to coerce this humanity when they turn to them as missionaries.

On the other hand, by believing that God already loves the people of this world we are not released from our responsibility to testify to them of God's love: speaking, listening, silent, acting, contradictory, reconciling, and taking sides. God's gift and our responsibility are to be distinguished. *Our* giving witness happens within the limitation that Christians cannot do what God alone accomplishes. They can *only* witness to it. Above all, they *themselves* have to do first what non-Christians have to do: they *themselves* always have to turn back to the One to whom the others also have to turn. Barth agrees here with Franz Rosenzweig: Christianity has the task of mission among the nonbelievers so that they convert, but she always must first be converted herself. Darrell Guder entitled his missiological text: *The Continuing Conversion of the Church.*[58]

In this way, according to Barth, Christians have to avoid a double danger. *On the one hand*, the danger of *neglecting* one's fellow human beings. Above all, this danger is that one can forget that it is essential for the Christian to communicate the Gospel with others, not from the top down, but in a way that they exist with them—in coexistence, in dialogue, not just speaking *to* them but *with* them. For "to begin again at the beginning" means, together with the other, relearning for oneself what God is telling us. A Christianity without the contemporary world is in mortal danger.[59]

On the other hand, Christians ought not to *patronize* their fellow human beings. This happens where the other becomes the material for the Christian's own art, where one approaches them in a know-it-all-manner and with a picture they have already made of the other.[60] "Patronization means the human exercise of power by people towards other people as though they were objects."[61] This becomes obsolete. If God in his incarnate Word is also present in a hidden way in religions before their followers recognize him, then Christians have to be open to the fact that he does not *only* have to be hidden from them. Barth concludes that "[a] witness will not intrude on [her or his] neighbor. . . . Witness can be given only when there is respect for the freedom of the grace of God, and therefore respect for the other [person] who can expect nothing from me but everything from God."[62]

NOTES

1. Franz Rosenzweig, "Atheistic Theology: From the Old to the New Way of Thinking," *Canadian Journal of Theology* 14, no. 2 (1968): 85.

2. Rosenzweig, 87, 85.

3. Rosenzweig, 88.

4. *CD* IV/3.2, 583; *KD* IV/3.2, 669. Revised translation.

5. *CD* IV/3.2, 826; *KD* IV/3.2, 946. Revised translation.

6. Darrell L. Guder, *Called to Witness: Doing Missional Theology* (Grand Rapids, MI: Eerdmans, 2015), 24–43.

7. *CD* IV/4, 96–97; *KD* IV/4, 106. Revised translation.

8. Hans Prolingheuer, *Der Fall Karl Barth, 1934–1935: Chronographie einer Vertreibung* (Neukirchen: Neukirchener Verlag, 1977), 41.

9. David J. Bosch, *Transforming Mission: Paradigm Shifts in Theology of Mission* (Maryknoll, NY: Orbis Books, 1991), 377.

10. *CD* IV/3.2, 767; *KD* IV/3.2, 877. Revised translation.

11. *CD* IV/3.2, 795–96; *KD* IV/3.2, 910. Revised translation.

12. *CD* IV/3.2, 762; *KD* IV/3.2, 872. Revised translation.

13. *CD* IV/4, 200; *KD* IV/4, 219. Revised translation.

14. *CD* IV/4, 37; *KD* IV/4, 41.

15. J. E. Lesslie Newbigin, *The Household of God: Lectures on the Nature of the Church* (London: SCM Press, 1953), 20.

16. "Dogmatic Constitution on the Church, *Lumen Gentium* (LG)," in *Vatican Council II: The Conciliar and Post Conciliar Documents*, ed. Austin Flannery (Northport, NY: Costello, 1996), 360–64, §10–12.

17. *Kirche der Freiheit: Perspektiven für die Evangelische Kirche im 21. Jahrhundert,* Ein Impulspapier des Rates der EKD, 2006, 54, accessed 19 June, 2018, https://www.ekd.de /ekd_de/ds_doc/kirche-der-freiheit.pdf.

18. Martin Luther, *Ausgewählte Werke* (München: Evangelischer Verlag Albert Lempp, 1948), 193.

19. Jean Calvin, *Institutes of the Christian Religion* (Louisville, KY: Westminster John Knox Press, 1960), 1289.

20. *CD* IV/4, 85; *KD* IV/4, 93.

21. *CD* IV/4, 201; *KD* IV/4, 221.

22. *CD* IV/4, 95, 100; *KD* IV/4, 104, 110.

23. *CD* IV/4, 201; *KD* IV/4, 221. Revised Translation.

24. *CD* IV/4, 201; *KD* IV/4, 221.

25. See *CD* IV/1, 157ff. *KD* IV/1, 171ff.

26. Guder, *Called to Witness*, 58.

27. *CD* IV/3.2, 764; *KD* IV/3.2, 874. Revised Translation.

28. *CD* IV/3.2, 763; *KD* IV/3.2, 873.

29. *CD* IV/2, 668; *KD* IV/2, 756.

30. *CD* IV/3.2, 762f; *KD* IV/3.2, 872f.

31. Guder, *Called to Witness*, 82.

32. *CD* IV/3.2, 789; *KD* IV/3.2, 903.

33. See Guder, *Called to Witness*, 63–77.

34. *CD* IV/3.2, 773; *KD* IV/3.2, 884.

35. Gilbert Cesbron, *Les Saints vont en enfer* (Paris: Robert Laffont, 1952). See, *CD* IV/3.2, 774; *KD* IV/3.2, 886.

36. Eberhard Busch, *Meine Zeit mit Karl Barth: Tagebuch 1965–1968* (Göttingen: Vandenhoeck & Ruprecht, 2011), 498 (November 4, 1967).

37. Editor's note: the word "dumm" here translated "stupid" is found within the 1912 Luther translation of Matt. 5:13.

38. Samuel Beckett, "Happy Days," in *The Complete Dramatic Works of Samuel Beckett* (London: Faber & Faber, 2006), 135–68.

39. Karl Barth, "Das Evangelium in der Gegenwart," *Theologische Existenz heute* 25 (1935): 18–36.

40. Dietrich Bonhoeffer, *Letters and Papers from Prison* (Fortress Press, 2010), 362.

41. David Friedrich Strauß, *Der alte und der neue Glaube: Ein Bekenntniß* (Leipzig: 1872), 141.

42. Karl Barth, "Das Christentum und die Religion," *Kirchenblatt für die reformierte Schweiz* 119, no. 12 (1963): 181–83.

43. Barth, 181–83.

44. See Karl-Wilhelm Dahm, *Beruf: Pfarrer. Empirische Aspekte zur Funktion von Kirche und Religion in unserer Gesellschaft* (München: Claudius, 1972).

45. Karl Barth, *Evangelical Theology: An Introduction*, trans. Grover Foley (London: Fontana Library, 1965), 119.

46. Barth, "Das Evangelium in der Gegenwart," 25, 35.

47. Barth, *Evangelical Theology*, 115.

48. Barth, 119.
49. Barth, 111.
50. Eberhard Busch, *Karl Barth: His Life from Letters and Autobiographical Texts* (Grand Rapids, MI: Eerdmans, 1994), 359.
51. Busch, 495, 247.
52. *CD* IV/3.2, 865–901; *KD* IV/3.2, 991–1034.
53. *CD* IV/3.2, 883; *KD* IV/3.2, 1012.
54. Friedrich-Wilhelm Marquardt, *Theologie und Sozialismus: Das Beispiel Karl Barths* (München: Chr. Kaiser, 1985), 87.
55. Busch, *Meine Zeit mit Karl Barth*, 326.
56. Karl Barth, *Dogmatics in Outline*, trans. George T. Thomson (New York: Philosophical Library, 1949), 32–33.
57. *CD* IV/3.2, 686; *KD* IV/3.2, 785.
58. Darrell L. Guder, *The Continuing Conversion of the Church* (Grand Rapids, MI: Eerdmans, 2000). The above text owes much to conversations with this missiologist. See also Darrell L. Guder, *Be My Witnesses: The Church's Mission, Message, and Messengers* (Grand Rapids, MI: Eerdmans, 1985); Darrell L. Guder, ed. *Missional Church: A Vision for the Sending of the Church in North America* (Grand Rapids, MI: Eerdmans, 1998).
59. *CD* IV/3.2, 827; *KD* IV/3.2, 947.
60. *CD* IV/3.2, 828; *KD* IV/3.2, 948.
61. *CD* IV/3.2, 829; *KD* IV/3.2, 950. Revised Translation.
62. *CD* I/2, 441.

BIBLIOGRAPHY

Barth, Karl. "Das Christentum und die Religion." *Kirchenblatt für die reformierte Schweiz* 119, no. 12 (1963): 181–83.

———. *The Doctrine of Reconciliation IV/1*. Edinburgh: T&T Clark, 1956.

———. *The Doctrine of Reconciliation IV/3.2*. Edinburgh: T&T Clark, 1962.

———. *The Doctrine of Reconciliation IV/4*. Edinburgh: T&T Clark, 1969.

———. *Dogmatics in Outline*. Translated by George T. Thomson. New York: Philosophical Library, 1949.

———. *Evangelical Theology: An Introduction*. Translated by Grover Foley. London: Fontana Library, 1965.

Beckett, Samuel. "Happy Days," in *The Complete Dramatic Works of Samuel Beckett,* 135–68. London: Faber & Faber, 2006.

Bonhoeffer, Dietrich. *Letters and Papers from Prison*. Fortress Press, 2010.

Bosch, David J. *Transforming Mission: Paradigm Shifts in Theology of Mission*. Maryknoll, NY: Orbis Books, 1991.

Busch, Eberhard. *Karl Barth: His Life from Letters and Autobiographical Texts*. Grand Rapids, MI: Eerdmans, 1994.

———. *Meine Zeit mit Karl Barth: Tagebuch 1965–1968*. Göttingen: Vandenhoeck & Ruprecht, 2011.

Calvin, Jean. *Institutes of the Christian Religion*. Louisville, KY: Westminster John Knox Press, 1960.

Cesbron, Gilbert. *Les Saints vont en enfer*. Paris: Robert Laffont, 1952.

Dahm, Karl-Wilhelm. *Beruf: Pfarrer; Empirische Aspekte zur Funktion von Kirche und Religion in unserer Gesellschaft*. München: Claudius, 1972.

"Dogmatic Constitution on the Church, *Lumen Gentium* (LG)," in *Vatican Council II: The Conciliar and Post Conciliar Documents*, edited by Austin Flannery, 350–426. Northport, NY: Costello, 1996.

Guder, Darrell L. *Be My Witnesses: The Church's Mission, Message, and Messengers*. Grand Rapids, MI: Eerdmans, 1985.

———. *Called to Witness: Doing Missional Theology*. Grand Rapids, MI: Eerdmans, 2015.

———. *The Continuing Conversion of the Church*. Grand Rapids, MI: Eerdmans, 2000.

————, ed. *Missional Church: A Vision for the Sending of the Church in North America* Grand Rapids, MI: Eerdmans, 1998.

Luther, Martin. *Ausgewählte Werke*. München: Evangelischer Verlag Albert Lempp, 1948.

Marquardt, Friedrich-Wilhelm. *Theologie und Sozialismus: Das Beispiel Karl Barths.* München: Chr. Kaiser, 1985.

Newbigin, J. E. Lesslie. *The Household of God: Lectures on the Nature of the Church.* London: SCM Press, 1953.

Prolingheuer, Hans. *Der Fall Karl Barth, 1934–1935: Chronographie einer Vertreibung.* Neukirchen-Vluyn: Neukirchener Verlag, 1977.

Rosenzweig, Franz. "Atheistic Theology: From the Old to the New Way of Thinking." *Canadian Journal of Theology* 14, no. 2 (1968): 79–88.

Strauß, David Friedrich. *Der alte und der neue Glaube: Ein Bekenntniß*. Leipzig: 1872.

Chapter Four

European Christianity Put to the Test

Observations Concerning the Use of the Term
"Christendom" in the Study of World Christianity

Christine Lienemann-Perrin

An observed shift of gravity of Christianity from the global North to the global South has come to dominate much missiological discussion. [1] It is also common for this discussion's interlocutors to distance themselves from the reality of Christianity in European history and present using the negatively connoted word "Christendom." The various academic titles with some formulation of "beyond/after/post Christendom" illustrate well both the negative appropriation of the term and its commonality. [2] In most of these publications, "Christendom" is juxtaposed to "Christianity" or "World Christianity." By way of example, Andrew Walls writes: "Christendom is dead, and Christianity is alive and well without it." [3] Another common juxtaposition is that of a "Post-Christian West" against a "non-Western Church." [4]

The Christendom/Christianity contrast is understood to mirror the southward shift of the majority of believers in World Christianity. [5] Usually, the term Christendom encapsulates those aspects considered to be aberrations with the history and present form of Christianity. Its historical roots are identified with the medieval idea of *christianitas* or *cristendome* and is manifested in its purest form in the European history of Christianity. This strong farewell addressed to the legacy of European Christian provides ample reason to give careful investigation to the included criticisms: in what respect and to what degree is such a stance necessary, justified, exaggerated, or untenable? The question is an important one, not the least because the term "Christendom" is itself a problem at a basic linguistic, semantic, and semiotic level: there exist no exact equivalents to the predominantly critical, if not polemic, undertones common in the Anglophone use of the word "Christendom" in other languages. Danish uses *Christendom* and *Kristendom* to express the true Christian faith and *Urkristendommen* to indicate the Apostolic Age. The Danish philosopher, theologian, and poet, Søren Kierkegaard, used *Christendom* in that sense and contrasted it with the state church of his time in Denmark (*Christenhed*), which in his view was a stumbling block for the access to the true faith in Jesus Christ. The German translation of "Christianity" is *Christentum*, but is subject to further differentiation: the word *Christenheit* can be used for "the people worldwide sharing the Christian faith" and this is distinguished from *Christentum* as a societal religious entity, including its doctrines, liturgies, and life styles.[6] It is obvious that these linguistic problems contribute to theological confusions concerning how one might today perceive European Christianity and its role in contemporary and future World Christianity. At stake is a significant ecumenical question: Are the past and present forms of the church and theological reflection in Europe meaningless for shaping the future of World Christianity, an assumption that has been evident within mission scholarship in the Global South and North America for quite some time?

How did this negative understanding of the term Christendom emerge in missiology? To answer this question, this chapter begins with a simple comparison of how the term is used in the period leading to the first World Mission Conference in Edinburgh 1910 and how it appears now, a century later, which illustrates the significant change in its meaning. For the architects of the World Missionary Conference in Edinburgh 1910, Christendom referred to an idealized understanding of European and North American Christianity, one properly contrasted not only to "Heathendom" but also to the small mission churches and ancient orthodox churches in the midst of "heathen lands." Second, mission scholars in the global South and North America trace the word Christendom back to the medieval concept of *christianitas/cristendome* and the presumed historical reality of a territorial, political, religious, and linguistic unity in Latin Europe. However, as recently demonstrated by medievalists, that interpretation is highly questionable. Third, to overcome the stalemate in missiological discourse it is time to explore new ways beyond the Christendom/post-Christendom binary. As one example of the problem, the text compares the criticisms of *Christendom* by Kwame Bediako (Ghana) and *verbürgerlichtes Christentum* by Karl Barth (Switzerland). Both share common theological concerns, but do so from different perspectives. Forth, this comparison encourages a new cross-continental and cross-lingual conversation, one that might enlarge the space of global missiological discourse.

CHANGES IN THE MEANING OF THE TERM *CHRISTENDOM*: A COMPARISON OF THE DISCOURSES SHAPING EDINBURGH 1910 AND MISSION STUDIES IN 2010

The pejorative meaning attributed to the word "Christendom" in many studies on World Christianity is in stark contrast to the affirmative and normative usage widespread in the realm of missions and missiology at the beginning of the twentieth century. Around 1900, 82 percent of all Christians worldwide lived in Europe and North America, while the remaining 18 percent inhabited Latin America, Africa, Asia, and Oceania.[7] Most churches living in the global South existed as small minorities in societies with majorities adhering to other religions. As one clear effect, these minorities churches were rarely recognized as distinct voices in their own right at the World Missionary Conference held in Edinburgh in 1910.[8] Unlike today, the term used as a contrast to Christendom was not (World) Christianity but "Heathendom."

The Christendom-Heathendom contrast played an eminent role during the years prior to the conference, and the final decision concerning the conference's format developed between divergent options. Planned as an ecumenical endeavor of the Protestant and Anglican churches and mission agencies, it risked being interpreted by Catholics and Orthodox churches as a hostile act of proselytism. To prevent such allegation, the representatives of Anglo-Catholicism in Britain proposed as the conference's theme: "Carrying the Gospel to All the *Non-Christian* World." That title was chosen against the original plan to dedicate the conference to the much broader theme of "Carrying the Gospel to *All* the World." This original proposal would have anticipated the phrase that became popular in the 1960s: "mission in six continents." This decision, taken with the intent not to damage relationships between neighbor churches in the global North, turned out to aggravate—maybe unintentionally—the gap between the "ecumenically" minded churches or mission agencies in the North and the churches in the global South. As a result, most of the conference debates were driven by the implicit premise that "mission from Christendom to Heathendom" was the challenge of the time.

Ironically, the final decision caused another problem: How might one define the realm of Christendom as distinguished from Heathendom, and where might one draw the line between the two? How might one classify territories where small Christian communities lived side by side with non-Christian neighbors? The dualist opposition of Christendom and Heathendom was simply assumed. This provided no space to develop a further category reliant on a notion of mixed territories. Heathendom indicated all those countries and regions whose habitants had not yet been fully evangelized. Likewise, it was undisputed that Europe embodied Christendom in its purest form, followed by the Christendom of North America. But, related to this is the question of how far "Europe" might extend East and South, and where bordered it with non-European Heathen lands?[9] Opinions about those questions diverged significantly. Geographical, historical, and qualitative arguments were brought forward to draw the lines. One opinion held that Europe ended where it bordered the Western parts of the Ottoman Empire and where Christians had lived for centuries as minorities among Muslim majorities. Whether the Orthodox parts of Eastern Europe should be regarded as part of Christendom or attributed to Heathendom remained a point of debate.[10] Even North America caused quite a headache. While the states that were founded by European settlers on the East Coast were regarded as reliable Christendom-territory, it was different with regions farther West, where Christian settlers lived side by side with First Nations who were either not yet evangelized or who were not yet considered to be fully Christianized.[11] In territories that had been missionized centuries ago, uncertainties about the classification were obvious as well. Some inclined to classify Brazil more as Christian, Goa more as Heathen.[12] In the years preparing the Edinburgh Conference, the opinion makers developed a set of implicit terms for defining Christendom: the unity of Christian faith, civilization, and culture in one specific territory, the unity of citizenship and church membership, the rootedness of Christian thinking in the European history of ideas, and the mature tradition of Christian teaching. Last but not least, sufficient financial and personal resources to missionize in heathen lands emerged as essential requirements for deserving the label Christendom.

In fact, the allocating of geographical areas to the territories of either Christendom or Heathendom was a side effect of more practical and strategic concern: which mission societies and churches involved in foreign mission should be invited to the first World Missionary Conference? This question propelled an investigation into the global missionary endeavor. The driving concern focused on deciding which regions should be included in such statistics and which might be ignored. The statistical question developed in pragmatic terms and without consideration of the implicit missional and ecclesiological aspects. Christendom served as the norm-giving center of Christianity. By contrast, the local churches which had emerged from Western foreign missions in Asia, Africa, and Latin America were classified as not yet sufficiently settled in doctrine and practice. It was presumed that those Christian communities remained weak due to the constant threat posed by non-European or non-Western religions, beliefs, and cultures. The fact that independent movements of native Christians rose and separated themselves from the established mission churches in the global South confirmed the missionary's suspicion that they were renegades on their way back to Heathendom.

The World Missionary Conference in Edinburgh marked the climax of a triumphalist concept of Christendom—but also its turning point. One of the delegates from Japan, Harada Tasuku (1863–1940), said that the European Christendom represented only insufficiently the body of Christ. For that reason, it should be complemented and enriched by Asian, African, and many other ways of being church in the South.[13] Those churches, Tasuku said, can give room for other facets of the Christian faith because they have incorporated the cultural-religious legacy of their societies. Some Americans and Europeans made critical comments against the evident Christendom-centrism, not only during the conference, but also in the decades before 1910 and increasingly afterwards.[14] Commission VI on *The Home Base of Missions* deplored the lack of missionary spirit in Christendom, and enlisted the Moravian Church as an ideal missionary church.[15] "Christendom is not yet missionary. . . . [T]he Church of the living God must arise as a great Missionary Society," stated W. H. T. Gairdner in his account of the conference,[16] and he called for taking "every phase of western Christian life in detail, and bring home to it . . . the *Moravian ideal.*"[17] Substantial doubts regarding the integrity of Christendom grew after the shock of the First World War. According to Joseph Oldham, one of the architects of the Edinburgh Conference, Christendom had discredited itself in a most damaging way. "Oldham looked back at 1910, and reflected that what had since changed was not so much the fracture of Christendom as the dissolution of the very notion."[18]

Christendom-centered criticism should be seen in context of the Western missionary movement around the turn of the nineteenth century. Such criticism can furthermore be traced back to the Wesleyan and Baptist identification of Christendom with state church Christianity, namely with churches supported by—and dependent on—the state. In contrast to "state churches," the "free church" model was perceived as a return to the authentic roots of Christian faith. For Helen Barrett Montgomery (1861–1934), the connection between the Baptist tradition, the missionary spirit, and the Edinburgh Conference was obvious.[19] In her book, *Western Women in Eastern Lands* (1910), she accused Christendom in the Western world of being perverted: "in Christendom, we have white-slave trade, the red-light district, and other hateful and debasing traffics of womanhood."[20] According to her, Western civilization was disconnected from the Gospel and had negative effects on the societies in the non-Western world.[21]

To sum up: at the beginning of the twentieth century, Christendom was a given concept in missionary discourse, though one can find mounting criticisms against it, especially in the assumption of its Christian nature. As a positive concept, it marginalized the churches in the global South, characterizing them either as misguided doctrinally and ecclesiastically or as irrelevant for the explication of the Christian faith and hence defined as being under the influence of—or belonging to—the realm of heathendom. Indirectly, the missionary conference intimated to the churches in the South that they were not fully-fledged parts of the ecumenical movement in the twentieth century.

There is no space here to recall the discussion by which Christendom ceased to be a positive concept through the twentieth century.[22] One hundred years later, only 38 percent of all Christians worldwide live in Europe and North America, compared with 62 percent living in all other regions of the globe. The self-confidence of ordinary Christians and particularly of theologians in the South has grown, even as church attendance and church membership has declined in the global North. The inversion of the numerical proportion and statistical weight stimulates, on the one hand, a fundamental critique of the concept and practice of Christendom. On the other hand, has encouraged a significant turn in Christian historiography: the focus has shifted away from Eurocentric church history to the history of World Christianity. Among the pioneers of that turn are theologians living in, or originating from, the global South and practitioners and theorists of foreign mission from the global North with long-term experiences in "their" mission fields. Andrew Walls's life journey is one of several examples. In the course of his commitment as a missionary in West Africa he distanced himself from his Western identity, criticizing what he perceives now as the demise of Western Christianity. In the same breath, he identifies with non-Western, mainly African, forms of Christianity. Walls, Lamin Sanneh, Jehu J. Hanciles, and others see Christianity becoming a non-Western religion.[23] According to them, Europe represents the post-Christian West more so than North America because here immigrants from Latin America, Asia, and other world regions have helped significantly to introduce and establish non-Western forms of Christianity. Critics forecast that secularism and its marks—for example, the privatization of religion, decline in church membership, and moral individualization—will continue to degrade Western Christendom. By contrast, the aspects of vitality, growth, and dynamism are taken as self-evident within non-Western Christianity. According to Hanciles, Christendom is bankrupt both, as idea and as reality.[24] He is convinced that if against all expectations, Europe might have a Christian future, it would do so only thanks to the migrant churches emerging in the West and which refuse to Westernize themselves.[25]

IS "CHRISTENDOM" A CONCEPT ROOTED IN EUROPE'S MEDIEVAL PERIOD?

Philip Jenkins opines that "Christendom" is not used in colloquial English today.[26] Rather it is an archaic term used only in intellectual circles. English speaking historians refer to it in a neutral sense in relation to medieval times. An idealized and normatively connoted meaning of the word Christendom was introduced by theologians, philosophers, and poets much later in the

European history. For some, the medieval period came to represent an ideal time and set this in contrast to the present, which they perceived as in a state of moral, cultural, and religious decline. In fact, the "Christendom" (Latin: *christianitas*) as a settled concept developed not in the Middle Ages, but in the European modern age. To give one example, Novalis (1772–1801) regarded the French Revolution and the Napoleonic wars as catastrophic and irreligious events. Against this trauma, he posited a political utopia rooted in the Middle Ages. In a cultural-historical essay titled *Die Christenheit oder Europa* (1799), he imagined a regenerated Europe, based on the renewed *Christenheit* and its capacity to bring about unity and freedom.[27] In the twentieth century, Pope Benedict XV, shocked by the First World War, called the church to bring the European nations back to their lost unity. His perception of medieval Christianity served as an alternate model to the fragmented, damaged, and disoriented society of his time.[28]

The same argument recurs repeatedly in the history of European Christianity: against a deteriorating present stands a possibility of transformation constructed out of an idealized past. Extremely critical diagnoses of Christianity in Europe occur frequently. In the 1850s, Søren Kierkegaard (1813–1855) accused *Christenhed* of becoming an obstacle barring the access to Jesus Christ. In his essay *Indøvelse I Christendom* (1850),[29] Kierkegaard uses the term *Christendom* or *Kristendom* in an affirmative way as *imitatio* Christi and modelled in the New Testament. What Kierkegaard explains as "practice" or "training" (*Indøvelse*) implies an explicit critique of the established order of the church as experienced by him in Denmark.[30]

Coming back to current Anglophone debates of Christendom in mission studies, these seem to be concerned with creating a theoretical space but display some distance from historical research. For Sanneh, the concept of Christendom is rooted historically in the early Middle Ages when the church was a domain of the state and the confession of faith was exploited for increasing political power.[31] In like manner, Walls understands that during the medieval period "territorial Christianity" came to mean the unity of territory, religion, political rule, Latin language, behavioral norm, and world view.[32] According to Hanciles, the concept of Christendom has been transmitted to—if not imposed on—the barbarian tribes at the geographical peripheries of Latin Europe. Later on, according to Hanciles, the concept was imposed on local churches in Africa, Asia, and Latin America by Western mission agencies.[33]

Medievalists would not affirm this position. Nora Berend (University of Cambridge, UK) and Tim Geelhaar (University of Frankfurt) are but two medievalists whose research studies the changing uses of the Latin term *christianitas*.[34] Thanks to a recently developed method of digitalization, Geelhaar has analyzed previously unavailable resources. He concludes that the prevailing ideas of medieval Europe, in general, and the idea and practice of medieval *christianitas*, in particular, require revision. From late Antiquity to the late medieval period, the term *christianitas*, occasionally translated as *cristendome* in the Middle English language, has undergone significant change in meaning, especially as it was adapted to particular religious and political aims and used by diverse actors for church politics, local and empire politics.[35] *Christianitas* could refer to Christianness, the Christian religion, Christian faith, to be a Christian, to administer the sacraments, power and jurisdiction of the church. *Christianitas* was also used as an honorary address for the kings of France. Last but not least, it referred either to the community of all Christians in Latin Europe or to Christianity of all nations worldwide.[36]

The usage of *christianitas* as the narrative expressing the unity of religion, territory, language, and political rule was only one of many others, neither the most frequent nor the predominate one. It was favored by popes and the highest representatives of the Holy Roman Empire. Political authorities of lower ranks used it strategically to pressure the pope in obtaining support when fighting against powers from outside Europe. The Hungarian king, Béla IV (1206–1270), tried to convince the pope in Rome that Mongolian attacks in 1241/1242 were not only threatening the Hungarian kingdom but also Europe and *christianitas* as a whole. In other respects, as for instance in economics and trade, Béla had no problems cooperating with the Mongols. He was not driven generally by the idea of a pan-European *christianitas* uniting religion, territory, language, and political rule.[37] As local rulers within Latin Europe tried to consolidate their power over against the political aspirations of other local rulers and against the religious center in Rome, their employment of the term *christianitas* suited disintegration and heterogeneity rather than the ideational and practical unity of a Christian Europe.

Another outcome of the research by medievalists is even more important. As Geelhaar demonstrated, middle and lower rank theologians used the term *christianitas* to distinguish the Christian faith, life, and liturgical rites from heresies, unsuitable accommodations to pagan cultures in the mission fields, and from mixing up Christian and non-Christian rituals. From late Antiquity to the late Middle Ages the discourses on *christianitas* reflect the struggle of maintaining continuity with the Early Church in face of the permanent changes of political, cultural, and religious circumstances. The perennial question concerned the innovations within the process of missionizing Europe and their relative adequacy to the Gospel. This is, to my mind, a genuinely ecumenical and missional concern and a proper deliberation concerning unity within legitimate diversity. In any case, Nora Berend, Tim Geelhaar, and other medievalists identify the outstanding mark of Latin Europe not in the homogenizing power of the Carolingian Empire and of the religious center in Rome, but rather in the political plurality in Europe manifested in many coexisting micro-Christianities. The idea of a territorial unity of Latin Europe—unified by religious and political powers—is misleading. I would like to go even a step further and say that critical self-examination with the intent of self-renewal was and remains one of the marks of European theology in late Antiquity, during the Middle Ages, in the centuries that followed during Modern Age, and to this present period.

"CHRISTENDOM" AND BOURGEOIS CHRISTIANITY PUT TO THE TEST: KWAME BEDIAKO'S AND KARL BARTH'S CRITICISMS COMPARED

The transmission and appropriation of the Gospel across cultural, linguistic, and contextual borders requires an ever-expanding and increasingly complex space of shared communication. The cultural-linguistic backgrounds of those who join that space become extremely diverse in terms of languages and the associated semantic rules and traditions. In extended theological communities, interlocutors use different languages, each with their own semiotics. Words that have a specific meaning in one local community living under particular circumstances have to be transposed into other communicative settings—or "semiotic systems" (Dietrich Ritschl).[38] That process is demanding, and all the more in regard to an ecumenical, multi-cultural, and multi-contextual community. Misunderstandings, equivocations, false allegations, and stereotypes are frequent and sometimes unavoidable. The southward shift of World Christianity has accelerated that challenge. A comparison of Kwame Bediako and Karl Barth, two theologians using different semiotic systems, may help illustrate some problems of translation and communication across cultural and linguistic diversities.

Both use different words for similar phenomena, namely, certain manifestations of Christianity in Europe, and criticize these phenomena in different ways. But one might question how close Bediako's (the younger of the two) own criticisms of Christendom were to those of Barth. When Barth died in 1968, Bediako (1945–2008) was only twenty-three years old. They never had a chance to meet and converse face to face. Since then, however, other theologians from Ghana, the United States, and Europe have started an intercultural conversation concerning both in the emerging global space of theological communication.[39] The following refers, in the main, to Timothy M. Hartman's doctoral thesis titled, "Revelation, Religion, and Culture in Kwame Bediako and Karl Barth."[40] Hartman analyzes Bediako's comprehensive work and places the themes that arise—revelation, religion, and culture—in constructive dialogue with Barth's Christology in *Church Dogmatics* IV.3, §69. Hartman himself seeks "cross-cultural theological comparisons to navigate contemporary theological and religious questions, including the complex nature of Christianity in the world today."[41]

Bediako was raised in a family belonging to the Presbyterian Church of Ghana (PCG) and was an ordained pastor. His grandfather had been a catechist in service of the Basel Mission, the founding institute of the PCG. During his first stay in Europe, Bediako refused what he perceived to be Western atheism while staying in France, while coincidentally developing an open mind to the African traditional religions. This "conversion" to the religion of his ancestors liberated Bediako to explore the Christian faith embedded in an African form. He returned to Ghana for theological studies before completing a doctoral thesis, in 1983, under the direction of Andrew F. Walls in Aberdeen, England. This dissertation compared doing theology in context of the second Christian century in the Mediterranean area and the same processes evident in late twentieth-century Africa.[42] During his many years of commuting between Ghana and Europe and by exchanging with interlocutors in North America, Bediako became one of the most creative African theologians in the context of contemporary Africa and World Christianity. His criticism of Europe became progressively severe, even to the point of labelling European Christendom a disaster: "the modern West has less to offer than may be readily recognized, unless it be the lessons from the disaster that was Christendom."[43] He countered the Christendom he found in Europe and North America with expressions of Christian faith embedded in African forms.[44] And, in Bediako's view, Karl Barth stood out as a prime example of a Western theologian representing a Christendom theology.[45] According to Hartman, Barth himself did not appear compelled to delve into the African theology that was emerging in the 1960s. Africa appeared to be, for him, a destination for missionaries—nothing more.[46]

It is beyond doubt that a European mission agency had paved the way for Bediako to communicate the Gospel in Ghana. Missionaries sent by the Basel Mission had initiated the translation of the Bible into Twi, the language used in Akropong-Aquapem, where Bediako was among the founders of the Akrofi-Christaller Institute of Theology, Mission and Culture in 1987. Thanks to these original efforts of translating the message, Bediako was able to assume that the Gospel can be translated into all languages, forms of thought, and human behavior. At the same time, he criticized that legacy as being only the first step of the translation process when the Gospel was articulated in European forms.

For rooting the Christian faith in the African soil, Bediako ignored "theologians from the sixth century to the twentieth in order to circumvent the theology of Christendom and the pernicious influence of Enlightenment philosophy."[47] He replaced the demonizing view of Africa's cultural legacy, shared for a long time by many missionaries, for an even-handed perspective of that legacy. He aimed at bringing the Christian faith to his African contemporaries in the very same way as the church fathers in the second century had transmitted it into the pagan cultures of their time. Bediako nevertheless approached the African cultures by means of selection, integration, reinterpretation as well as with criticism and rejection, if such seemed necessary. Inspired by the Gospel, something new ought to arise that was also rooted in "the primal imagination as the substructure of African Christianity."[48]

At first sight, this theological journey distances Bediako from Barth's own theological profile. Was his approach not exactly the kind of theology criticized by Barth as "hyphenated theology"? Was he not looking for "points of contact" in Africa's religious and cultural traditions? Bediako's jump from Antiquity into the present time by omitting the large stream of faith witnesses and theological consideration in between would certainly have estranged Barth. On closer inspection, however, some clear commonalities emerge between the two. Both, for example, express evident criticisms of Christianity in the history of Europe, and maintain the centrality of Jesus Christ in their theological thinking. Both affirm that God's revelation is accessible only in human language and not beyond human forms of expression; that no language can be called holy and of higher value than others. They also understand the potential of religion(s) to reduce to human attempts that distort Christ and his Gospel.[49]

Barth's remarks on European Christianity have to be seen in the frame of his ecclesiology and Christology. He uses the word *Christentum* (1) usually in the sense of *the amount of all phenomena that are related to the "religion" named according to Jesus Christ*. It has sometimes a neutral, other times a negative connotation, the latter especially when the adjective *verbürgerlicht* is added (*verbürgerlichtes Christentum* = Christianity having become bourgeois). In distinction to this first usage, the same word *Christentum* can refer to (2) a sense of "genuine/pure/true/ultimate" (*eigentlich/echt*) Christianity, qualified by the call and witness of the community of believers based on Jesus Christ alone. More often, however, *Christentum* is juxtaposed to Jesus Christ or the Gospel. Barth avoids the dualism of a corrupt *Christentum* ("Christendom") over against a doubtlessly identifiable "true" *Christentum* ("Christianity"). Similarly, Barth uses the word *Christenheit* sometimes in neutral, other times affirmative or critical ways. As to which of these definitions might be attributed to any particular usage of *Christentum* or *Christenheit*, this is dependent on the context in which they occur.[50] To avoid misinterpretation, I will use these words as they appear in Barth's German original without translating them.[51]

Looking at Barth's lifework, there is both continuity and discontinuity in how he uses *Christentum*. In the early, militant period of Barth's writing his criticisms on *Christentum* are formulated in a sharp, uncompromising way, and refer in the main to the *verbürgerlichtes Christentum* in Europe of his time. In his last years, however, these harsh judgments on *Christentum* take a back seat in context of his teaching about reconciliation. The continuity of Barth's thinking on *Christentum* throughout his life can be illustrated quite adequately by a speech presented in 1935. In that year, Barth was banned from teaching in Germany due to his criticism of national socialism. Shortly afterwards he gave a public lecture in Bern and Basel titled "Das Evangelium in der Gegenwart" (The Gospel in the present time).[52] It was a critical appraisal of *Christentum* in Europe and North America in general, and in Germany in particular. To paraphrase: *Christentum*, as it has long existed, is in a process of decline. Its end is near; it has no future: "[T]he *Christian*-bourgeois or the bourgeois-Christian age has come to an end [. . .] Christianity in the form we have known has come to an end."[53] Signs of its end are already visible: it has become vacuous in London, distorted in Germany through it sympathies with national socialism, ignored in Zurich, and persecuted in Russia. European *Christentum* failed by making itself dependent on earthly powers in order to survive, to enjoy a comfortable life in society, and to gain influence in politics and over social life. By compromising with secular powers throughout its one thousand five hundred years, it lost its credibility in the "world." "Right after the first centuries of its existence, *Christenheit* took refuge in the arms of a great fiction, an illusion or, quite bluntly, of a great lie."[54] As a consequence of this, the state and society rejected *Christentum*. This is not a tragedy, however, because it liberates *Christentum* from its worldly bondages; the opportunity now exists for it to return to its genuine mission before the world without becoming like the world.[55]

Immediately after developing this position, however, Barth relativizes and questions his own diagnosis of *Christentum* in past and present Europe. That scenario is nothing but one hypothesis among many others that he writes.[56] More precisely, he puts a question mark behind it and adds another hypothetical diagnosis: Could it not be that the last one thousand five hundred years of European *Christentum* bear signs of God's grace and patience? Were there not in the midst of the *corpus christianum* also manifestations of the coming kingdom of Christ? With greatest precaution Barth posits the following with regards to the medieval age: "It was necessary to bind Satan for a while. In the meantime, it was adequate to see nature and grace, Antiquity and *Christentum*, reason and revelation, state and church as united like being under the arch of a second Noachian covenant." That union "was embodied in the quaint and at the same time meaningful idea and reality of the 'Holy Roman Empire of the German Nation.'"[57] That era of Christian history has maybe not been useless, concludes Barth. It probably had some magnitude and dignity even though it could not last in that form and even though it is not supposed to reappear in some future form.[58]

Barth assumes that there may be some truth in both hypotheses. He leaves the final judgment to God, however, and does not opt for one against the other. Nor is he juxtaposing "false" and "true" forms of *Christentum*. Instead, he observes *Christentum* as being placed in front of "the gospel"—challenged, questioned, and judged, but also justified by it.[59] Likewise, Barth avoids contrasting the visible, imperfect over against an invisible, spiritualized church. In fact, the Gospel creates signs of true church, here and now, past and present, inside and outside of *Christentum*. Since the church-building process is led by the Holy Spirit who blows where it wills, the Spirit may not be damped and hampered, that is, new forms of being church, or *Christentum*, wherever, whenever, and in whatever manifestations, should be given the freedom to emerge and flourish.[60] Even if they occur in the most unexpected ways, they should not be prejudged and controlled according to established doctrines.

Barth's life ended before the public awareness of these new churches in six continents and the southward shift of Christianity. He had no chance to comment on these new developments nor participate in a global dialogue on the Christianity of today. But if we try to extrapolate his arguing into the present, the first task to achieve in an enlarged ecumenical community is openness toward new forms of being church, inspired by the Holy Spirit. The encounter between old and new forms of being church would not stop there, however. Mutual questioning about how the interlocutors see the essentials of the Christian faith would follow, accompanied by critical self-reflection, careful listening to other witnesses, and raising questions addressed to other partners in dialogue. Those who participate in such interlocution will together read anew the Holy Scripture and learn what the Gospel is saying to them in view of the challenges of the day.

CONCLUSIONS FOR THE STUDY OF WORLD CHRISTIANITY

(1) In many studies on World Christianity, the criticism on "Christendom" focuses on its explicit or implicit claim to be normative for Christian life in all parts of the globe. There is certainly truth in such criticism: unless the Gospel is given space to adopt new forms in new cultural, linguistic, societal, and political contexts (instead of imposing one form in all other settings), the Christian faith cannot be appropriated faithfully, nor can new ways of being church be acknowledged by the worldwide ecumenical community as legitimate expressions of the one common witness. New facets of the Gospel are made visible and new potentials released. New insights in what the fullness (*pleroma*) of Christ means come to the fore. Such fullness is described in Ephesians 4:11–13 as follows: "And he gave the apostles, the prophets, the evangelists, the shepherds and teachers to equip the saints for the work of ministry, for building up the body of Christ, until we all attain to the unity of the faith and of the knowledge of the Son of God, *to mature manhood, to the measure of the stature of the fullness of Christ*" (emphasis mine). When in a certain time at the peripheries of the established forms of Christianity emerge new Christian faith communities, this is neither a distortion nor a danger to

the faith and its institutional expressions. They rather signal a gain of matureness of the body of Christ and a further step in the insight into the "full-grown humanity of Christ."[61] In other words: "[T]he more Christ is translated into various thought forms and life systems which form our various national identities, the richer all of us will be in our Christian identity."[62] From this it follows that if Christianity quits transcultural communication it ends up in a cultural captivity, becoming (self-)satisfied with a closed theological horizon. However, one difficulty with an extended criticism of Christendom lies in replacing this with an uncritically idealized (World) Christianity as can appear to be the case with phrases like "Christianity beyond Christendom." One key question, of course, concerns if, how, and by whom questions and critical remarks may be raised in regard to the myriads of new emerging faith expressions. A critical questioning in light of the Gospel cannot work unilaterally from the global North to the global South or vice versa. This has to be a mutual process, irrespective of who and from where the interlocutors are.[63]

(2) Unlike Bediako I do not view the fading out of sight one and a half thousand years of European history as a precondition to develop locally rooted theologies outside Europe. The Middle Ages, taken as a history of mission, reveal amazing correspondences between the forms of transcultural transmission of faith then and now. Between the time of the Western Roman Empire and the Carolingian Empire until the beginning of the Modern Age the transmission and appropriation of the Christian faith lead time and again to new situations of disintegration and reintegration. The common space of communication was fragile and fragmentary; numerous micro-Christianities emerged and coexisted side by side. Due to the constant growth of Christianity in the global South, similar processes occur there today—although in a far greater extent than throughout the whole preceding history of Christianity.[64] It could be a chance to learn from medieval European Christianity for today's multiplication of micro-Christianities, with its many disintegrations, but also with its new ways of ecumenical community. In turn, contemporary experiences of mission from everywhere to everywhere could assist in the understanding of medieval Christianity.

(3) The translatability of the Gospel into human language and culture is an indispensable postulate in missiology, but not at all easy to apply in practice. Simple words of everyday language can mutate to terms, from terms to notions, from notions to concepts, and all of them are not immune against regressing into clichés. In the translation process, words can develop a dynamism and make themselves independent from former intentions and meanings. This is amply illustrated by the word "Christendom" in missiological discourse. The meaning given to that word cannot be translated satisfyingly into other languages. We might even complicate the issue: in other languages expressions with a similar sound are "occupied" by other meanings and

produce confusion when used to express the English term "Christendom." My conclusion is this: at the linguistic level, it is not possible to gain sufficient clarity of meaning when using the term Christendom in missiological discourse. Would it not be helpful to avoid altogether that term at least for a while and replace it by describing the intended phenomena as precisely as possible? Of course, it is useful in international discourse to opt for a *lingua franca* as a language of communication. In the medieval period, Latin held that function, being used for doctrine, theology, and liturgy. Today, English occupies a similar role. However, ecumenical English as *lingua franca* includes the danger of producing asymmetries of expression, along with asymmetries of participation and linguistic power. The saying that "God speaks in dialect" acts as a counterbalance to any *lingua franca* that dominates other idioms. In search of a global theology suitable to the complexity of contemporary World Christianity the question remains as to how to develop an ecumenical language that can be understood and shared by all in their own idioms—a Pentecostal endeavor indeed!

(4) As we have seen, the medieval period used the word *christianitas* primarily in context of new mission fields in Europe where questions were raised concerning how, in other cultural and linguistic settings, the marks of the Christian faith and confession, of church, liturgy, and behavior might be distinguished from hypocrisy, heresy, apostasy, and ethical wrongdoing. Likewise, it is a concern of the study of World Christianity today to explore the marks of Christian faith in midst of myriads of new and increasingly disparate faith expressions. I can see here a broad common concern across time and space. This is a chance to enlarge the space of communication between Christian expressions of past and present, across North and South, East and West. More than ever the ecumenical principle coined by Pope John Paul II in the Encyclical *Ut unum sint* should apply also in missiology: "What unites us is greater than what divides us."[65]

NOTES

1. This article is a revised and enlarged version of Christine Lienemann-Perrin, "Europäisches Christentum auf dem Prüfstand: Was folgt daraus für die Missionswissenschaft?," *Interkulturelle Theologie* 42, no. 2–3 (2016): 252–70.

2. Ryan K. Bolger, *The Gospel after Christendom: New Voices, New Cultures, New Expressions* (Grand Rapids, MI: Baker Academic, 2012); Thomas J. Curry, *Farewell to Christendom: The Future of Church and State in America* (Oxford: Oxford University Press, 2001); Jehu J. Hanciles, *Beyond Christendom: Globalization, African Migration, and the Transformation of the West* (Maryknoll, NY: Orbis Books, 2008); Lloyd Pietersen, *Reading the Bible after Christendom* (Harrisonburg, VA: Herald Press, 2012); David Smith, *Mission after Christendom* (London: Darton, Longman & Todd, 2003). Paternoster, a publisher in Milton Keynes, UK, provides many further titles in the "After Christendom Series." See, for example, Stuart Murray, *Post-Christendom: Church and Mission in a Strange New World* (Milton Keynes: Paternoster, 2004).

3. Andrew F. Walls, *The Cross-Cultural Process in Christian History: Studies in the Transmission and Appropriation of Faith* (Maryknoll, NY: Orbis Books, 2002), 34.

4. Wesley Granberg-Michaelson, *From Times Square to Timbuktu: The Post-Christian West Meets the Non-Western Church* (Grand Rapids, MI: Eerdmans, 2013).

5. Global South and global North are a classification of all countries worldwide, introduced by the United Nations and usually applied in modified ways in studies on World Christianity. Global North and South do not accord exactly with the northern and southern hemispheres along the equator. Russia East of Ural is attributed to the global South, West of Ural to the global North, China to the global South, New Zealand to the global North, etc.

6. In French, *chrétienté* can be used for the institutionalized church, imposed by political powers, and in this sense is close to the usage of Christendom in English. *Christianisme* refers to the religion as an organized social entity in a neutral sense. *Christianitude* and *christianité* are more recent neologisms to express the true Christian community in Kierkegaard's sense of *Christendom*. See Gabriel Monet, *L'Église émergente: Être et faire Église en postchrétienté* (Berlin: Lit Verlag, 2014), 180–82. The French lay theologian, Jacques Ellul, proposed the formula "X" to refer to the marks of true Christian community in distinction to all wrong forms of Christianity. "X" stands for three aspects: "D'une part, la Révélation et l'Oeuvre de Dieu accomplies en Jésus-Christ; en second lieu, l'Être vrai de l'Église en tant que corps du Christ; en troisième lieu, la foi et la vie du chrétien, dans la vérité et dans l'amour." Jacques Ellul, *La subversion du Christianism* (Paris: Seuil, 1995), 18 (quoted in Monet, *L'Église émergente*, 182). In Dutch, *Christendom* can be the translation of both English words, *Christendom* and *Christianity*.

7. Philip Jenkins, "Ein globaler religiöser Klimawandel—Wie die demographische Entwicklung die christliche Mission verändert," *Interkulturelle Theologie* 44, no. 1 (2016): 55–70, here 57.

8. For the following, see Brian Stanley, *The World Missionary Conference, Edinburgh 1910* (Grand Rapids, MI: Eerdmans, 2009), especially chapter 3, "Carrying the Gospel to *All* the World? Defining the Limits of Christendom," 49–72, 303–7.

9. There were debates on the question: "What percentage of Christians . . . shall be deemed sufficient to change the country from the non-Christian to the Christian class?" Stanley, *The World Missionary Conference*, 62.

10. Stanley, 50. Churches with historical roots in Antiquity living in Muslim countries or India, e.g., the Assyrian churches in Near East and Persia, the Thomas Christians in India, and the Copts in Egypt, were categorized as belonging to the peripheries of Christendom, if not outright to Heathendom.

11. That was the opinion of Bishop Henry H. Montgomery representing the British Anglo-Catholics, who was opposed by the Americans. Stanley, 65–66.

12. Stanley, 64. However, missionaries from continental Europe, such as Julius Richter, declared Catholic South America as a half-Christian or pagan territory. Therefore, they were in favor of inviting Protestant missionaries from South America to participate at the conference. They failed to convince the majority. See Stanley, 52. By contrast, the Portuguese colonies in India and Africa as well as Madagascar, where Catholic Christians outnumbered the Protestants, were regarded as insufficiently evangelized and therefore classified as Protestant mission territories.

13. The title of his paper was "The Contribution of Non-Christian Races to the Body of Christ." Stanley, *The World Missionary Conference*, 113.

14. As an example, Robert E. Speer, an American missiologist, remarked that paganism develops in the midst of Christendom.

15. *Report of Commission VI: The Home Base of Missions* (Edinburgh/London: Oliphant, Anderson and Ferrier, 1910).

16. William Henry Temple Gairdner, *Echoes from Edinburgh, 1910: An Account and Interpretation of the World Missionary Conference* (New York: Fleming H. Revel, 1910), 240.

17. Gairdner, 241–42.

18. Stanley, *The World Missionary Conference*, 305.

19. In the follow-up of the conference in Edinburgh 1910, she became a member of the Education Commission of Continuation Committee. Her name is connected with the worldwide

women's missionary movement. See Kendal P. Mobley, *Helen Barrett Montgomery: The Global Mission of Domestic Feminism* (Waco, TX: Baylor University Press, 2009).

20. Helen Barrett Montgomery, *Western Women in Eastern Lands: An Outline Study of Fifty Years of Women's Work in Foreign Missions* (New York: Macmillan, 1910), quoted in Mobley, *Helen Barrett Montgomery*, 216.

21. After the second World Mission Conference in Jerusalem (1928), Montgomery praised the mission churches in the South who "emphasized the autonomy of indigenous Christians and even their resistance to the negative aspects of Western civilization." Mobley, *Helen Barrett Montgomery*, 239, referring to Helen Barrett Montgomery, *From Jerusalem to Jerusalem: "Fly Abroad, Thou Mighty Gospel"* (Cambridge, MA: The Central Committee on the United Study of Foreign Missions, 1929). Montgomery's hope was that the missionary spirit of Christianity in the global South may trigger a renewing effect in Western Christianity.

22. The history of that gradual shift has still to be written. Two of the critics were Hendrik Kraemer, *The Christian Message in a Non-Christian World* (London: Harper and Brothers, 1938) and Christiaan J. Hoekendijk, "Die Welt als Horizont," *Evangelische Theologie* 25 (1965): 467–84. See John G. Flett, *Apostolicity: The Ecumenical Question in World Christian Perspective* (Downers Grove, IL: IVP Academic, 2016), 190–91, 217–19.

23. "At a time when Christianity is itself increasingly marginal to Western intellectual discourse, that discourse needs to come to terms with Christianity as a non-Western religion." Andrew F. Walls, *The Missionary Movement in Christian History: Studies in the Transmission of Faith* (Maryknoll, NY: Orbis Books, 1996), xix.

24. Hanciles, *Beyond Christendom*, 84–111.

25. Hanciles, 276–302.

26. Said Philip Jenkins in an oral exchange with the author (Sept. 2015 at Basel) on the usage of the term in the United States. The same was confirmed to the author by Paul and Jennifer Jenkins regarding England. Other participants at a missiological conference in Bad Boll in October 2015 opined that, e.g., in India and the Philippines "Christendom" is not common as an English term.

27. Novalis, "Die Christenheit oder Europa: Ein Fragment (1799)," in *Das Philosophische Werk II*, ed. Richard Samuel (Stuttgart: Kohlhammer, 1968), 507–24.

28. Pope Benedict XV, *Pacem, Dei munus Pulcherrimum*, May 23, 1920.

29. Anti-Climacus (pseudonym). *Indøvelse I Christendom. No. I. II. III*, ed. Søren Kierkegaard (Copenhagen, 1850). Translated into English as Søren Kierkegaard, *Training in Christianity* (London: Oxford University Press, 1941). In a recent article, Philip Jenkins refers to that title and without reference to potential translation problems, he uses the English *Christianity* where Kierkegaard uses the Danish term *Christendom*. See Philip Jenkins, "The Legacy of Christendom," in *The Wiley-Blackwell Companion to World Christianity*, ed. Lamin Sanneh, and Michael McClymond (Oxford: Wlley-Blackwell, 2016), 131–41, here 134.

30. Kierkegaard's harsh diagnosis of European forms of Christianity has left its mark on Karl Barth, such as in Karl Barth, *The Epistle to the Romans*, trans. Edwyn C. Hoskyns (London: Oxford University Press, 1933). Barth remained true to Kierkegaard's wake-up call (*Weckruf*) for the rest of his life. In other respects, however, he had reservations about Kierkegaard's theology; see Karl Barth, "Dank und Reverenz," *Evangelische Theologie* 23, no.7 (1963): 337–42.

31. Lamin O. Sanneh, *Whose Religion is Christianity? The Gospel beyond the West* (Grand Rapids, MI: Eerdmans, 2003), 23.

32. Walls, *The Cross-Cultural Process*, 35–45.

33. Hanciles, *Beyond Christendom*, 90–100.

34. Nora Berend, "Frontiers of Christendom: The Endurance of Medieval and Modern Constructs," in *Das Sein Der Dauer*, ed. Andreas Speer, and David Wirmer (Berlin: Walter de Gruyter, 2008), 27–40; Nora Berend, "The Concept of Christendom: A Rhetoric of Integration or Disintegration," in *Hybride Kulturen im Mittelalterlichen Europa/Hybrid Cultures in Medieval Europe*, ed. Michael Borgolte, and Bernd Schneidmüller (Berlin: Akademie Verlag, 2010), 51–61; Tim Geelhaar, *Christianitas: Eine Wortgeschichte von der Spätantike bis zum Mittelalter* (Göttingen: Vandenhoeck & Ruprecht Academic, 2015).

35. The term *cristendome* was introduced as a Middle English neologism in the 9th century. There were no exact equivalents to *cristendome* in Greek and Latin. Judith Herrin, *The Formation of Christendom* (Princeton, NJ: Princeton University Press, 1989), 8.

36. Geelhaar, *Christianitas*, 305–37.

37. For further examples, see the Polish king, Kazimierz the Great (1310–1370) in battles with the Mongols and Lithuanians, and Scanderberg (1403–1468) of Albany in conflicts with the Turks when they expanded their territories on the Balkan peninsula. Berend, "Frontiers of Christendom," 28–35.

38. Dietrich Ritschl, *Theorie und Konkretion in der Ökumenischen Theologie: Kann es eine Hermeneutik des Vertrauens inmitten differierender semiotischer Systeme geben?* (Münster: LIT Verlag, 2003).

39. Charles Sarpong Aye-Addo, *Akan Christology: An Analysis of the Christologies of John Samuel Pobee and Kwame Bediako in Conversation with the Theology of Karl Barth* (Eugene, OR: Wipf & Stock, 2013); Alan Thomson, *Culture in a Post-secular Context* (Eugene, OR: Pickwick, 2014); Bernhard Dinkelaker, "How is Jesus Christ Lord? Perspectives on Intercontextual Theological Encounters in the Work of Kwame Bediako," diss., (Heidelberg University, 2016).

40. Timothy M. Hartman, "Revelation, Religion, and Culture in Kwame Bediako and Karl Barth," diss., (University of Virginia, 2014).

41. Hartman writes: "Both theologians maintain a Christological focus in revelation that in turn penetrates culture and redefines religion. Their conclusions, illuminated through this comparison of divergences and convergences, can guide the work of contemporary constructive theology that seeks to navigate questions of the interrelationship of revelation, religion, and culture now and in the future." Hartman, 261.

42. Kwame Bediako, *Theology and Identity: The Impact of Culture upon Christian Thought in the Second Century and Modern Africa* (Oxford: Regnum Books, 1992). For Bediako's further publications, see Gillian Mary Bediako, Benhardt Y. Quarshie, and J. Kwabena Asamoah-Gyadu, eds., *Seeing New Facets of the Diamond: Christianity as a Universal Faith— Essays in Honour of Kwame Bediako* (Oxford: Regnum, 2014).

43. Kwame Bediako, "Africa and Christianity on the Threshold of the Third Millennium: The Religious Dimension," *African Affairs* 99 (2000): 303–23, here 316, cited in Hartman, "Revelation, Religion, and Culture," 117. According to Bediako, the problem of Christendom is that "all possible religious alternatives are presumed to be non-existent, or in a secularized environment in which specifically religious claims are held to be no longer decisive." Kwame Bediako, "Biblical Exegesis in the African Context: The Factor and Impact of Translated Scriptures," *Journal of African Christian Thought* 6, no.1 (2003): 15–23, here 20, cited in Hartman, "Revelation, Religion, and Culture," 117.

44. Hartman, "Revelation, Religion, and Culture," 15. "Bediako's corpus is an example of writing from the margins of the empire back to the center of theological power and production in the West." Hartman, 18.

45. Bediako had only sparse knowledge of Barth's oeuvre. He accused Barth of having a deficient sensibility when in contact with people of color—an allegation that was based on rumors spread during his stay in England. Eberhard Busch, biographer of Karl Barth, for example, notes Barth's comment after his encounter with Christian Baëta and his wife from Ghana as follows: "jet-black, but very likable." Eberhard Busch, *Karl Barths Lebenslauf: Nach seinen Briefen und autobiographischen Texten* (München: Chr. Kaiser, 1975), 410.

46. The suspicion that each theologian had of the other was mutual—"for Bediako, of Western theology as insular with a history of oppression; and for Barth, of Africans not being serious interlocutors." Hartman, "Revelation, Religion, and Culture," 18. "Barth did not concern himself with Africa, or things African (aside from as a destination for missionaries)." Hartman, 245.

47. Hartman, 244.

48. Hartman, 100.

49. Hartman, 10f.

50. Another case is the word *Christlichkeit*, which has a qualifying character in Barth's texts: A critical scrutiny of what is called "Christian" can either entail the conclusion that it is

only a sham; or, in a more eschatological sense, it is something that will be revealed as genuinely Christian only at the end of the times. See Karl Barth, *Karl Barth–Eduard Thurneysen: Briefwechsel: Band I, 1913–1921* (Zürich: Theologischer Verlag Zürich, 1973), 207–9. Barth invites Thurneysen to join him in his attack on false *Christlichkeit*. Barth, 208.

51. The translation of the German is mine.

52. Karl Barth, "Das Evangelium in der Gegenwart," *Theologische Existenz heute* 25 (1935): 18–36. For the political, church-related, professional and private circumstances of Barth in 1935, see Busch, *Karl Barths Lebenslauf*, 268–75, here 274.

53. Barth, 33.

54. Barth, 30. See also Karl Barth, *Predigten 1915* (Zollikon-Zürich: TVZ, 1996), especially "Sermon no. 277" (Safenwil, 30 June, 1915), 242f; "Sermon no. 283" (Safenwil, 1 August, 1915), 306f., and *CD* IV/3.2, 513, 524–25, 744; *KD* IV/3.2, 590; 602–4; 856.

55. Barth, "Das Evangelium in der Gegenwart," 18–22, 34.

56. Barth, 35. See also, *CD* IV/3.2, 514; *KD* IV/3.2, 591.

57. Barth, 32f.

58. Barth, 33. "The Gospel Is Not Identical to *Christentum*." Barth, 22.

59. Barth, 22–26.

60. Barth, 23.

61. "The full-grown humanity of Christ requires all the Christian generations, just as it embodies all the cultural variety that six continents can bring." Walls, *The Missionary Movement*, xvii.

62. Walls, 54.

63. That issue has been treated as a question of different hermeneutics: the hermeneutics of suspicion, coherence and confidence. See Ritschl, *Theorie und Konkretion in der Ökumenischen Theologie*; Rudolf von Sinner, *Reden vom dreieinigen Gott in Brasilien und Indien* (Tübingen: Mohr Siebeck, 2003), 338f.

64. According to the *World Christian Database*, there exists about 40,000 denominations worldwide, defined as organized Christian faith communities in every country worldwide, distinguishing themselves from other autonomous denominations, churches and traditions, see "The World Christian Database," accessed, 11 January 2019, http://www.world christiandatabase.org/.

65. John Paul II, *Ut unum sint: On Commitment to Ecumenism* (Boston, MA: Pauline Books and Media, 1995), §20. Pope John XXIII first coined this phrase.

BIBLIOGRAPHY

Aye-Addo, Charles Sarpong. *Akan Christology: An Analysis of the Christologies of John Samuel Pobee and Kwame Bediako in Conversation with the Theology of Karl Barth.* Eugene, OR: Wipf & Stock, 2013.

Barth, Karl. "Dank und Reverenz." *Evangelische Theologie* 23, no.7 (1963): 337–42.

———. "Das Evangelium in der Gegenwart." *Theologische Existenz heute* 25 (1935): 18–36.

———. *The Epistle to the Romans.* Translated by Edwyn C. Hoskyns. London: Oxford University Press, 1933.

———. *Karl Barth–Eduard Thurneysen: Briefwechsel: Band I, 1913–1921.* Zürich: TVZ, 1973.

———. *Predigten 1915.* Zollikon-Zürich: TVZ, 1996.

Bediako, Gillian Mary, Benhardt Y. Quarshie, and J. Kwabena Asamoah-Gyadu, eds. *Seeing New Facets of the Diamond: Christianity as a Universal Faith—Essays in Honour of Kwame Bediako.* Oxford: Regnum, 2014.

Bediako, Kwame. "Africa and Christianity on the Threshold of the Third Millennium: The Religious Dimension." *African Affairs* 99 (2000): 303–23.

———. "Biblical Exegesis in the African Context: The Factor and Impact of Translated Scriptures." *Journal of African Christian Thought* 6, no.1 (2003): 15–23.

———. *Theology and Identity: The Impact of Culture upon Christian Thought in the Second Century and in Modern Africa.* Oxford: Regnum Books, 1992.

Berend, Nora. "The Concept of Christendom: A Rhetoric of Integration or Disintegration," in *Hybride Kulturen im Mittelalterlichen Europa/Hybrid Cultures in Medieval Europe*, edited by Michael Borgolte, and Bernd Schneidmüller, 51–61. Berlin: Akademie Verlag, 2010.

———. "Frontiers of Christendom: The Endurance of Medieval and Modern Constructs," in *Das Sein Der Dauer*, edited by Andreas Speer, and David Wirmer, 27–40. Berlin: Walter de Gruyter, 2008.

Bolger, Ryan K. *The Gospel after Christendom: New Voices, New Cultures, New Expressions.* Grand Rapids, MI: Baker Academic, 2012.

Busch, Eberhard. *Karl Barths Lebenslauf: Nach seinen Briefen und autobiographischen Texten.* München: Chr. Kaiser, 1975.

Curry, Thomas J. *Farewell to Christendom: The Future of Church and State in America.* Oxford: Oxford University Press, 2001.

Dinkelaker, Bernhard. "How is Jesus Christ Lord? Perspectives on Intercontextual Theological Encounters in the Work of Kwame Bediako." PhD diss., Heidelberg University, 2016.

Ellul, Jacques. *La subversion du Christianism.* Paris: Seuil, 1995.

Flett, John G. *Apostolicity: The Ecumenical Question in World Christian Perspective.* Downers Grove, IL: IVP Academic, 2016.

Gairdner, W. H. T. *Echoes from Edinburgh, 1910: An Account and Interpretation of the World Missionary Conference.* New York: Fleming H. Revel, 1910.

Geelhaar, Tim. *Christianitas: Eine Wortgeschichte von der Spätantike bis zum Mittelalter.* Göttingen: Vandenhoeck & Ruprecht, 2015.

Granberg-Michaelson, Wesley. *From Times Square to Timbuktu: The Post-Christian West Meets the Non-Western Church.* Grand Rapids, MI: Eerdmans, 2013.

Hanciles, Jehu J. *Beyond Christendom: Globalization, African Migration, and the Transformation of the West.* Maryknoll, NY: Orbis Books, 2008.

Hartman, Timothy M. "Revelation, Religion, and Culture in Kwame Bediako and Karl Barth." PhD diss., University of Virginia, 2014.

Herrin, Judith. *The Formation of Christendom.* Princeton, NJ: Princeton University Press, 1989.

Hoekendijk, J. C. "Die Welt als Horizont." *Evangelische Theologie* 25 (1965): 467–84.

The Home Base of Missions. Report of Commission VI: With Supplement: Presentation and Discussion of the Report in the Conference on 23rd June 1910. Edinburgh and London: Oliphant, Anderson & Ferrier, 1910.

Jenkins, Philip. "Ein globaler religiöser Klimawandel—Wie die demographische Entwicklung die christliche Mission verändert." *Interkulturelle Theologie* 44, no. 1 (2016): 55–70.

———. "The Legacy of Christendom," in *The Wiley-Blackwell Companion to World Christianity*, edited by Lamin Sanneh, and Michael McClymond, 131–41. Oxford: Wiley-Blackwell, 2016.

Kierkegaard, Søren. *Training in Christianity* (London: Oxford University Press, 1941).

Kraemer, Hendrik. *The Christian Message in a Non-Christian World.* London: Harper and Brothers, 1938.

Mobley, Kendal P. *Helen Barrett Montgomery: The Global Mission of Domestic Feminism.* Waco, TX: Baylor University Press, 2009.

Monet, Gabriel. *L'Église émergente: Être et faire Église en postchrétienté.* Berlin: Lit Verlag, 2014.

Montgomery, Helen Barrett. *From Jerusalem to Jerusalem: "Fly Abroad, Thou Mighty Gospel."* Cambridge, MA: The Central Committee on the United Study of Foreign Missions, 1929.

———. *Western Women in Eastern Lands: An Outline Study of Fifty Years of Women's Work in Foreign Missions.* New York: Macmillan, 1910.

Murray, Stuart. *Post-Christendom: Church and Mission in a Strange New World.* Milton Keynes: Paternoster, 2004.

Novalis. "Die Christenheit oder Europa: Ein Fragment (1799)," in *Das Philosophische Werk II*, edited by Richard Samuel, 507–24. Stuttgart: Kohlhammer, 1968.

Paul II, John. *Ut unum sint: On Commitment to Ecumenism.* Boston, MA: Pauline Books and Media, 1995.

Pietersen, Lloyd. *Reading the Bible after Christendom.* Harrisonburg, VA: Herald Press, 2012.

Ritschl, Dietrich. *Theorie und Konkretion in der Ökumenischen Theologie: Kann es eine Hermeneutik des Vertrauens inmitten differierender semiotischer Systeme geben?* Münster: LIT Verlag, 2003.

Sanneh, Lamin O. *Whose Religion is Christianity? The Gospel beyond the West.* Grand Rapids, MI: Eerdmans, 2003.

Smith, David. *Mission after Christendom.* London: Darton, Longman & Todd, 2003.

Stanley, Brian. *The World Missionary Conference, Edinburgh 1910.* Grand Rapids, MI: Eerdmans, 2009.

Thomson, Alan. *Culture in a Post-secular Context.* Eugene, OR: Pickwick, 2014.

von Sinner, Rudolf. *Reden vom dreieinigen Gott in Brasilien und Indien.* Tübingen: Mohr Siebeck, 2003.

Walls, Andrew F. *The Cross-Cultural Process in Christian History: Studies in the Transmission and Appropriation of Faith.* Maryknoll, NY: Orbis Books, 2002.

———. *The Missionary Movement in Christian History: Studies in the Transmission of Faith.* Maryknoll, NY: Orbis Books, 1996.

Chapter Five

From Praxis to Reflection

The Development of Integral Mission in Latin America

Samuel Escobar

In the year 2000, Ediciones Kairós from Buenos Aires published the book *Ser testigos de Jesucristo* by Darrell L. Guder. It is the Spanish translation of Guder's classic *Be My Witnesses* (1985). I still remember that when I first read it in English, its structure and style resonated with my own effort to reflect missiologically about my practice as an evangelist in Latin American universities. As I look back to years of collegial reflection with Darrell in the American Society of Missiology and the Overseas Ministries Study Center, I appreciated his awareness of the post-Christendom situation in which Christians live and do theology in Europe and the West. In the preface of that book Darrell gives us an autobiographical record of the circumstances in which the book was written. It is good to keep this in mind in order to evaluate better his proposal for a missional church.

To conceive the church as a missional church has been the starting point of Evangelical missiological reflection in Latin America. Right at the start of Protestant missionary work in this region the pioneers of the early nineteenth century were aware that in Latin America the background of their missionary practice was a continent in which Christendom in its Roman Catholic version was in decline, and that for Evangelical Protestants the churches they were trying to establish would only grow and become stable if they were missional churches.

One of the books that provoked missiological reflection and even debate in the 1980s and 1990s was *Christ Outside the Gate* by Puerto Rican missiologist Orlando Costas. The subtitle the author chose for it was "Mission Beyond Christendom." We could say that this collection of essays reflects well the author's role as a provocative debater in missiological circles of

North America and the world. Referring to his pastoral and teaching experience among Hispanics in the United States and his missionary years as an evangelist in Latin America, Costas introduced his book saying: "these essays reflect the 'thinking out loud' of an 'outsider'—one who not only belongs to a marginalized community in the American metropolis and has lived and worked in an oppressed continent, but who has also situated himself in the periphery of history."[1] The two parts in which the book is divided reflect well the agenda of the articles, sermons, and academic essays that Costas put together in the midst of an intense activism: (1) from the Latin American Periphery, and (2) from the Periphery of the American Metropolis.

Spain, where I presently live, is a society that is experiencing the decline of Christendom and gaining awareness about it. The Roman Catholic Church is still a powerful institution, committed to the Christendom mentality. However, there is a slow though continuous decline in the number of citizens that declare themselves Roman Catholic in the census, and the opinion of the church has less weight every day in the shaping of private and public morality. In addition, religious freedom has made possible the growth of religious minorities such as Protestant evangelicals, Jews, Muslims, Orthodox, and Jehovah Witnesses.

THE END OF CHRISTENDOM AND MISSION

When, as a Latin American Protestant, I consider the end of Christendom, one fact that comes to my mind is the famous Edinburgh 1910 Missionary Conference and its decision to exclude Latin America as a mission field for Protestants because supposedly it was already Christian. The policy behind the decision reflected a typical Christendom perspective. Later historical developments placed such perspective in a critical transition, questioning its presuppositions. In 1914, just four years after Edinburgh, European nations that defined themselves as Christians embarked in a disastrous war in which there were Christian chaplains blessing the troops on both sides. The unprecedented scale and cruelty of the First World War brought a crisis to Christian conscience and undermined the Christendom perspective. Sometimes I have the impression that there are missionary enthusiasts and even missiologists who have not yet grasped the nature of the crisis and its consequences.

In the centennial celebration at Edinburgh 2010, of the three hundred participants that attended, sixteen Latin American men and women, all of them Protestants, had been invited and eight of them were among the presenters of the seventy-seven papers and presentations in the program.[2] Some of them, like Bertil Ekstrom or Antonia Van der Meer from Brazil, are involved in the training and sending of Latin American Evangelical missionaries to Europe, Asia, and Africa. This fact lends itself to the kind of reflection on practice that is at the core of missiology.

The legitimacy of a Protestant missionary presence in Latin America had been acknowledged by the time of the Jerusalem meeting of the International Missionary Council in 1928. In fact, American Protestant missionary enthusiasts corrected the refusal of Edinburgh 1910 to accept Latin American Protestantism by forming a Committee of Cooperation in Latin America and sponsoring the first continental gathering of Latin American Protestants known as the Panama Congress on Christian Work, in 1916.[3] With a program patterned after the model of Edinburgh 1910, the Panama Congress became a milestone of Protestant advance. It was preceded by a careful study of the missionary situation, based on reports sent by correspondents throughout the continent. That material served as the basis for ten working groups.[4] The three volumes that sum up the studies of the congress provide a clear idea of the scope of the Protestant mission in those lands, and the results that it had achieved by the second decade of the twentieth century. The congress also reflected the self-critical attitude of the participating missions, which recognized the flaws in their work and were looking for new forms of cooperation and coordination.[5]

A more polemical and missiological interpretation of the exclusion of Latin American Protestants from Edinburgh 1910 came some years later from Gonzalo Báez-Camargo, a respected Mexican ecumenist, journalist, and Bible scholar, who interpreted this exclusion as a sign of the prevailing mindset among European Protestants in 1910, which was still shaped by Victorian-era complacency and paternalism.[6] They saw the human race as divided into a "Christian world" that included Europe and the Americas and a "non-Christian" world encompassing Asia, Africa, and the Pacific islands. "In other words," says Báez-Camargo, "there were grouped on one side and on the other a bloc of Christian civilized, missionary 'sending' countries, and a bloc of non-Christian, uncivilized, 'receiving' mission fields."[7] He believed that this global classification was too naive and had paved the way for blatant inconsistencies, such as placing Latin America in the first bloc and excluding from Edinburgh Protestant missionaries who had been working there for over a half century.

Briefly, Latin America was then regarded by influential Protestant leaders of both sides of the Atlantic (especially in Europe) as the exclusive private hunting ground of the historic church that had been predominant to the south of the Rio Grande for over four hundred years. Thus recognition was denied to the struggling and growing Protestant minority in that part of the world. For a moment it seemed as if the Evangelical Christians in Latin America, then already numbering about a million, would become permanent outcasts from the ecumenical movement.[8]

In the intense missiological debates around this issue, some Protestant missionary statesmen from Great Britain and North America described the spiritual condition of Latin America in somber tones. The appeal to send Protestant missionaries was accompanied by a description of social, moral, and spiritual conditions that were considered as a call to action. Thus, Robert Speer, the well-known American Presbyterian mission statesman, wrote in 1913:

> The first test of religious conditions is to be found in the facts of social life. No land can be conceded to have a satisfactory religion where the moral conditions are as they have been shown to be in South America. If it can be proved that the conditions of any European or North American land are as they are in South America, then it will be proved also that that land needs a religious reformation. [9]

RELIGION AND ETHICS

Speer's observation reflected an Evangelical conviction about the relationship between faith and ethics, between religion and morality, which is also found in other authors of missionary literature in those days: "Christianity is not opinion or ritual. It is life and that life must utter itself in moral purity and strength. No amount of theological statement or devout worship can avail to take the place of ethical fruitage in social purity and victory over sin." [10] For Speer the situation was not a matter of concern only to Protestants, but also to Catholics in North America.

We find a similar approach in John A. Mackay, a Scottish Presbyterian who had been a missionary in Peru since 1916 and later on in Mexico, before becoming president of Princeton Theological Seminary in 1936. His book *The Other Spanish Christ* is still considered a classic and valid analysis of the religious condition of Latin America. [11] Well known for his friendship with several liberal and socialist leaders of Latin America, Mackay had come to the conviction that most of them rejected the Catholic religion out of moral motives related to social justice. [12] Twelve years after the Panama Congress, at the initial meeting of the International Missionary Council in Jerusalem (1928), Mackay made it very clear the legitimacy of a Protestant missionary presence in Latin America.

Sometimes those who are interested in Christian service in South America are apt to be regarded as religious buccaneers devoting their lives to ecclesiastical piracy, but that is far from being the case. The great majority of men to whom we go will have nothing to do with religion. They took up this attitude because religion and morality had been divorced throughout the whole history of religious life in South America. [13]

Interpreting what happened in this meeting in Jerusalem, Báez-Camargo holds that it represented a significant change of mindset: "Jerusalem gave recognition to a new fact in the realm of world missions—the emergence of indigenous churches out of the pioneer 'mission stations' and their growing acting role in the evangelization of [hu]mankind." He goes on to add that "this time Latin America was given free access and the validity of Protestant missions in that vast area was quietly accepted."[14] Elsewhere in his analysis he notes that people had become aware that it was impossible to speak of Christian mission without taking into account the social context in which it was taking place. "So the assembly launched itself into an earnest study of social and economic questions as they affect missionary work. It also aimed at awakening and strengthening of the sense of the Christian's responsibility for social justice."[15] In Jerusalem it was also noted that a wave of secularism had invaded the countries that sent missionaries as well as those that received them. According to Báez-Camargo, acknowledgment of this fact had major consequence for both missiology and theology:

> This proved to be a revolutionary admission, for it meant that, after all, the formerly self-designated "Christian world" was also a mission field itself. It meant again—and this was still more important—that the Kingdom of God cannot be defined in terms of mere territorial accretion, but that the whole of life everywhere must be brought under the Lordship of Jesus Christ.[16]

Thus starting from convictions established by Protestant missionary practice in Latin America, serious questions were raised about the Christianizing process that had accompanied the Iberian conquest in the sixteenth century. This perspective is well summarized by Argentine Methodist theologian José Míguez Bonino, who was the only Latin American Protestant observer at Vatican II. Míguez wrote,

> Latin America was never "Christian" in the sense that Europe or even North America can be said to be so. What took place here was a colossal transplantation—the basic ecclesiastical structures, disciplines, and ministries were brought wholesale from Spain, and were expected to function as a Christian order: a tremendous form without substance.[17]

Without confirming Míguez Bonino's radical conclusion, some Catholic historians and theologians have also criticized the Christianization process in the Americas during the sixteenth century. I limit myself to mention only one author at this point, but the subject is today an important field of research. Liberation theologian Gustavo Gutiérrez has written a massive critical study of the Iberian conquest and evangelization based on a careful analysis of the work of the Dominican missionary Bartolomé de las Casas (1484–1556). In this book, Gutiérrez identifies and evaluates the historical circumstances in which an Iberian theology of mission and missionary practice shaped the conquering process and developed a religious ideology that justified it. It shows the contradictions between the Gospel and the methods of the Iberian enterprise in America.[18] It also proves that there were in those days missionaries that criticized the conquest approach and tried to find a more biblical model.

This long process of critical reflection about the religious condition of Latin America explains why, for Protestant missionaries and missiologists, it was possible to speak of Latin America as a mission field that turned out to be fertile terrain for the growth of evangelical Protestantism. A Catholic observer said in 1989 that if current growth rates at that point would continue, Latin America would have an evangelical majority in the early twenty-first century. Actually, in terms of church participation, "practicing" evangelicals may already outnumber "observant" Catholics.[19] The continuous numerical growth of Protestants in the second half of the twentieth century led other Catholic observers to refer back not to the first century, but to the sixteenth. Bishop Boaventura Kloppenburg, for example, has noted how in terms of changing religious affiliation, what is happening in Latin America surpasses what happened during the Protestant Reformation in the sixteenth century. In the twentieth century, the Catholic Church lost more faithful who have become Protestants than it lost in the age of Luther and Calvin.

I have studied elsewhere the way in which, during the second part of the twentieth century, some Roman Catholic missionaries and missiologists changed their perspective on Latin American Protestantism.[20] While many of the bishops, even today, hold an attitude that I call the "police approach"—how can we stop the Protestants?—these missiologists have a more "pastoral approach"—what can we learn from them? It would be worth to pursue the missiological significance of what Jesuit historian Jeffrey Klaiber, an American missionary in Peru, wrote in 1970:

> It may be one of the ironies of history that the final contribution of Latin American Protestantism will have been to awaken and revitalize a dormant Catholic Church. If indeed it does awake and come to life, it will not be because the Church rose from slumber to fight a hostile force, as in the days of the Reformation, but because that new force taught the Church urgently needed lessons about what its own prime task in the future must be.[21]

INTEGRAL MISSION

The course followed by Evangelical missionary practice and the theological reflection that accompanied it in Latin America may be summarized as the development of a missiological approach that has come to be known as Integral Mission. It has an evangelistic thrust nourished by the conviction that evangelization is a key component of the mission of the church in a continent that has a nominal kind of Christianity but has never been truly Christian. But it also has a socially transformative agenda that is based on a Christological missionary pattern. The numerical growth of Protestantism in Latin America is the outcome of the presence and action of churches that have kept evangelization at the heart of their missionary activity. And at the same time the social impact of this church growth is undeniable. The third element that is equally important is that mission has to be carried on with integrity that derives from its Christological pattern. My book *The New Global Mission* is an introduction to missiology from the perspective of Integral Mission.[22]

At this point, almost half a century after the beginning of the theological reflection from which Integral Mission has developed, we have at our disposal systematic studies about the process and its main actors written by scholars of a younger generation. Colombian theologian Daniel Salinas published, in 2009, his doctoral dissertation "Latin American Evangelical Theology in the 1970s: The Golden Decade."[23] On the other hand, Irish scholar Sharon E. Heaney has covered a wider chronological period in her doctoral dissertation, "Contextual Theology for Latin America," published in 2008.[24] In this chapter I am limiting myself to a personal account of the initial period.

The relationship between theology and mission was forcefully stated by Orlando Costas: "Theology enables evangelization to transmit the faith with integrity by clarifying and organizing its content, analyzing its context and critically evaluating its communication. Evangelization enables theology to be an effective servant of the faith by relating its message to the deepest spiritual needs of humankind."[25] In fact, in the case of Integral Mission, the Latin American Congresses of Evangelism (CLADE) have been the platform for theological reflection from the first in Bogotá (1969), to the fifth in San José, Costa Rica (2012). This emphasis makes Evangelical theologizing different from the forms of Protestant theology that come from churches that are not concerned with evangelization, and from the Catholic approach in which the sacramental presence of the Roman Catholic Church in Latin America is taken as the basis for assuming that the population is already Christian.

This evangelistic thrust wants to be guided by a Christological model for the way Jesus carried on his mission, providing a programmatic structure: incarnation, sacrificial service, crucifixion, and resurrection. A contextual reading of the New Testament and a Trinitarian awareness provide key guidelines for the way of carrying on mission in the contemporary situation. In the 1960's René Padilla and this author had been working in this Christological model as the basis for our own ministry to university students in Latin America.[26] Then historian and theologian Justo L. González used a study of the Johannine material in the New Testament as a way of calling Evangelicals to become aware of the kind of docetic Christology into which they had fallen.[27] Christ was proclaimed as the Savior whose death in the cross gave us salvation. But the reference to the life of Jesus as an example for us today was absent and thus theology was proving sterile especially in relation to social ethics.

González's book was a call to develop a social ethics that would use a Christological paradigm as a foundation, and a contextual interpretation of Christology as a way to figure out the nature and mission of the church. For González, Evangelicals should agree to reject the docetism of those who see no more task than that of saving souls for a future life, as well as the ebionism of those who imagine that their action in society and in history is going to establish the Kingdom of God. He deepened the analysis of Christological themes, working from the concerns of the Hispanic context in the United States and he concludes, "In the last analysis, what docetism denied was not only the reality of the incarnation and the suffering of Jesus but the very nature of a God whose greatest victory is achieved through suffering and whose clearest revelation is in the cross."[28] Docetism among Evangelicals could be traced back to the negative effect of post-World War II independent missionaries from North America, that were heavily influenced by Dispensationalism, the mentality of the Cold War with its suspicion about social change, and the delayed effects of the Liberal-Fundamentalist debates of the first decades of the twentieth century.

The Latin American missionary involvement in other parts of the world has brought a need to rediscover and expound the concrete actions of Jesus as they were reported by the evangelists so that they may be grasped, contemplated, and understood as the shaping patterns for contemporary discipleship and missionary activity, a challenging task that Mortimer Arias describes as recovering "the subversive memory of Jesus" for evangelization.[29] This theological task goes to the wealth of biblical data that lies behind the creedal systematizations in which "the Christian message was cast into philosophical categories, and the historical dimension of revelation was completely overshadowed by dogma."[30]

In the 1974 Lausanne Congress of Evangelism, René Padilla presented his paper "Evangelism and the World." With a rich biblical background, he criticized what he called Secular Christianity and Culture Christianity and showed how they were shaping Western, especially American, Evangelical missionary practices. Then he outlined a form of evangelism that would return to a biblical and Christological pattern. The debates around his paper showed that he had touched sensitive areas in the self-image of a missiological enterprise that needed correction and new directions. Several points of Padilla's criticism were incorporated in the *Lausanne Covenant*. Right after the Lausanne Congress in 1976, Padilla edited an international symposium about the Lausanne Covenant with contributions from around the world.[31] A good sample of pieces that he contributed to the Lausanne movement may be appreciated in his book *Mission between the Times.*[32] He has also edited several volumes about the biblical basis for mission, and about models of Integral Mission.[33]

Emilio A. Núñez acknowledges the fact that Latin American Evangelicals received an Anglo-Saxon Christology that was the result of the liberal-fundamentalist debate: "We were presented with a divine-human Christ in the theological formula; but in practice he was far removed from the stage of this world, aloof to our social problems."[34] Orlando Costas chose Jesus's pattern of a missionary effort starting from Galilee, from the margins, as a significant pattern for the Hispanic minorities in the United States and for Latin Americans at a global level.[35] Brazilian Valdir Steuernagel has shown the renewed and continued relevance of historical models of missionary obedience patterned after Jesus.[36]

A TRINITARIAN APPROACH WITH A CHRISTOLOGICAL DISCERNMENT

The significant growth of Pentecostalism around the world has brought the work of the Holy Spirit and the relationship of Word and Spirit to the agenda of Evangelical theology. Pentecostal theologians Norberto Saracco from Argentina, Ricardo Gondim from Brazil, and Bishop Darío López from Perú, are among those that have worked at articulating a self-critical reflection that looks to Christology as the basis for discernment in evaluating the Pentecostal experience.[37] From the Hispanic church in the United States, Eldin Villafañe has worked in the development of a Pentecostal social ethic.[38] The memory of Jesus and the centrality of the Kingdom of God in his teachings are to enrich the traditional Evangelical soteriology of popular Protestantism with its emphasis on the atonement. They will provide also guidelines for the evangelistic and pastoral tasks of the church as well as for the social and political participation of believers at a time of social transitions. In the twenty-first century in Latin America, postmodern culture and the rise of so-called post-denominational mega churches pose the question of how the work of the Spirit is to be distinguished from what could be simply a manipulative purely human religious enterprise. Latin American Evangelical thinkers continue their theological task with a strong Christological foundation and frame. What comes from the Spirit will transform human lives and create living communities modeling them after the pattern of Jesus Christ.

From a sociological perspective, British-Brazillian sociologist Paul Freston says that: "The British diaspora and Anglo-Saxon missions responsible for much worldwide expansion of Protestantism since the eighteenth century have now been overtaken by other diasporas (African, Caribbean, Latin American, Chinese and Korean) and by other missions."[39] This growth is not just an imitation of the Western churches or a response to the mobilizing techniques that Western agencies may have developed. The spiritual vitality of persons, churches, and denominations has nourished the vision and the willingness to obey, which made possible great steps of advance in mission. Revival has been the cradle for missionary vocations. Howard Snyder who was a missionary in Brazil has offered a very convincing analysis that also shows that spiritual revival has been the kind of environment in which new structures for mission have been imagined and developed.[40] The sheer numerical weight of a church does not produce missionary vocations naturally or following human logic. Catholics in Latin America are concerned by the fact that though close to half of the Catholics of the world live in Latin America, only 2 percent of the Catholic missionary force comes from that region.[41]

The Holy Spirit seems to be at work especially in the periphery of the world giving Christian people a vision and mobilizing them for local and global mission in spite of poverty, lack of experience, and absence of training. Almost in every continent, migration movements have brought to cities and industrial or commercial centers a legion of mission minded lay people from majority world churches that enter into contact with old established forms of Christendom. These are being rejuvenated by the spiritual warmth and the sacrificial commitment of persons whose parents or grandparents had been recent converts from other faiths or from a dead nominal form of Christianity. If this is the way the Spirit is moving, what needs to be done in order to walk in step with his reviving and transforming activity? What kinds of global partnerships have to be imagined and developed for this new stage of mission history? Obedience to Christ's commission and the Spirit's missionary drive will keep Christian mission advancing in the twenty-first century, but it will also demand a humble and reflective missiological expertise to propose avenues of obedience to biblical imperatives about *the way and the style* in which such advance is to take place.

My observation of the missionary dynamism of churches in Asia and Latin America, but also among minorities in the United States and Spain, is that they live in the world of poverty. Newly formed churches experience life together in Christian community as a continuous effort to prolong the possibility of survival. As missiologists we cannot fall into the trap of idealizing these churches but neither can we afford to bypass them as we think of global partnerships for mission in the future. Their missionary dynamism is the expression of a thankful response to the experience of the power of the Holy Spirit and the love of Jesus Christ. The marginal, the lonely, the displaced and the refugee find in these churches a home for the homeless and they experience *koinonia*. The oppressed who are "nobodies" because they do not have a name, money or education, find a community where they may unburden their hearts or express their joy in their own way without censorship.

Those desperate because neither psychology nor the fear of police can deliver them from alcohol or drugs experience the liberating power of the Holy Spirit in the name of Jesus. One can then understand the joyful response by which out of their poverty they become stewards of God's grace and their churches are born with a special ability to be self-sufficient.

What is distinctive about the stewardship of these churches of the poor is what we could call a stewardship for survival. Popular churches planted among the poor cannot depend on a tradition, on the help of the state, on the endowment of rich benefactors, or on a body of professional ministers. They have to be fellowships where members join forces to make the community live, grow, propagate the faith, and survive. The stewardship of the totality of life is experienced as total missionary mobilization. What seems to be more difficult to obtain in the case of developed and old established churches is lay mobilization, total participation in the holistic welfare of the Christian community. Among the churches of the poor that mobilization is the normal lifestyle of the community. No other form of life and ministry is possible. After the reality of survival has been possible for a certain time, then it is also possible to speak of patterns of stewardship that will project the community to the great tasks of centrifugal mission. But that experience of voluntary contribution for the survival and growth of the church creates a discipline, a pattern of timing and budgeting that is new, a foundational experience.

As we are well into the twenty-first century, paragraph 9 of the *Lausanne Covenant* has a new relevance: "All of us are shocked by the poverty of millions and disturbed by the injustices that cause it. Those of us who live in affluent circumstances accept our duty to develop a simple life style, in order to contribute more generously to both relief and evangelism." On the one hand, an accelerated globalization process has facilitated communication to the point that we could say that material and technological means are available for the creation and development of transnational and transcontinental partnership for the recruitment, training, and sending of missionaries. On the other hand, that globalization process is generating a world of economic and social disparities that militate against the possibility of effective and legitimate global partnerships for mission. Within this ambivalent situation it is a timely missiological exercise to ask about what is implied in the development of new global partnerships for a mission that is carried on having Jesus as a model.

NOTES

1. Orlando E. Costas, *Christ Outside the Gate: Mission beyond Christendom* (Maryknoll, NY: Orbis Books, 1982), xiv.

2. Manuel López, "La presencia latinoamericana en Edimburgo 2010 se acerca a la veintena de delegados," *ALC Noticias*, June 3, 2010.

3. An exhaustive study of these two conferences is included in the first volume of *Evangelización Protestante en América Latina*, by Costa Rican historian, Quito Arturo Piedra (Ecuador: CLAI, 2000).

4. Juan Kessler and Wilton M. Nelson, "Panamá 1916 y su impacto sobre el Protestantismo latinoamericano," *Pastoralia* 2 (1978): 5–21.

5. This was noted particularly by the Catholic historian, Prudencio Damboriena, SJ, *El Protestantismo en América Latina* (Bogotá-Friburgo: FERES, 1962), 1:23.

6. I have written about this subject in chapter 3 of my book. Samuel Escobar, *Changing Tides: Latin America and World Mission Today* (Maryknoll, NY: Orbis Books, 2002), 23–34.

7. Gonzalo Baez-Camargo, "Mexico—A Long Stretch from Edinburgh," *The Ecumenical Review* 16, no. 3 (1964): 266–73, here 267.

8. Gonzalo Baez-Camargo, "The Place of Latin America in the Ecumenical Movement," *The Ecumenical Review* 1, no. 3 (1949): 311–19, here 311.

9. Robert E. Speer, *South American Problems* (New York: Student Volunteer Movement for Foreign Missions, 1913), 145.

10. Speer, 145.

11. John A. Mackay, *The Other Spanish Christ: A Study in the Spiritual History of Spain and South America* (New York: Macmillan, 1932).

12. John A. Mackay, *That Other America* (New York: Friendship Press, 1935), 69–73, 107–16. For a brief appraisal of Mackay's work see Samuel Escobar, "The Missionary Legacy of John A. Mackay," *International Bulletin of Missionary Research* 16, no. 3 (1992): 116–22. A biography of Mackay was published recently, John Mackay Metzger, *The Hand and the Road: The Life and Times of John A. Mackay* (Louisville, KY: Westminster John Knox Press, 2010).

13. John A. Mackay, "The Power of Evangelism," in *Addresses and Other Records: Report of the Jerusalem Meeting of the International Missionary Council, March 24th–April 8th, 1928* (London: Oxford University Press, 1928), 121.

14. Baez-Camargo, "Mexico—A Long Stretch from Edinburgh," 268.

15. Baez-Camargo, 267.

16. Baez-Camargo, 268.

17. José Míguez Bonino, "Latin America," in *The Prospects of Christianity throughout the World*, ed. M. Searle Bates and Wilhelm Pauck (New York: Scribner, 1964), 168.

18. Gustavo Gutiérrez, *Las Casas: In Search of the Poor of Jesus Christ* (Maryknoll, NY: Orbis, 1993).

19. John McCoy, "La embestida evangélica," *Noticias Aliadas* 26, no. 24 (1989): 2.

20. See "Popular Protestantism and Catholic Missiology" in chapter 8 in my book *Changing Tides*.

21. Jeffrey Klaiber SJ, "Pentecostal Breakthrough," *America* 122, no. 4 (1970): 99–102.

22. Samuel Escobar, *The New Global Mission: The Gospel from Everywhere to Everyone* (Downers Grove, IL: IVP Academic, 2003).

23. Daniel Salinas, "Latin American Evangelical Theology in the 1970s: The Golden Decade"(Leiden: Brill, 2009).

24. Sharon E. Heaney, "Contextual Theology for Latin America: Liberation Themes in Evangelical Perspective" (Eugene, OR: Wipf & Stock, 2008).

25. Orlando E. Costas, *Liberating News: A Theology of Contextual Evangelization* (Grand Rapids, MI: Eerdmans, 1989), 1.

26. I have offered a summary of that theological development in Samuel Escobar, "Doing Theology on Christ's Road," in *Global Theology in Evangelical Perspective: Exploring the Contextual Nature of Theology and Mission*, ed. Jeffrey P. Greenman, and Gene L. Green (Downers Grove, IL: IVP Academic, 2012), 67–85.

27. Justo L. Gonzalez, *Revolución y encarnación* (Rio Piedras, Puerto Rico: Libería La Reforma, 1965).

28. Justo L. González, *Mañana: Christian Theology from a Hispanic Perspective* (Nashville, TN: Abingdon Press, 1990), 143.

29. Mortimer Arias and Alan Johnson, *The Great Commission: Biblical Models for Evangelism* (Nashville, TN: Abingdon Press, 1992); Mortimer Arais, *Announcing the Reign of God: Evangelization and the Subversive Memory of Jesus* (Philadelphia: Fortress Press, 1984).

30. René Padilla and Mark Lau Branson, eds., *Conflict and Context: Hermeneutics in the Americas: A Report on the Context and Hermeneutics in the Americas Conference* (Grand Rapids, MI: Eerdmans, 1986), 81.

31. René Padilla, ed., *New Face of Evangelicalism: An International Symposium on the Lausanne Covenant* (Downers Grove, IL: InterVarsity Press, 1976).

32. René Padilla, *Mission between the Times: Essays on the Kingdom* (Grand Rapids, MI: Eerdmans, 1985).

33. See for instance, René Padilla and Tetsunao Yamamori, eds., *The Local Church, Agent of Transformation: An Ecclesiology for Integral Mission* (Buenos Aires: Ediciones Kairos, 2004).

34. Emilio A. Núñez, *Liberation Theology* (Chicago, IL: Moody Press, 1985), 236.

35. Orlando E. Costas, *The Church and Its Mission: A Shattering Critique from the Third World* (Wheaton, IL: Tyndale House, 1974); Costas, *Christ Outside the Gate*; Costas, *Liberating News: A Theology of Contextual Evangelization*.

36. Valdir Steuernagel, *Obediência missionária e prática histórica: Em busca de modelos* (Sao Paulo: ABU Editora, 1993).

37. See the contributions from Saracco and Gondim to the volume *CLADE III: Tercer Congreso Latinoamericano de Evangelización, Quito, 24 de agosto a 4 de septiembre de 1992* (Buenos Aires: FLT, 1993). See further Darío López Rodriguez, *The Liberating Mission of Jesus: The Message of the Gospel of Luke* (Eugene, OR: Pickwick, 2012).

38. Eldin Villafañe, *The Liberating Spirit: Toward an Hispanic American Pentecostal Social Ethic* (Grand Rapids, MI: Eerdmans, 1993).

39. Paul Freston, "The Transnationalization of Brazilian Pentecostalism: The Universal Church of the Kingdom of God," in *Between Babel and Pentecost: Transnational Pentecostalism in Africa and Latin America*, ed. André Corten and Ruth R. Marshall-Fratani (Bloomington: Indiana University Press, 2001), 196–215, here 196.

40. Howard A. Snyder, *Signs of the Spirit: How God Reshapes the Church* (Eugene, OR: Wipf & Stock, 1997); Howard A. Snyder, *The Radical Wesley and Patterns for Church Renewal* (Downers Grove, IL: InterVarsity Press, 1980).

41. *Memorias del COMLA 4: Minutes of the Fourth Latin America Missionary Congress, Lima Feb. 3–8, 1991* (Lima: Ediciones Paulinas, 1991), 267.

BIBLIOGRAPHY

Arais, Mortimer. *Announcing the Reign of God: Evangelization and the Subversive Memory of Jesus*. Philadelphia: Fortress Press, 1984.

Arias, Mortimer, and Alan Johnson. *The Great Commission: Biblical Models for Evangelism*. Nashville, TN: Abingdon Press, 1992.

Baez-Camargo, Gonzalo. "Mexico—A Long Stretch from Edinburgh." *The Ecumenical Review* 16, no. 3 (1964): 266–73.

———. "The Place of Latin America in the Ecumenical Movement." *The Ecumenical Review* 1, no. 3 (1949): 311–19.

Bonino, José Míguez. "Latin America," in *The Prospects of Christianity throughout the World*, edited by M. Searle Bates and Wilhelm Pauck, 168. New York: Scribner, 1964.

CLADE III: Tercer Congreso Latinoamericano de Evangelización, Quito, 24 de agosto a 4 de septiembre de 1992. Buenos Aires: FLT, 1993.

Costas, Orlando E. *Christ Outside the Gate: Mission beyond Christendom*. Maryknoll, NY: Orbis Books, 1982.

———. *The Church and its Mission: A Shattering Critique from the Third World*. Wheaton, IL: Tyndale House, 1974.

———. *Liberating News: A Theology of Contextual Evangelization*. Grand Rapids, MI: Eerdmans, 1989.

Escobar, Samuel. *Changing Tides: Latin America and World Mission Today*. Maryknoll, NY: Orbis Books, 2002.

——. "Doing Theology on Christ's Road," in *Global Theology in Evangelical Perspective: Exploring the Contextual Nature of Theology and Mission*, edited by Jeffrey P. Greenman, and Gene L. Green, 67–85. Downers Grove, IL: IVP Academic, 2012.

——. "The Missionary Legacy of John A. Mackay." *International Bulletin of Missionary Research* 16, no. 3 (1992): 116–22.

——. *The New Global Mission: The Gospel from Everywhere to Everyone*. Downers Grove, IL: IVP Academic, 2003.

Freston, Paul. "The Transnationalization of Brazilian Pentecostalism: The Universal Church of the Kingdom of God," in *Between Babel and Pentecost: Transnational Pentecostalism in Africa and Latin America*, edited by André Corten and Ruth R. Marshall-Fratani, 196–215. Bloomington, IN: Indiana University Press, 2001.

González, Justo L. *Mañana: Christian Theology from a Hispanic Perspective*. Nashville, TN: Abingdon Press, 1990.

——. *Revolución y encarnación*. Rio Piedras, Puerto Rico: Libería La Reforma, 1965.

Gutiérrez, Gustavo. *Las Casas: In Search of the Poor of Jesus Christ*. Maryknoll, NY: Orbis, 1993.

Heaney, Sharon E. *Contextual Theology for Latin America: Liberation Themes in Evangelical Perspective*. Eugene, OR: Wipf & Stock, 2008.

Klaiber SJ, Jeffrey. "Pentecostal Breakthrough." *America* 122, no. 4 (1970): 99–102.

Mackay, John A. *That Other America*. New York: Friendship Press, 1935.

——. *The Other Spanish Christ: A Study in the Spiritual History of Spain and South America*. New York, Eugene, OR: Macmillan, Wipf & Stock, 1932.

——. "The Power of Evangelism," in *Addresses and Other Records: Report of the Jerusalem Meeting of the International Missionary Council March 24th–April 8th, 1928*, 1928.

McCoy, John. "La embestida evangélica." *Noticias Aliadas* 26, no. 24 (1989): 2.

Memorias del COMLA 4: Minutes of the Fourth Latin America Missionary Congress, Lima Feb. 3–8, 1991. Lima: Ediciones Paulinas, 1991.

Metzger, John Mackay. *The Hand and the Road: The Life and Times of John A. Mackay*. Louisville, KY: Westminster John Knox Press, 2010.

Núñez, Emilio A. *Liberation Theology*. Chicago, IL: Moody Press, 1985.

Padilla, René. *Mission between the Times: Essays on the Kingdom*. Grand Rapids, MI: Eerdmans, 1985.

——, ed. *New Face of Evangelicalism: An International Symposium on the Lausanne Covenant*. Downers Grove, IL: Intervarsity Press, 1976.

Padilla, René, and Mark Lau Branson, eds. *Conflict and Context: Hermeneutics in the Americas: A Report on the Context and Hermeneutics in the Americas Conference*. Grand Rapids, MI: Eerdmans, 1986.

Padilla, René, and Tetsunao Yamamori, eds. *The Local Church, Agent of Transformation: An Ecclesiology for Integral Mission*. Buenos Aires: Ediciones Kairos, 2004.

Rodriguez, Darío López. *The Liberating Mission of Jesus: The Message of the Gospel of Luke*. Eugene, OR: Pickwick, 2012.

Salinas, Daniel. *Latin American Evangelical Theology in the 1970's: The Golden Decade*. Leiden: Brill, 2009.

Snyder, Howard A. *The Radical Wesley and Patterns for Church Renewal*. Downers Grove, IL: Intervarsity Press, 1980.

——. *Signs of the Spirit: How God Reshapes the Church*. Eugene, OR: Wipf & Stock, 1997.

Speer, Robert E. *South American Problems*. New York: Student Volunteer Movement for Foreign Missions, 1913.

Steuernagel, Valdir. *Obediência missionária e prática histórica: Em busca de modelos*. Sao Paulo: ABU Editora, 1993.

Villafañe, Eldin. *The Liberating Spirit: Toward an Hispanic American Pentecostal Social Ethic*. Grand Rapids, MI: Eerdmans, 1993.

Chapter Six

Gospel and Culture Conversations about Biblical Interpretation

James Brownson

More than thirty years ago Darrell Guder published the foundational book *Be My Witnesses*, developing a new approach to thinking theologically about the church's mission.[1] Shortly after this time, Darrell became involved in the Gospel and Our Culture Network (or GOCN), an attempt to deepen the church's missionary engagement with its cultural context, and Darrell has been an active participant in this movement for many years. This network has sought to reframe the church's ecclesiological thinking more deeply around mission, and in so doing, to transform not only the church's witness, but also its identity, and its way of reading Scripture. Darrell and I met in that context, and I have benefited from his friendship over many years.

I want to explore what has happened since that movement began, particularly around a missional reading of Scripture. Where has the discussion moved, and what are its results? I myself have been a participant in these conversations, publishing a number of articles, and in 1998, offering my own attempt at a missional hermeneutic entitled *Speaking the Truth in Love: New Testament Resources for a Missional Hermeneutic*,[2] as well as collaborating on another published project a few years later entitled *Storm Front: The Good News of God*.[3]

In particular, I want to explore two different themes or issues that have emerged since those original publications that continue to bear on the question of missional hermeneutics. As we look ahead, and seek to determine how a missional hermeneutic should continue to shape our reading of Scripture, these are two questions that the movement must address, if it is going to continue to be effective and relevant.

The first of these questions concerns the tension between universality and particularity/contextuality in a missional hermeneutic. On the one hand, we have seen a variety of books come out in the last ten years that attempt to engage in a comprehensive or universal reading of Scripture from a missional perspective. One thinks of Richard Bauckham's book, *Bible and Mission: Christian Witness in a Postmodern World*,[4] or Christopher Wright's *The Mission of God: Unlocking the Bible's Grand Narrative*,[5] as examples of this sort of inquiry. These are useful attempts to engage in a comprehensive sort of interpretive inquiry focusing on mission, but precisely because such inquiries are so comprehensive, they run the risk of downplaying the cultural or contextual dimension of missional hermeneutics, in favor of a grand narrative encompassing a variety of times and places, perhaps even a universalized sort of reading.

We have also seen the balancing sort of inquiry, which is more focused and contextual. The Missional Hermeneutics Forum of the GOCN continues to hold annual meetings in conjunction with the gathering of the Society of Biblical Literature every fall, and has invited a variety of papers over the years that focus on more particular hermeneutical questions (as well as the broader and sweeping ones). Recently, studies have emerged that focus on particular segments of the biblical witness, such as Michael Gorman's work, *Becoming the Gospel: Paul, Participation, and Mission*,[6] which focuses on a missional reading of the Pauline literature, in particular.

In addition to this focus on particular contexts within the canon, the missional hermeneutics conversation has also become more deeply contextualized in a variety of denominational traditions, including Reformed, Presbyterian, Mennonite, Episcopalian, and many others. This is not surprising. None of us comes to the Bible as a "blank slate." Instead, we read the scripture in light of the particular tradition in which we are located. We also read the Bible, located in a particular tradition, with a view to discerning how such a reading leads us across cultural boundaries in new contexts. But one of the learnings of the GOCN over the years is that this factor of "tradition" is an extremely important one for missional readings of scripture. Even though mission is a common task of the whole church, it is also a particular task of specific churches, who read the Bible in particular ways. And until a specific church discerns how its own call to mission invites a cross-cultural encounter that has a particular shape, it is unlikely that missional readings will have a transformative effect in such churches. We all sit on our own three-legged stool, drawing upon scripture, tradition, and context.

This has been an important learning of the GOCN. It is not sufficient to speak merely about Gospel and about culture. We must also be clear and explicit about the specific tradition(s) in which we are located, and explicit in exploring how those traditions shape the Gospel/culture conversation. This has deepened and enriched GOCN conversations about contextuality.

These have been productive conversations about contextuality and universality, that have furthered our grasp of multiple sides of the missional hermeneutics conversation, and I expect them to continue. Because the church offers the good news *of God*, it must always engage the universalizing implications of the Gospel. Because the God whom the church proclaims became human in the incarnation and spawned a missionary gospel, this good news always has a particular shape, depending on its local context and its particular tradition, which must be factored into discussions about its beliefs and identity.

A second issue that has emerged since those original publications has been more complex, and has posed a greater challenge to the GOCN as a movement. I am speaking here of the role of *rationality* in a missional hermeneutic. I think that, by and large, participants in the GOCN missional hermeneutics conversation have operated under the assumption that rational discourse represents the most helpful way to engage in hermeneutical conversations that cross-cultural boundaries. The GOCN movement has been, in large part, an *academic* movement—a movement which therefore thrives on rational discourse and rational analysis. I have fully participated in these assumptions in my own work.

But more recently, I have been forced to confront what many involved in the mission of the church have known for some time: missional hermeneutics is not entirely or exclusively a *rational* enterprise. At one level, of course, this is not at all surprising. Participants in the GOCN have, for some time, spoken of the contemporary mission movement as a step past the rationalism of the Enlightenment, where it was simply assumed that rational discourse could resolve all issues. Craig Van Gelder writes in one of the chapters found in *The Church between Gospel and Culture* entitled "Mission in the Emerging Postmodern Condition," about how more recent postmodern analysis has exposed the many ways in which so-called "rational" discourse is, in reality, dependent on a host of local and contextual factors, including language, money, and experience.[7]

But it is one thing to affirm this at a very lofty conceptual level, using categories like "postmodernism." It is another to engage these dynamics at the more specific level of biblical interpretation, known as "missional hermeneutics."

One of the missional issues where this has emerged involves the question of racism and racial bias. This has been a deeply disturbing and contentious issue in my own country, the United States, for some time now. In the face of repeated and sometimes inexplicable uses of violence against black folks by police, the "Black Lives Matter" movement has sought to bring focused attention to this problem. And yet the country has also seen a reaction against the "Black Lives Matter" movement, which uses "All Lives Matter" as a slogan, with the implicit assertion that it is wrong to single out black lives for any specific and focused attention.

On the surface, it is hard to see where the problem lies. If it is true that "all lives matter," then specific attention needs to be devoted to those lives that are treated as if they do not matter, which in many contexts means black lives in particular. But the fact that this issue continues to be contentious suggests that there are factors operating here that extend beyond rational analysis.

Willie James Jennings has explored these meta-rational categories in his insightful book, *The Christian Imagination: Theology and the Origins of Race.*[8] Jennings introduces two helpful categories into the conversation on race. One of them is the notion of "imagination." For Jennings, imagination concerns the possibilities we allow ourselves to contemplate. He notes how, prior to the thirteenth century, there was not even a word for "race" in European languages. Instead, people were identified with the places from which they came. But as land began to be bought and sold in an emerging European colonialism, this way of identifying people seemed increasingly relativized, and so Europeans developed the category of "race" to identify people instead. And, of course, this new category became a device to classify people according to their economic interest to an emerging European coloni-alism, thus dehumanizing people on the basis of their skin color or general appearance.

Jennings also asks a further important question: What is it that disrupts this socially constructed imagination, in order to invite a deeper and wider perception of reality? His answer is *intimacy*. When we get to know someone well who does not fit into our socially constructed categories, what we had always taken for granted becomes subject to more careful analysis, and the gate is opened to a wider imagination, shaped by new categories. We sudden-ly find ourselves contemplating possibilities that had not even appeared on the horizon before.

Something like this clearly happened in the mission of the early church. For centuries, the people of God had identified themselves by particular practices, namely circumcision and kosher eating. Those who engaged in these practices were part of the people of God; those who did not were outsiders. Yet the book of Acts records the dilemma faced by the early disciples of Jesus—as gentiles responded to the Gospel they seemed to be transformed by receiving the Holy Spirit, but yet they failed to observe the core practices, which had always, in the disciples' memory, defined the people of God. Acts 10–11 narrates how Peter came to recognize, based on his intimate encounter with the gentile Cornelius, that God's categories in this new gospel were not the same categories he had always assumed and taken for granted. As the word from heaven stated, "What God has made clean, you must not call profane" (Acts 10:15).

Hence, in light of Jennings's analysis, merely rational analysis, even in the service of mission, misses two vital elements. On the one hand, rational analysis by itself will not always address possibilities beyond those that we simply take for granted as self-evident. On the other hand, rational analysis will often fail, at least initially, to adequately integrate the results of intimate encounters that disrupt our world and complicate our vision.

I want to apply this analysis to another area in the church's life that has been the source of great disagreement and controversy. I am referring to the widespread disagreement in the church over the inclusion of LGBTQ folks within the life of the church, as well as disagreements over how to respond to the Supreme Court's recent *Obergefell* decision legalizing same-sex marriage in the United States. Several years ago, I wrote a book on this topic.[9] I do not intend to rehearse all the arguments from that book here. Rather, I want to focus on some aspects of my experience dealing with responses to the book.

Although there are some notable exceptions, I have noticed a general pattern in my interactions with people surrounding the book. I have found that there is a core question that tends to determine, in most instances, the nature of the conversation. That question goes something like this: "Do you know well and care deeply about someone who is LGBTQ?" If the answer to that question is "no," the conversation about the interpretation of biblical passages found in my book will follow a very different trajectory, and it will be far more difficult to find common ground in interpretation.

I take this to be at least roughly analogous to Jennings's category of "intimacy" noted above. Simply put, we are taught the meaning of our gender before we can even speak. Consequently, assumptions about the meaning of gender are often so self-evident to us that it seems absurd even to contemplate alternatives. Until these assumptions are disrupted by some sort of close encounter with someone who doesn't fit these assumptions, they will continue to be regarded by most people as simply self-evident.

From this traditional perspective, to welcome LGBTQ folks without requiring them to submit to heterosexual norms is to buy into one of our culture's worst characteristics, specifically the idolatry of impulse and passion. It is to accept an assumption that Christians have never embraced—the assumption that we have a moral obligation to follow all our passions and desires (so long as no one else is hurt in the process).

So here, then, is the problem that seems to emerge from the analysis up to this point. Many folks who lack intimate encounters with LGBTQ folks assume that the privileging of such a personal encounter would actually represent a distortion of Christian faith, the idolatry of desire. This raises the basic question of the role of intimacy in theological, missiological, and ethical reflection. Is such a move simply the replacement of objective norms with subjective experience, or is something deeper at work here?

I do not believe that such appeals to intimacy are necessarily appeals to inappropriate subjective factors in missiological or ethical deliberation. But I do believe that it is necessary to clarify exactly what, more constructively, is at stake in these appeals to intimacy. I believe that two dynamics are at work here. The first one is the dynamic of disruption. Just as an intimate encounter with someone from a different race can often disrupt our assumptions about that other person, so a deep personal engagement with an LGBTQ person can disrupt our assumptions about the nature of the experience of these people. The world we have taken for granted can no longer be taken for granted; it must be tested and analyzed more deeply. This, of course, does not mean that deeper assumptions must necessarily change, but they are "on the table" after such encounters in ways that they were not, prior to the encounter. We encounter a problem with our assumptions that we didn't know existed, before that time. Intimacy is a necessary condition for the identification of a problem with assumptions that we have simply taken for granted before that moment.

This leads directly to a second role of intimacy in missiological or ethical deliberation: the hard work of constructing an alternative paradigm. Perhaps an analogy from the past may be illuminating here. For one thousand eight hundred years of the church's history, the church had critiqued abuses of slavery, but had never spoken collectively about the institution of slavery itself. Likewise, even though the Bible encouraged people to avoid becoming slaves (e.g., 1 Cor. 7:23), it never rejected the institution itself, and offered advice at multiple points toward a humanizing of the institution (e.g., Eph. 6:5ff., Col. 3:22ff., 1 Tim. 6:1). This perspective was never deeply called into question until the nineteenth century, when the slave trade became so com-mercialized and morally repugnant that Christians began to ask deeper ques-tions. The result was a deeper realization that there is something incompat-ible between the radical value that the Gospel places on each human life, and the practice of buying and selling, under any conditions, these same human lives. In other words, an intimate encounter with a practice that wasn't work-ing led to a deeper analysis of the tradition and Scripture itself, and a refor-mulation of the Gospel in new terms that shed light on the institution of slavery itself.

In this light, then, it is not that the experience of intimacy is trumping or displacing Scripture; rather, we simply won't do the hard work of reformulat-ing our reading of Scripture until the disruption of our experience forces us to develop a new paradigm for the reading and interpretation of Scripture. In this context, then, the disruption of intimacy does not replace Scripture; it drives us back to read Scripture more deeply.

We find this happening in the New Testament itself, with respect to circumcision and kosher eating. It is evident from the pages of the New Testament that this issue was not immediately resolved; Paul writes about it in many of his letters, and the entire New Testament seems deeply concerned about developing a new way of reading the Hebrew Scriptures that would accommodate the experience of gentiles more fruitfully. The actual experience with gentile Christians drove the leadership back, over an extended period of time, to their Bible, to read it more deeply, and to develop new paradigms for interpreting it. Without the experience of dealing with gentile Christians, the early church simply wouldn't have done the hard work to develop a new paradigm.

This is the point at which, for the present, I would like to leave my discussion of LGBTQ issues in this exploration. I am not suggesting that intimacy should replace Scripture. Instead, I am suggesting that close relationships with LGBTQ folks will disrupt our current paradigms, and force us back to the text, to interpret it more deeply. We shall have to wait and see what the results of that activity look like, when the dust has settled.

So we return again to the question with which we began: the state of the conversation about the Gospel and our culture as it pertains to biblical interpretation. As I have tried to argue, this is a complex question, both because of the particularity of our diverse traditions, and also because of the meta-rational elements that infuse many of the Gospel/culture/context conversations. But I believe that the core reality remains the same: the Gospel constantly invites us to cross cultural boundaries with good news, and that activity constantly draws us more deeply into the reality of the Gospel, expanding our grasp of its scope and its implications. May it always be so.

NOTES

1. Darrell L. Guder, *Be My Witnesses: The Church's Mission, Message, and Messengers* (Grand Rapids, MI: Eerdmans, 1985).

2. James V. Brownson, *Speaking the Truth in Love: New Testament Resources for a Missional Hermeneutic* (Grand Rapids, MI: Eerdmans, 1998).

3. James V. Brownson et al., *Storm Front: The Good News of God* (Grand Rapids, MI: Eerdmans, 2003).

4. Richard Bauckham, *Bible and Mission: Christian Witness in a Postmodern World*,(Grand Rapids, MI: Baker, 2003).

5. Christopher J. H. Wright, *The Mission of God: Unlocking the Bible's Grand Narrative* (Downers Grove, IL: IVP, 2006).

6. Michael Gorman, *Becoming the Gospel: Paul, Participation, and Mission* (Grand Rapids, MI: Eerdmans, 2015).

7. George R. Hunsberger, and Craig Van Gelder, eds. *The Church between Gospel and Culture: The Emerging Mission in North America* (Grand Rapids, MI: Eerdmans, 1997), 113–38.

8. Willie James Jennings, *The Christian Imagination: Theology and the Origins of Race* (New Haven, CT: Yale University Press, 2010).

9. James V. Brownson, *Bible, Gender, Sexuality: Reframing the Church's Debate on Same-Sex Relationships* (Grand Rapids, MI: Eerdmans, 2013).

BIBLIOGRAPHY

Bauckham, Richard. *Bible and Mission: Christian Witness in a Postmodern World.* Grand Rapids, MI: Baker, 2003.

Brownson, James V. *Bible, Gender, Sexuality: Reframing the Church's Debate on Same-Sex Relationships.* Grand Rapids, MI: Eerdmans, 2013.

———. *Speaking the Truth in Love: New Testament Resources for a Missional Hermeneutic.* Grand Rapids, MI: Eerdmans, 1998.

Brownson, James V., Inagrace T. Dietterich, Barry A. Harvey, and Charles C. West. *Storm Front: The Good News of God.* Grand Rapids, MI: Eerdmans, 2003.

Guder, Darrell L. *Be My Witnesses: The Church's Mission, Message, and Messengers.* Grand Rapids, MI: Eerdmans, 1985.

Hunsberger, George R., and Craig Van Gelder, eds. *The Church between Gospel and Culture: The Emerging Mission in North America.* Grand Rapids, MI: Eerdmans, 1997.

Jennings, Willie James. *The Christian Imagination: Theology and the Origins of Race.* New Haven, CT: Yale University Press, 2010.

Wright, Christopher J. H. *The Mission of God: Unlocking the Bible's Grand Narrative.* Downers Grove, IL: IVP, 2006.

Chapter Seven

Demythologizing as an Intercultural Hermeneutic

David W. Congdon

Nearly eighty years have passed since Rudolf Bultmann delivered his programmatic lecture on demythologizing in Alpirsbach in the spring of 1941.[1] This chapter argues that the key to a new perspective on his controversial program comes from the burgeoning field of intercultural hermeneutics. The work in this field is the result of an interdisciplinary (and increasingly also interreligious) dialogue between missiology, cultural anthropology, and biblical studies. The issues and questions raised by scholars in this field would seem to be miles away from—not to mention, at times sharply opposed to—the concerns operative in Bultmann's work. A careful look again at his writings on demythologizing, however, proves this initial impression to be misguided. The program of demythologizing is best understood as a *hermeneutic of intercultural encounter*—in this case, the encounter between the ancient culture of the biblical text and the contemporary culture of its readers today.

THE PROGRAM OF INTERCULTURAL HERMENEUTICS

Intercultural hermeneutics is still relatively unknown in anglophone theology and missiology.[2] When it comes to the intersection of mission and interpretation, the North American conversation has focused on the idea of "missional hermeneutics," for which James Brownson and Darrell Guder are the leading representatives. Recent work in intercultural theology and hermeneutics, however, expands and nuances the effort to think hermeneutically about mission and culture. The term "intercultural theology" is an increasingly common way of clarifying the field of missiology.[3] As Klaus Hock notes in his recent introduction to intercultural theology, too often the field of mission studies is "positioned beyond or outside of the theological disciplines."[4] Intercultural theology thus recognizes that the questions raised by intercultural research are crucial for the entire theological curriculum and for the nature of theological discourse as such. In this sense, the term "intercultural theology" serves the same function as "missional theology," while avoiding the pejorative connotations of the word "mission."

Intercultural theology, as the name suggests, gives more sustained and sophisticated attention to the theory of culture itself and the relation between theology and culture. As a normative enterprise it seeks to address the problem of cultural imperialism, which we can define theologically as the binding of the Christian norm (i.e., the Gospel) to specific cultural norms, thus leading to the absolutizing of a particular culture. According to Hollenweger, "intercultural theology is that scientific, theological discipline that operates in the context of a given culture without absolutizing it."[5] It avoids cultural absolutization by making its object of theological inquiry the "processes of translation, adaptation, reformation, and appropriation that are produced in the encounter between persons of different cultural backgrounds."[6] Intercultural theology, we might say, is the process of understanding our talk about God in the context of encountering those who are culturally foreign. As a process of understanding, such theology is perpetually engaged in the act of interpretation. Intercultural theology is therefore essentially intercultural *hermeneutics*, or, to put it another way, hermeneutics forms the underlying logic of intercultural theology. This represents the most significant advance upon traditional work in missiology.

As Theo Sundermeier notes, "'hermeneutics' was not a theme of mission studies." The only real question was one of "communication," not interpretation, since "there was obviously no doubt about *what* was to be proclaimed," only *how* to proclaim it.[7] The problem with this model of communication—and thus with related terms like contextualizing and indigenizing—is that it does not recognize the way interpretation and contextualization are already involved from the very start:

> Contextualizing thus does not take place afterwards, after the [biblical] text is fixed, but is already involved in the initial witness, because it is inherent in the process of understanding and passing on. It is therefore inadequate to speak of "contextualizing" . . . since it is in truth a matter of *re*contextualizing in the particular appropriation of a text. Recontextualizing is less a problem of communication; it rather belongs centrally to hermeneutics.[8]

The work of contextualization is internal to the very message of the Gospel, and thus theology cannot but be hermeneutical. Intercultural theology aims to overturn this misconception of mission as a merely secondary and "practical" discipline by redefining mission as the task of understanding and interpretation, and thus redefining theology itself as an exercise in hermeneutical reflection.

The hermeneutical problem of mission thus does not merely concern the *form* of theology but also and especially its *content*. Whereas an imperialistic understanding of mission promotes a unidirectional movement of a fixed content *from* the cultural-linguistic form of the missionaries *to* the cultural-linguistic form of the recipients, intercultural theology locates Christian self-understanding within a *multidirectional* context of intercultural dialogue. "An intercultural hermeneutic is essentially relational," according to Sundermeier. "It is a process of understanding in the context of a relation between people who are strangers to each other."[9] Borrowing from recent research in communication studies, Sundermeier points out the way "the receiver as hearer of the message is not an object of the sender, not even just an object of the message, but is at the same time the subject and corresponding sender."[10] The hermeneutical problem of intercultural understanding requires rethinking the very nature of Christian witness. Missionary witness "does not mean the delivery of a message, like the way the mail carrier passes on a package," but involves "concern for and loving treatment" of others.[11] Theology is thereby defined as an enterprise of mutual understanding in which each dialogue partner is, in effect, a missionary to the other. This process of understanding has significant ethical implications. A theology of intercultural understanding aims at a "free living-together" that Sundermeier calls *Konvivenz* or *convivencia*, a term he takes from Latin American liberation theology.[12] In contrast to a colonial mission that was often "culture-destroying," a mission of *Konvivenz* leads to ongoing "cultural innovation" through intercultural dialogue and engagement.[13] Such a mission necessitates hermeneutical reflection since it is already an interpretive process: it is an understanding of the other that leads toward a liberating life together.

Sundermeier defines the hermeneutics of mission in terms of understanding (*Verstehen*) and translation (*Übersetzung*).[14] Understanding takes place in an encounter with the cultural other that dialectically maintains both distance and nearness. The two culturally distinct subjects are simultaneously separate and together. Strangeness and sameness exist "in a relational, interdependent relationship," and for this reason an intercultural hermeneutic is "essentially relational."[15] Sundermeier calls the process by which understanding occurs "appropriation," which he clarifies does not mean the annexation, expropriation, or assimilation of the other, but rather involves a critical self-distancing—a distinction of oneself from one's cultural presuppositions—that frees one for new understandings and translations.[16] Translation then names the process of inculturation, in which the Christian message or kerygma takes on new forms. Heinrich Balz calls this process "transpropriation" (*Übereignung*) as a counterpart to "appropriation" (*Aneignung*).[17] Whichever term we use, transpropriation or translation is "not the transporting of cargo unchanged from one shore to another. New pictures, new idioms, new comparisons must be found, which transfer the subject matter in such a way that it can be received on the other shore." This process of translation, he says, necessarily involves syncretism.[18] An intercultural hermeneutic embraces this creative pluralism, recognizing that the truth is found precisely in the "interplay of different interpretations."[19]

The program of intercultural hermeneutics therefore has a twofold character. Negatively, intercultural hermeneutics rejects the absolutizing of culture. Positively, intercultural hermeneutics takes place within the dynamic space of understanding and translation, of appropriation and transpropriation. As we will see, this is precisely the space that Bultmann's program of demythologizing opens up and in which it operates.

THE PROGRAM OF DEMYTHOLOGIZING

To understand how Bultmann's program of demythologizing is a program of intercultural hermeneutics, we must begin by looking at the twofold definition of demythologizing that he provides in his 1952 essay, "Zum Problem der Entmythologisierung": "Negatively, demythologizing is *criticism of the world-picture of myth* insofar as it conceals the real intention of myth. Positively, demythologizing is *existentialist interpretation*, in that it seeks to make clear the intention of myth to talk about human existence."[20] The negative and positive aspects of demythologizing correspond, respectively, to (a) the criticism of cultural absolutization and (b) the intercultural hermeneutic of appropriation and transpropriation.

The Criticism of the Mythical World-Picture

Bultmann defines myth as an objectifying thinking situated within an antiquated world-picture (*Weltbild*). Myth "is an objectifying thinking like that of science," he says in 1952,[21] while in 1941 he begins his programmatic essay by stating that "the world-picture of the New Testament is a mythical world-picture" and thus "mythological speech . . . is hard for people to believe, because for them the mythical world-picture is a thing of the past."[22] Both parts of this composite definition are significant and merit close attention. In order to clarify the intercultural aspect of Bultmann's program, we will focus our attention on the idea of the mythical world-picture. Ulrich Körtner rightly points out that "the concept of world-picture is a key to Bultmann's concept of myth."[23] Unfortunately, many scholars—including Körtner himself—have misunderstood Bultmann's use of *Weltbild*, often confusing it with the notion of objectification (*Objektivierung*).[24]

The reason for this confusion seems to be the overestimation of Heidegger's significance for Bultmann, and in this case, the assumption that Heidegger's 1938 essay, "Die Zeit des Weltbildes," determines the meaning of the term *Weltbild*.[25] But Bultmann's development of *Weltbild* predates Heidegger by well over a decade. Moreover, Bultmann specifically differentiates between world-pictures and objectifying modes of thought, whereas Heidegger collapses them. The more important source for Bultmann's work is Wilhelm Dilthey's worldview theory (*Weltanschauungslehre*), according to which *Weltbild* refers to the general perceptions and representations of the world that are derived from one's cultural context, and which form the underlying basis for the more systematic evaluation of meaning that constitutes a *Weltanschauung*.[26] Bultmann employs this distinction between a cultural world-picture and an ideological worldview in his 1925 essay on speaking of God, and it remains operative throughout the rest of his career.[27] Especially notable in this regard is a conversation that took place on July 31, 1953, between Bultmann, Günther Bornkamm, and Friedrich Karl Schumann, where Bultmann made the following statement:

> I am of the opinion that all people, whether they live in a mythical age or an enlightened age, have a *Weltbild*, live in a *Weltbild*, by which I naturally do not mean that this *Weltbild* must be a closed and systematic *Weltbild*. The fact that people can go about their daily activities and communicate with their fellow human beings all presupposes that a definite *Weltbild* is taken for granted.[28]

The category of *Weltbild*, as Bultmann uses it, thus refers to the general cultural framework—the shared assumptions, practices, customs, and concepts—that people presuppose in their everyday lives. A world-picture is the native milieu into which one is born. While it shapes how one exists in the world, it is spatially and temporally relative and open to change and hybridization. No world-picture—whether mythical or scientific, ancient or modern, Western or non-Western—is ever final or secure. As Bultmann puts it, everyone "knows that all of the results of science are relative and that any world-picture worked out either yesterday, today, or tomorrow can never be definitive."[29]

Because the *Weltbild* is as natural to us as our mother tongue, it is easy to absolutize what is in fact relative and provisional. We are constantly prone to shielding ourselves from cultural pluralism and avoiding intercultural encounters with those who seem foreign, because of the threat such pluralism poses to our traditional and self-enclosed plausibility structures. Wolfgang Gantke thus warns against absolutizing "culturally-conditioned partial truths about the world," which leads to a lack of openness to new and foreign experiences and reduces religion to political ideology.[30] Following Gantke, we can thus define *Weltbild* as a culturally-conditioned perspective on the world. While there is no acultural standpoint from which a person can survey the world as a neutral observer, we must be careful not to absolutize our

standpoint and so close ourselves off from what is culturally alien and historically new.

Bultmann's criticism of the mythological *Weltbild* aims to prevent this
cultural absolutization. What distinguishes myth qua myth is not the objectification of the divine—which occurs in every age, both ancient and
modern—but the fact that this objectification is naively bound up with an
antiquated *Weltbild*, that is, a set of cultural assumptions from a *foreign*
historical situation. The encounter with scripture is therefore analogous to the
encounter with the stranger: both are intercultural engagements in which
understanding and translation are necessary moments in the interpretive
enterprise. The intercultural dialogue can be both chronological and geographical in nature. Bultmann's differentiation between kerygma and myth is
simply a way of saying that the kerygma can no more be conflated with the
cultural situation of the prophets and apostles any more than it can be conflated with one of the various cultures of the present day. Negatively, his
claim is that the kerygma is free *from* the processes of cultural formation and
hybridization in the sense that the truth of the kerygma is irreducible to the
matrix of cultural forces. This negative point then serves the positive claim
that the kerygma is free *for* culture in the sense that the truth of the kerygma
is always translatable into new cultural contexts. If the *negative* aspect of
demythologizing maintains the kerygma's openness to foreign and new experiences, then the *positive* side of demythologizing—namely, existentialist
interpretation—provides the hermeneutical method for this intercultural
translation.

Existentialist Interpretation: Preunderstanding as Appropriation

The first thing to say about existentialist interpretation is that, despite the
semantic kinship with existentialism, the two are "not the same thing."[31]
Existentialist interpretation has nothing to do with conforming scripture to a
new metaphysics or Heideggerian ontology. Bultmann's method of hermeneutical translation instead has two aspects, what he terms "preunderstanding" (*Vorverständnis*) and "self-understanding" (*Selbstverständnis*). These
correspond to what he calls in his Gifford lectures the "two points of view in
historiography": the first is "the perspective or viewpoint" of the historian,
while the second is "the existential encounter with history."[32] I will demonstrate that these aspects constitute the Bultmannian parallel to the intercultural method of appropriation and transpropriation.

The concept of preunderstanding is not unique to Bultmann, but he employs it in a way that is distinctive to his project. Preunderstanding serves as
shorthand for Bultmann's participatory epistemology. His 1955 essay, "Wissenschaft und Existenz," describes two ways of knowing the world: the way
of objectifying science and the way of participatory existence. Scientific

knowledge is a neutral observation or "disinterested *seeing*" of things in the world that captures "a certain side of the historical process," such as "that and when this or that battle took place, this or that catastrophe happened."[33] Existential understanding, by contrast, recognizes that there is no ahistorical location from which to survey history as a whole. Each perspective sees something "objective"—something that is actually already *there* in the object—but it can only see this object *in a certain way*. The truth of the object is, in a sense, relative to the context in which the object is revealed and comes to expression. Historical meaning "is only possible for the one who does not stand over against [history] as a neutral, nonparticipating spectator, but rather stands within it and shares in the responsibility for it."[34] This entails the paradoxical claim that "the 'most subjective' interpretation of history is precisely the 'most objective.'"[35] Understanding history demands an ongoing recognition of the historicity and sociocultural embeddedness of both the text and ourselves. Our participation in the existential understanding of history therefore requires the responsible *appropriation* of ever new conceptualities—that is, modes of thinking specific to particular cultural-historical contexts—that correspond to both the human subject and the historical subject matter. The exegete who exists historically "will understand the old word ever anew. Ever anew the word will reveal who we are and who God is, and the exegete must state this in an ever new conceptuality."[36]

Bultmann refers to appropriation as the task of translation. The exegete encounters "a strange language" in the text that uses concepts from "a strange *Weltbild*." In order to make sense of this language and to engage the text responsibly, however, "it must be *translated*."[37] Hermeneutical inquiry recognizes that the meaning of a text is never self-evident or internal to the text itself. To interpret the text is necessarily to move beyond it, but always in dialogue with it. "Each translation signals the incompleteness of a text," according to Sundermeier. In the same way that a person finds her identity extended and enlarged through a communal coexistence with others, so too "the text finds in translation its continuation and a secondary restating."[38] The culturally alien form of speech has to be interpreted and stated anew, meaning that the hearer of the text must relate to it in such a way that she can appropriate resources from her own cultural situation for the sake of establishing a mutual understanding between past and present. The interpreter must so thoroughly participate in the subject matter of the text that she is able to hear the message of the past as a message that concerns her personally. Translation is the process by which the participating, empathetic reader *recontextualizes* the message of the text, and in so doing creates a space of mutuality between the ancient *Weltbild* and the contemporary *Weltbild*. Translation therefore consists in constructing a hermeneutical *Konvivenz* between the reader and the strangers who meet us in the text. In order to carry this out appropriately, the interpreter must reflect on the present cultural situation in order to properly recognize the real strangeness of the text. This requires assessing the distinctiveness of one's own preunderstanding.

The term, "preunderstanding names," the fact that the interpreting subject exists in a particular historical situation that conditions her reading of the text and demands new conceptual categories. There is no "presuppositionless exegesis," he argues in 1957, in part because "every exegete is determined by his or her individuality in the sense of special biases and habits, gifts and weaknesses."[39] More importantly, the exegete is unique by virtue of her location within a specific cultural context, which conditions her way of seeing the world and makes an authentic understanding of history possible: "The individual historian is guided by *a particular way of asking questions, a particular perspective.*"[40] This perspective gives the interpreter a relation to (i.e., a particular understanding of) the "subject matter that comes to expression (directly or indirectly) in the text."[41] The specific relation of the interpreter to the subject matter is the preunderstanding. According to Bultmann, this preunderstanding is "grounded in the *life-context* [*Lebenszusammenhang*] in which the interpreter stands."[42] The concept of *Lebenszusammenhang* only appears several times in Bultmann's writings but functions as a synonym for *Weltbild*. In his 1950 essay on the problem of hermeneutics, while commenting on Dilthey's hermeneutics, Bultmann says that "every interpretation includes a particular preunderstanding, namely that which grows out of the life-context to which the subject matter belongs."[43] And in 1933 he says that "understanding presupposes the life-context in which the one who understands and what is understood belong together from the outset."[44] Both *Lebenszusammenhang* and *Weltbild* thus refer to the cultural situation that conditions our thinking and speaking.

The point in clarifying these concepts is to disabuse readers of Bultmann of the widespread assumption that his talk of preunderstanding refers to a particular *philosophical* perspective. To be sure, Bultmann does speak of philosophy in relation to preunderstanding, but this is misleading since Bultmann understands philosophy, in this context, as phenomenology, namely, the conceptual analysis of one's cultural life-context. This is the only sense in which he is willing to embrace philosophy within theology. To appropriate existentialist philosophy is simply to appropriate the resources available in a particular cultural situation; a different situation would thus demand a different conceptuality. Bultmann nowhere makes the existentialist appropriation the final and universally valid translation of the kerygma. He in fact states explicitly that the historical picture achieved by any translation "is falsified only if a particular way of asking questions is declared to be the only way possible," that is to say, it "would be falsified if the exegete takes his or her preunderstanding to be a definitive understanding."[45] In other words, the cultural appropriation that is a necessary aspect of hermeneutical translation is only rightly carried out in the constant awareness that no cultural form is superior to another or universally valid. Faith recognizes that it "has not found in our age the right forms of expression."[46] The task of understanding the culturally alien past within the present situation demands, at the very same time, the recognition that our own situation is relative and provisional, subject to perpetual reevaluation in light of new intercultural encounters.

The hermeneutical task of appropriation that lies at the heart of Bultmann's program of demythologizing is a dialectical task. It requires, on the one hand, an ongoing readiness to discern anew the conceptualities available in a particular situation and to assess their fittingness for the proclamation of the kerygma. On the other hand, the task of appropriation demands a refusal to assimilate the kerygma into the cultural life-contexts of either the past or the present; neither the preunderstanding of the ancient apostles nor the preunderstanding of contemporary readers is a definitive understanding. This dialectical mode of appropriation—with its critical freedom with respect to both past and present, both stranger and self—is a fruit of the kerygma itself as the word of one who "always remains beyond what has once been grasped."[47] As an eschatological event, the kerygma demands not only appropriation but also *transpropriation* in light of "the real strangeness of Christian faith."[48]

Existentialist Interpretation: Self-Understanding as Transpropriation

A participatory epistemology must attend not only to the existential *location* of the interpreter, but also to the interpreter's existential *encounter* with history. An authentic understanding of history—of that which is historically foreign—occurs as an encounter that transforms one's own existence. This occurs in a paradigmatic way in the encounter with the kerygmatic Christ, namely, an encounter with what is *eschatologically* foreign.

If preunderstanding addresses the question of one's given perspective within history, then self-understanding concerns what lies *beyond* the given. Historical occurrences, as well as those who participate in them, are not defined solely by their cultural embeddedness. History is at the same time open to the *future*. A historical phenomenon has no "being-in-itself."[49] Events in the past, occurrences that are strictly *historisch*, are not truly historical or *geschichtlich* in themselves, Bultmann argues, but rather become historical "only *in their relatedness to the future*." The future of each event is constitutive of the event itself: "to every historical phenomenon belongs its own future in which it first shows itself for what it is."[50] This future only appears to the historian "who is open for historical phenomena due to his or her responsibility for the future." In a certain sense, therefore, history always already involves eschatology.[51]

The simultaneity—or rather, to use Bultmann's preferred term, paradoxical identity—of history and eschatology that characterizes historical understanding, in general, corresponds to the simultaneity of history and eschatology that characterizes the singularly decisive eschatological event of Jesus Christ. Whereas other historical occurrences are self-involving, this event alone grants a new self-understanding. Whereas other occurrences are *related* to the future, this event comes to us *from* the future; it is the eschatological reality that alone makes possible our freedom for the future. A philosophical theory or worldview is incapable of providing or replacing this eschatological self-understanding, since a *Weltanschauung* remains confined within the limits of one's cultural horizon. True historicity is only ever a gift—"a gift from the future," Bultmann says—while a *Weltanschauung* "serves as a flight from historicity."[52] According to Christian faith, the freedom from the past—from being enclosed within the self—that is required for authentic historical decisions is only possible when a person understands herself as someone future, and this self-understanding can only come from the future; in more traditional terms, it is an act of divine grace. Bultmann thus argues that the gift of a new self occurs in the event of a radical "deworldizing" (*Entweltlichung*).[53] Deworldizing is the soteriological basis for the hermeneutical transpropriation that constitutes demythologizing.

Bultmann adapts the concept of deworldizing from his studies in gnosticism.[54] Whereas gnosticism, he argues, cosmically and ontologically divides humanity into those who are worldly and those who are separated from the world, the Christianity of the Gospel of John existentially divides between two modes of existence: belief and unbelief. Unbelief denies the possibility of a new existence freed from the past, while belief, for John, is an existence that remains fully in the world while being existentially distinct from it. Bultmann finds in both Paul and John a dialectical and paradoxical conception of deworldizing in which those who have faith are taken out of the world precisely in their worldliness; the believer is deworldized *within* the world. The person justified before God is simultaneously a sinner. The true church is an eschatological community that paradoxically exists as one worldly society among others. Bultmann finds this deworldized existence exemplified in the Pauline "as if not" (ὡς μή) from 1 Corinthians 7:29–31. For Paul the justified sinner is a new creation who exists paradoxically within "the present form of this world [that] is passing away" (1 Cor. 7:31). Such a person lives as if what is the case (history) were in fact not the case (eschatology). To be deworldized is to live out of the future—that is, to live within the eschatological moment of decision in which God's futurity breaks in upon a person in the word of the kerygma. A deworldized person sees the world and thus herself in light of God's eschatological proximity. Faith is therefore an eschatological existence within historical existence, and this paradox scandalously disturbs all worldly norms, expectations, and demands for proof: "faith is not flight from the world or asceticism but *deworldizing* as the breaking to pieces of all human standards and assessments."[55] In this way faith corresponds to its object, that is to say, "the paradox of Christian existence corresponds to the paradox of 'the word made flesh.'" The inner connection between these two paradoxes consists in the fact that "both are an offense to the human pursuit for security."[56]

If self-understanding means deworldizing, then we cannot agree with Sundermeier's criticism of this notion as a monological "conversation with oneself."[57] The new self-understanding of faith that corresponds to the kerygmatic word is not at all a solipsistic turning in upon oneself. On the contrary, it is in fact a self-displacement and self-dispossession, in the sense that God's eschatological action in Christ interrupts our bondage to the world and to ourselves and breaks us open to that which arrives on the scene from God's future—and thus what meets us in the face of the neighbor and stranger. The new self-understanding is a freedom from the world that makes us newly free *for* the world. Bultmann states explicitly that "eschatological existence is not flight from the world, but rather the attitude of the 'as if not,' and in such an attitude it is service to the world in love; those who are liberated and under obligation live no longer for themselves but for the Lord. Faith works through love."[58] Those who exist eschatologically do not thereby disdain the cultures, societies, and institutions of the world. Instead, they relate to the world in a new way, no longer regarding others "according to the flesh" (2 Cor. 5:16). They are freed for new relationships with others, both neighbors and strangers, without conflating the kerygma or the eschatological community with their particular cultural situation.

The concept of deworldizing lies at the very heart of Bultmann's theological project: it names both the justifying action of God and the faithful mode of existence that corresponds to this action.[59] As such it is also the heart of his hermeneutical project. Demythologizing and deworldizing form a conceptual pair. Both have a positive content within a negative form: deworldizing means to exist in faith and love within the world, while demythologizing means to translate the kerygma within the present situation. The theological connection between these two concepts becomes most evident at the end of his 1951 Shaffer and Cole lectures. After quoting 1 Corinthians 7:29–31, he adds the closing line: "Let those who have a modern worldview [*Weltanschauung*] live as though they had none."[60] The use of *Weltanschauung* can be misleading, and throughout these lectures the word is mostly used as a synonym for *Weltbild*, a distinction he is more careful about in other writings.[61] His point is that those who exist out of God's future relate to their modern culture as if they did not belong to this culture. This, of course, does not mean believers are to adopt some acultural identity. Bultmann's statement can no more be taken literally than Paul's original. The claim rather refers to the eschatological relativization of all cultural situations; justified sinners are liberated by God from enslavement to sin for the sake of loving the neighbor (*Entweltlichung*) and translating the kerygma (*Entmythologisierung*). Those who live by faith thus have a dialectical existence that prevents them from being confined within their context. They are now open to perspectives and preunderstandings other than their own; they are freed for an authentic intercultural encounter with the stranger. That holds as true for people within modernity as it does for those in antiquity. Faith thus demands "to be liberated from all worldviews that arise from human thought, whether they are mythological or natural-scientific."[62]

We are now in a position to see the hermeneutical significance of Bultmann's eschatological interpretation of Christian existence. Demythologizing is existentialist interpretation in the sense that it interprets the kerygma in light of the eschatological existence of faith, which is simultaneously concretized in a particular historical situation and deworldized in the face of God's coming future.[63] We have already demonstrated that his concept of preunderstanding affirms the *appropriation* of a particular culture for the understanding of the kerygma. Now we can see that his concept of self-understanding—in which the one who encounters the eschatological event of Christ is liberated from her self-enclosed bondage to the world and thus from her cultural myopia—is the basis for the hermeneutical *translation* or *transpropriation* of the kerygma to new cultural contexts. Bultmann understands the deworldizing event of the kerygma as a divine power that eschatologically frees us from our cultural situation and so makes us open for new intercultural encounters. The kerygma is freed from the ancient culture of the text just as we are freed from our modern culture, and this eschatological freedom makes possible an intercultural encounter with scripture. The eschatological deworldizing of the believer is not a denial of cultural particularity; it is rather the condition for the possibility of intercultural understanding. The one who exists in faith is able to understand the stranger because she herself now lives a strange existence within the world in correspondence to the divine Stranger. The dialectical nature of the Christ-event as simultaneously historical and eschatological translates into a dialectical hermeneutic that simultaneously appropriates the kerygma to a specific historical context and transpropriates the kerygma to ever new contexts. The twin aspects of demythologizing as preunderstanding and self-understanding thus constitute Bultmann's distinctively existentialist intercultural hermeneutic.

CONCLUSION: DEMYTHOLOGIZING
AS MISSIONARY EXISTENCE

In his account of missionary existence, Theo Sundermeier defines mission as a way of being in the world that corresponds to the fact that "the Son comes to his own, and yet it is a way into the unknown," that is, into what is alien and strange. "Mission describes a way, a movement, a transgression toward what is other, into the strange unknown."[64] Mission is always a journey "into the far country," to borrow from Karl Barth. It is crucial to see that it is the transgression into the unknown itself that constitutes a missionary existence. There is no aim to convert the unknown to the known, the foreign into the familiar. Any such attempt would violate the paradoxical and eschatological event of Christ that commissions us as God's ambassadors. The kerygma is permanently unfamiliar, ungraspable, and unsettling, and this demands that those who become agents of the kerygma constantly open themselves to what is unsettling. For this reason, the missionary task—as redefined within an existential, intercultural framework—is always a *conversion of oneself to the other*, and never a conversion of the other to oneself. It is the "missionary," so to speak, who is the one being evangelized. The missionary encounter with the other therefore necessarily "signals a readiness to always keep open anew the question of identity. . . . Distance and coexistence, difference and convivence, are essential elements of the practice of missionary existence."[65]

It is certainly true that Bultmann does not present his program of demy-thologizing in terms of encountering and understanding the cultural stranger. He does not reflect on the problem of coexistence within a pluralistic society. What he does instead is to put forward a hermeneutic—in truth, a soteriology that functions as a hermeneutic—that provides the condition for the possibil-ity of authentic intercultural encounters. Bultmann's program of demytholo-gizing *thinks toward* missionary existence and thus functions as a necessary precondition for an intercultural theology that *thinks from* missionary exis-tence. Demythologizing serves this function by accomplishing two primary tasks: as criticism of the mythical world-picture, it frees the kerygma from its assimilation to an ancient cultural context; as existentialist interpretation, it translates the kerygma into new contexts through the appropriation of our preunderstanding, while precluding future assimilations of the kerygma through the deworldizing power of transpropriation given in the new self-understanding of faith. Negatively, demythologizing rejects the confining of the kerygma to the known and the familiar, whether this is the world-picture of the early Christian community or that of the contemporary church. Posi-tively, demythologizing keeps the kerygma open to ever new cultural situa-tions and contextual conceptualities. And it does this by keeping those called to proclaim the kerygma continually open to the inbreaking future of God, and thus open to the neighbor in one's midst. Just as "every moment has the possibility of being an eschatological moment," so too every context, every encounter, has the possibility of being the occasion for the proclamation of the kerygma.[66] Bultmann conceptualizes this possibility as an event of God's eschatological address that elicits the decision of faith. It is this deworldizing address that ensures "the church is always a missionary church."[67]

Bultmann recognizes that the encounter with scripture is an encounter with a cultural stranger. He further recognizes that the condition for a proper coexistence with this stranger is a theological interrogation of one's own existence. Hermeneutical *Konvivenz* between the culturally alien scriptures and the reader can only occur through a decision of personal responsibility, that is to say, through an act of faithful receptivity to the word of the Bible within the parameters of one's historical situation. But this act of receptivity must occur ever anew. In a lecture given in Alpirsbach on June 5, 1941, the day after presenting his programmatic essay on demythologizing, Bultmann states that "even the most accurate translation itself needs to be translated again in the following generation." For there is no "ideal type of the kerygma," but rather every translation "is formulated for today and only for today."[68] Demythologizing, as a missionary hermeneutic of translation, never results in a *demythologized* kerygma. There is no final outcome, no permanent interpretation. That would, in fact, be a contradiction. Since Bultmann defines myth precisely as the conflation of the kerygma with a particular context or world-picture, a program of demythologizing can only be the repeated unsettling of the sinful human attempt to turn the kerygma into a doctrinal law, philosophical worldview, or cultural institution that has a stable and permanent form.[69] In a way that anticipates contemporary work in intercultural theology, demythologizing refuses to secure Christian identity "within a traditional theological frame of reference."[70] Indeed, according to Bultmann, "there is neither a definitive form of the Christian kerygma nor a definitive version of Christian self-understanding, but both must always appear in a new form in correspondence to each historical situation." Demythologizing embraces the radical contextuality of the kerygma for the sake of "preventing a petrifaction of the kerygma."[71]

Demythologizing has been widely misunderstood as the reduction of theology to philosophy and the confinement of the Christian Gospel to the limits of a Heideggerian ontology. Such assumptions prove quite alien to Bultmann's actual project. His stated aim is nothing less than to recover the true scandal of the Gospel message, a message that remains scandalous by resisting every attempt to secure or stabilize it. His hermeneutic is instead the method of interpretation that corresponds to the Christ "who always destroys every security, who always irrupts from the beyond and calls into the future," with the consequence that his disciples "can never hold on to whatever served as the occasion for the encounter with revelation, whether it was an experience of the soul, Christian knowledge, or culture."[72] Demythologizing is therefore a hermeneutic for the "continuing conversion of the church."[73] Demythologizing is not merely a hermeneutical task; it is a mode of faithful Christian existence. Specifically, it is a *missionary* mode of existence in the sense that it seeks to understand the kerygma in the context of each new intercultural encounter, but always in the relativizing light of God's future.

Demythologizing thus obeys the commission of Jesus Christ by confronting every tradition, community, and individual with the challenge to participate anew in the eschatological mission of God.

NOTES

This chapter contains material previously published in David W. Congdon, *The Mission of Demythologizing: Rudolf Bultmann's Dialectical Theology* (Minneapolis: Fortress, 2015).

1. He first gave the lecture on April 21 at a regional meeting of the Society for Protestant Theology (*Gesellschaft für evangelische Theologie*) in Frankfurt/Main, and then he gave it again before the entire society on June 4 at Alpirsbach. See Konrad Hammann, *Rudolf Bultmann: Eine Biographie* (Tübingen: Mohr Siebeck, 2009), 308. The Gesellschaft für evangelische Theologie was a group of theologians of the Confessing Church who gathered to discuss questions related to academic theology and the work of the church in order to combat the rise of Nazi ideology.

2. This is changing due to the recent English translation of Henning Wrogemann's magisterial three-volume work on intercultural theology, beginning with Henning Wrogemann, *Intercultural Theology, Volume 1: Intercultural Hermeneutics* (Downers Grove, IL: IVP Academic, 2016).

3. See Wissenschaftliche Gesellschaft für Theologie and Deutsche Gesellschaft für Missionswissenschaft, "Mission Studies as Intercultural Theology and Its Relationship to Religious Studies," *Mission Studies* 25, no. 1 (2008): 103–8.

4. Klaus Hock, *Einführung in die Interkulturelle Theologie* (Darmstadt: WBG, 2011), 9.

5. Hollenweger, *Interkulturelle Theologie*, 3 vols. (München: Kaiser, 1979–1988), 1:50.

6. Hock, *Einführung in die Interkulturelle Theologie*, 51.

7. Theo Sundermeier, "Erwägungen zu einer Hermeneutik interkulturellen Verstehens," in *Konvivenz und Differenz: Studien zu einer verstehenden Missionswissenschaft*, ed. Volker Küster (Erlangen: Verlag der Ev.-Luth. Mission, 1995), 87–101, here 87. Emphasis added.

8. Sundermeier, 88.

9. Theo Sundermeier, *Mission—Geschenk der Freiheit: Bausteine für eine Theologie der Mission* (Frankfurt am Main: Lembeck, 2005), 82.

10. Sundermeier, "Erwägungen zu einer Hermeneutik interkulturellen Verstehens," 89.

11. Sundermeier, 90.

12. Sundermeier, *Mission*, 29.

13. Sundermeier, 118–19.

14. Sundermeier, 77–104.

15. Sundermeier, 83, 82.

16. Sundermeier, 84.

17. Heinrich Balz, "Hermeneutik und Mission," *Zeitschrift für Mission* 14, no. 4 (1988): 206–20. Technically, Balz identifies appropriation and transpropriation as the two sides of translation: "Mission is translation in a double sense: the transpropriation of the gospel to others, and at the same time the appropriation of other human languages and cultures for the gospel" (Balz, 207).

18. Sundermeier, *Mission*, 85, 88.

19. Sundermeier, "Erwägungen zu einer Hermeneutik interkulturellen Verstehens," 99.

20. Rudolf Bultmann, "Zum Problem der Entmythologisierung," in *Kerygma und Mythos, Band II: Diskussion und Stimmen zum Problem der Entmythologisierung*, ed. Hans-Werner Bartsch (Hamburg-Volksdorf: H. Reich, 1952), 184.

21. Bultmann, 183.

22. Rudolf Bultmann, *Neues Testament und Mythologie: Das Problem der Entmythologisierung der neutestamentlichen Verkündigung*, ed. Eberhard Jüngel (Munich: Chr. Kaiser Verlag, 1985), 12, 14.

23. Ulrich H. J. Körtner, "Glaube und Weltbild: Die Bedeutsamkeit des Kreuzes im Konflikt der Interpretationen von Wirklichkeit," in *Kreuz und Weltbild: Interpretationen von Wirklichkeit im Horizont des Todes Jesu*, ed. Christof Landmesser and Andreas Klein (Neukirchen-Vluyn: Neukirchener, 2011), 15–34, here 23.

24. See Ulrich H. J. Körtner, "Arbeit am Mythos?: Zum Verhältnis von Christentum und mythischem Denken bei Rudolf Bultmann," *Neue Zeitschrift für systematische Theologie und Religionsphilosophie* 34, no. 2 (1992): 163–81, here 172–73.

25. Martin Heidegger, "Die Zeit des Weltbildes [1938]," in *Holzwege* (Frankfurt am Main: Klostermann, 1950), 69–104.

26. See Wilhelm Dilthey, "Die Typen der Weltanschauung und ihre Ausbildung in den metaphysischen Systemen," in *Gesammelte Schriften, Bd. 8. Weltanschauungslehre: Abhandlungen zur Philosophie der Philosophie*, ed. Bernard Groethuysen (Stuttgart: Teubner, 1931), 75–118.

27. Rudolf Bultmann, "Welchen Sinn hat es, von Gott zu reden?," in *Glauben und Verstehen: Gesammelte Aufsätze*, 4 vols. (Tübingen: Mohr, 1933–1965), 1:26–37, here 31–33.

28. Rudolf Bultmann, *Die christliche Hoffnung und das Problem der Entmythologisierung* (Stuttgart: Evangelisches Verlagswerk, 1954), 46–47.

29. Bultmann, "Zum Problem der Entmythologisierung," 181.

30. Wolfgang Gantke, "Weltbild: Religionsgeschichtlich," in *Theologische Realenzyklopädie*, vol. 35, ed. Gerhard Krause, Gerhard Müller, and Siegfried Schwertner (Berlin: Walter de Gruyter, 2003), 562–69, here 563.

31. Ernst Fuchs, "Was ist existentiale Interpretation? A," in *Zum hermeneutischen Problem in der Theologie: Die existentiale Interpretation* (Tübingen: J.C.B. Mohr, 1959), 66.

32. Rudolf Bultmann, *Geschichte und Eschatologie* (Tübingen: Mohr, 1958), 131.

33. Rudolf Bultmann, "Wissenschaft und Existenz," in *Glauben und Verstehen*, 3:107–21, here 108, 110.

34. Rudolf Bultmann, "Ist voraussetzungslose Exegese möglich?," in *Glauben und Verstehen*, 3:142–50, here 147.

35. Bultmann, "Wissenschaft und Existenz," 115.

36. Bultmann, "Ist voraussetzungslose Exegese möglich?," 150.

37. Bultmann, 145.

38. Sundermeier, *Mission*, 100.

39. Bultmann, "Ist voraussetzungslose Exegese möglich?," 143.

40. Bultmann, 146.

41. Bultmann, 146–47.

42. Bultmann, 147.

43. Rudolf Bultmann, "Das Problem der Hermeneutik," in *Glauben und Verstehen*, 2:211–35, here 218.

44. Rudolf Bultmann, "Das Problem der 'natürlichen Theologie,'" in *Glauben und Verstehen*, 1:294–312, here 296.

45. Bultmann, "Ist voraussetzungslose Exegese möglich?," 146, 147.

46. Rudolf Bultmann, *Jesus Christus und die Mythologie: Das Neue Testament im Licht der Bibelkritik* (Hamburg: Furche, 1964), 99.

47. Bultmann, "Wissenschaft und Existenz," 121.

48. Rudolf Bultmann, "Das Befremdliche des christlichen Glaubens," in *Glauben und Verstehen*, 3:197–212, here 202.

49. Bultmann, "Wissenschaft und Existenz," 114.

50. Bultmann, 113.

51. Bultmann, *Geschichte und Eschatologie*, 137. In discussing R. G. Collingwood's position, Bultmann states: "every now is an eschatological now, and history and eschatology are identical" (Bultmann, 161).

52. Bultmann, 178–79.

53. I follow Roger Johnson in translating *Entweltlichung* as "deworldizing," though he spells it as "deworldlizing." In my previous work I followed his spelling, but I have since changed my position in agreement with the philosophical literature on Heidegger's concept of *Entweltlichung*. See Roger A. Johnson, *The Origins of Demythologizing: Philosophy and*

Historiography in the Theology of Rudolf Bultmann (Leiden: Brill, 1974), 118. While awkward, the word is a necessary neologism, because it brings out the semantic connection between *Entweltlichung* and *Entmythologisierung*.

54. Bultmann's historical scholarship on gnosticism is quite dated and widely criticized. It does not follow, however, that his theological interpretation of John is thereby discredited. Bultmann's theology does not depend on the veracity of his work on the history of religions.

55. Rudolf Bultmann, *Theologie des Neuen Testaments*, 2nd ed. (Tübingen: J. C. B. Mohr, 1954), §50, 422. See Bultmann, *Geschichte und Eschatologie*, 183–84: "The paradox that Christian existence is at the same time one that is eschatological, unworldly, and historical is synonymous with the Lutheran statement: 'Simul iustus simul peccator.'" In a 1956 essay in honor of C. H. Dodd, Bultmann says that "the deworldizing of believers is certainly a paradox. For as long as they still live 'in the flesh,' those who are deworldized stand at the same time within a history and hear the call of God in each case within their concrete situation." Rudolf Bultmann, *Theologie als Kritik: Ausgewählte Rezensionen und Forschungsberichte*, ed. Matthias Dreher and Klaus W. Müller (Tübingen: Mohr Siebeck, 2002), 479. In 1958 Bultmann writes: "eschatological existence is *deworldized existence within the world*" (Bultmann, "Das Befremdliche des christlichen Glaubens," 207). Regarding the church, Bultmann says "the essence of the church consists in being the eschatological, deworldized community [*Gemeinde*] *within* the world," and thus "they are to realize their *deworldized* being as a *worldly* community [*Gemeinschaft*]." See Rudolf Bultmann, *Das Evangelium des Johannes*, 10th ed. (Göttingen: Vandenhoeck & Ruprecht, 1941), 389, 384.

56. Bultmann, "Das Befremdliche des christlichen Glaubens," 204, 211.

57. Sundermeier, "Erwägungen zu einer Hermeneutik interkulturellen Verstehens," 91.

58. Rudolf Bultmann, "Der Mensch und seine Welt nach dem Urteil der Bibel," in *Glauben und Verstehen*, 3:151–65, here 165.

59. The fact that Bultmann uses the term *Entweltlichung* positively also highlights the sharp difference between his theology and Heidegger's philosophy. For Heidegger the goal is authentic being-in-the-world, and the term *Entweltlichung*, sometimes translated as "unworlding," refers to when an object loses its proper worldliness and becomes a mere object of nature to be grasped as something present-at-hand. See Magda King, *A Guide to Heidegger's Being and Time*, ed. John Llewellyn (Albany: State University of New York Press, 2001), 73, 269.

60. Bultmann, *Jesus Christus und die Mythologie*, 101. Cf. Rudolf Bultmann, *Jesus Christ and Mythology* (New York: Scribner, 1958), 85.

61. See Congdon, *The Mission of Demythologizing*, 782n221.

62. Bultmann, *Jesus Christus und die Mythologie*, 98.

63. Some may question whether this counts as "existentialist interpretation" since it does not seem sufficiently existentialist or Heideggerian, but that is to assume Bultmann's Heideggerianism when the truth is that he is only existentialist in the most formal and minimal way. Existentialist philosophy, as appropriated by Bultmann, serves little purpose other than to provide a way of speaking about the importance of our personal responsibility as historical creatures: "We would learn little if existentialist philosophy—as many people assume—in fact attempted to provide an ideal picture of human existence. The notion of 'authenticity' provides no such picture. Existentialist philosophy does not say to me: 'In such and such a way you must exist.' It says only: 'You must exist!' . . . While existentialist philosophy does not answer the question regarding my own existence, it makes my own existence a matter of my personal responsibility, and by doing so it makes me open to the word of the Bible" (Bultmann, 63–64). Existentialist philosophy makes it clear "that the hearing of the word of the Bible can only take place in personal decision" (Bultmann, 65–66).

64. Sundermeier, *Mission*, 97.

65. Sundermeier, 98.

66. Bultmann, *Geschichte und Eschatologie*, 183.

67. Rudolf Bultmann, "Der Arier-Paragraph im Raume der Kirche," *Theologische Blätter* 12 (1933): 359–70, here 365.

68. Rudolf Bultmann, "Theologie als Wissenschaft," *Zeitschrift für Theologie und Kirche* 81, no. 4 (1984): 447–69, here 460–61.

69. "The statements of scripture cannot be taken over as a doctrinal law; for God's revelation does not mean God's revealedness, i.e., God is not given directly in God's revelation, but rather God's revelation is only present *in actu*, as occurrence, an occurrence that is not available for observation as a world-occurrence but is only perceptible for the one who participates in it" (Bultmann, 461).

70. Hock, *Einführung in die Interkulturelle Theologie*, 11.

71. Bultmann, "Theologie als Wissenschaft," 466.

72. Bultmann, *Das Evangelium des Johannes*, 431–32.

73. See Darrell L. Guder, *The Continuing Conversion of the Church* (Grand Rapids, MI: Eerdmans, 2000).

BIBLIOGRAPHY

Balz, Heinrich. "Hermeneutik und Mission." *Zeitschrift für Mission* 14, no. 4 (1988): 206–20.

Bultmann, Rudolf. "Das Befremdliche des christlichen Glaubens [1958]." In *Glauben und Verstehen: Gesammelte Aufsätze*, 4 vols., 3:197–212. Tübingen: Mohr, 1933–1965.

———. *Das Evangelium des Johannes*. 10th ed. Göttingen: Vandenhoeck & Ruprecht, 1941.

———. "Das Problem der Hermeneutik [1950]." In *Glauben und Verstehen: Gesammelte Aufsätze*, 4 vols., 2:211–35. Tübingen: Mohr, 1933–1965.

———. "Das Problem der 'natürlichen Theologie' [1933]." In *Glauben und Verstehen: Gesammelte Aufsätze*, 4 vols., 1:294–312. Tübingen: Mohr, 1933–1965.

———. "Der Arier-Paragraph im Raume der Kirche." *Theologische Blätter* 12 (1933): 359–70.

———. "Der Mensch und seine Welt nach dem Urteil der Bibel [1957]." In *Glauben und Verstehen: Gesammelte Aufsätze*, 4 vols., 3:151–65. Tübingen: Mohr, 1933–1965.

———. *Die christliche Hoffnung und das Problem der Entmythologisierung*. Stuttgart: Evangelisches Verlagswerk, 1954.

———. *Geschichte und Eschatologie*. Tübingen: Mohr, 1958.

———. "Ist voraussetzungslose Exegese möglich? [1957]." In *Glauben und Verstehen: Gesammelte Aufsätze*, 4 vols., 3:142–50. Tübingen: Mohr, 1933–1965.

———. *Jesus Christ and Mythology*. New York: Scribner, 1958.

———. *Jesus Christus und die Mythologie: Das Neue Testament im Licht der Bibelkritik*. Hamburg: Furche, 1964.

———. *Neues Testament und Mythologie: Das Problem der Entmythologisierung der neutestamentlichen Verkündigung*. Edited by Eberhard Jüngel. Munich: Chr. Kaiser Verlag, 1985.

———. *Theologie als Kritik: Ausgewählte Rezensionen und Forschungsberichte*. Edited by Matthias Dreher and Klaus W. Müller. Tübingen: Mohr Siebeck, 2002.

———. "Theologie als Wissenschaft." *Zeitschrift für Theologie und Kirche* 81, no. 4 (1984): 447–69.

———. *Theologie des Neuen Testaments*. 2nd ed. Tübingen: J. C. B. Mohr, 1954.

———. "Welchen Sinn hat es, von Gott zu reden? [1925]." In *Glauben und Verstehen: Gesammelte Aufsätze*, 4 vols., 1:26–37. Tübingen: Mohr, 1933–1965.

———. "Wissenschaft und Existenz [1955]." In *Glauben und Verstehen: Gesammelte Aufsätze*, 4 vols., 3:107–21. Tübingen: Mohr, 1933–1965.

———. "Zum Problem der Entmythologisierung." In *Kerygma und Mythos, Band II: Diskussion und Stimmen zum Problem der Entmythologisierung*, edited by Hans-Werner Bartsch, 179–208. Hamburg-Volksdorf: H. Reich, 1952.

Dilthey, Wilhelm. *Gesammelte Schriften, Bd. 8. Weltanschauungslehre: Abhandlungen zur Philosophie der Philosophie*. Edited by Bernard Groethuysen. Stuttgart: Teubner, 1931.

Fuchs, Ernst. "Was ist existentiale Interpretation? A [1952]." In *Zum hermeneutischen Problem in der Theologie: Die existentiale Interpretation*, 65–90. Tübingen: J.C.B. Mohr, 1959.

Gantke, Wolfgang. "Weltbild: Religionsgeschichtlich." In *Theologische Realenzyklopädie*, vol. 35, edited by Gerhard Krause, Gerhard Müller, and Siegfried Schwertner, 562–69. Berlin: Walter de Gruyter, 2003.

Guder, Darrell L. *The Continuing Conversion of the Church*. Grand Rapids, MI: Eerdmans, 2000.

Hammann, Konrad. *Rudolf Bultmann: Eine Biographie.* Tübingen: Mohr Siebeck, 2009.

Heidegger, Martin. "Die Zeit des Weltbildes [1938]." In *Holzwege,* 69–104. Frankfurt am Main: Klostermann, 1950.

Hock, Klaus. *Einführung in die Interkulturelle Theologie.* Darmstadt: WBG, 2011.

Hollenweger, Walter J. *Interkulturelle Theologie.* 3 vols. München: Kaiser, 1979–1988.

Johnson, Roger A. *The Origins of Demythologizing: Philosophy and Historiography in the Theology of Rudolf Bultmann.* Leiden: Brill, 1974.

King, Magda. *A Guide to Heidegger's Being and Time.* Edited by John Llewellyn. Albany: State University of New York Press, 2001.

Körtner, Ulrich H. J. "Arbeit am Mythos?: Zum Verhältnis von Christentum und mythischem Denken bei Rudolf Bultmann." *Neue Zeitschrift für systematische Theologie und Religionsphilosophie* 34, no. 2 (1992): 163–81.

———. "Glaube und Weltbild: Die Bedeutsamkeit des Kreuzes im Konflikt der Interpretationen von Wirklichkeit." In *Kreuz und Weltbild: Interpretationen von Wirklichkeit im Horizont des Todes Jesu,* edited by Christof Landmesser and Andreas Klein, 15–34. Neukirchen-Vluyn: Neukirchener, 2011.

Sundermeier, Theo. "Erwägungen zu einer Hermeneutik interkulturellen Verstehens." In *Konvivenz und Differenz: Studien zu einer verstehenden Missionswissenschaft,* edited by Volker Küster, 87–101. Erlangen: Verlag der Ev.-Luth. Mission, 1995.

———. *Mission—Geschenk der Freiheit: Bausteine für eine Theologie der Mission.* Frankfurt am Main: Lembeck, 2005.

Wissenschaftliche Gesellschaft für Theologie and Deutsche Gesellschaft für Missionswissenschaft. "Mission Studies as Intercultural Theology and Its Relationship to Religious Studies." *Mission Studies* 25, no. 1 (2008): 103–8.

Chapter Eight

For the Fitness of Their Witness

Missional Christian Practices

Benjamin T. Conner

As the primary apologist for "missional theology," Darrell Guder has recovered and promoted the notion that the animating activity of God's redemptive mission in the world must be the starting point for theological reflection, biblical interpretation, and evaluating the faithfulness of the concrete life and practices of the congregation. In this career-long project, the biblical theme of "witness" has served as his orienting and unifying leitmotif for engaging contemporary ecclesiology. Both theology and the congregation exist for the sake of witness, with witness serving as the nexus concept that brings together service, proclamation, and the communal identity of a congregation. In his words,

> The term *witness* integrates the who, the what, and the how of Christian mission. The Christian individual is defined as Christ's witness; the entire community is defined as a witnessing community; its impact upon the world into which it is sent is observable witness; all of its activities are, in some way, a form of witness—demonstration of the gracious rule of the risen Lord. [1]

At the heart of his theology of witness is a vision for discipleship in service of the mission of God, enacted through Christian practices (my term applied to his concepts) that shape a witnessing community's "observable activities" in order to support them in more faithfully demonstrating the Kingdom of God. The one element of his theology of discipleship in witness that remains underdeveloped is his articulation of missional Christian practices. [2]

The entire *Missional Church* conversation, to which Guder was a key contributor, has, at times, been accused of being too abstract, technical, academic, and removed from the concrete life of the congregation.[3] That critique was answered, in part, by *Treasure in Clay Jars: Patterns of Missional Faithfulness*,[4] a book that, while lacking any articulated theory or theology of Christian practices, distinguished practices like proclamation, discernment, reconciliation, and hospitality as vital indicators of a missional church.[5] Nonetheless, bringing the contemporary discussion about the role of Christian practices in discipleship together with Guder's vision for missional discipleship can provide some concepts and language to speak more concretely about how congregations are shaped to "walk worthily."

The purpose of this chapter is to draw out and develop Guder's practical theology of missional Christian practices, which I characterize as being both for the sake of forming congregations for witness as well as enactments of that witness for the world. I will, first, advance a theology of Christian practices in conversation with Guder's theology of witness making the claim, with Kathryn Tanner's support, that striving for faithful witness is what unites our diverse practices as Christian. Next, I will make the case that Guder understands Christian practices to be an expression of Christian discipleship that serves the fitness of congregational witness. Finally, I will suggest that Christian practices provide a way of embodied and spirit-enabled witness that takes many forms and, as such, provide an inclusive way for understanding how people with intellectual disabilities are indispensable for the fitness of our witness.

MISSIONAL CHRISTIAN PRACTICES

Conceptually and concretely, Christian practices provide a way to evaluate and participate in Christian discipleship in the empirical church. There is a movement among theologians, especially practical theologians, to turn away from ideals and "models of the church" and to, instead, examine ecclesiology in terms of observable practices.[6] A recent series, *Studies in Ecclesiology and Ethnography*,[7] is representative of this shift. Clare Watkins's contribution to that series succinctly summarizes one of its central arguments—that theologians need to be able to "speak truthfully about concrete realities, and faithfully about the historical and present promise of the work of the Spirit, enlivening what we understand to be 'the body of Christ,' the church."[8] Similar concerns motivated the *Practicing Our Faith* discussion of Christian practices led by Craig Dykstra, Dorothy Bass, and others. The need to address "concrete realities" led Serene Jones to interrogate Christian practices in her contribution to *Practicing Theology*. She asks, from within her own Reformed faith tradition, "How are we concretely 'saved by grace' and what does this say about the shape of our daily patterns of living, our collective and individual practices?"[9]

Darrell Guder, also, demonstrated concern for "concrete realities" and "patterns of living" in his earliest articulation of missional theology, *Be My Witnesses*. Drawing upon the influential work of Avery Dulles, *Models of the Church*, an approach to ecclesiology representative of those mentioned above that theologians are moving beyond today, Guder frames his discussion of missional ecclesiology by expanding Dulles's models to include a sixth model, "the equipping community model." This model shifts the focus from the ideal church (institutional, mystical, sacramental, herald and servant) to emphasize enfleshing witness through actions and practices through a "ministry for incarnational witness."[10] In Guder's approach, a central role of the church is to form congregants to be faithful witnesses to the Gospel in words and actions (or *practices*). His term "incarnational," which has received some critique as not being appropriate theologically for a "model" of ministry,[11] is, in fact, less a model than a way of communicating the importance of the embodied, corporeal witness of the church in the world. What Guder is attempting to communicate through his concept of incarnational witness shares much in common with the contemporary practices discussion.

The discussion of Christian practices, associated with *Practicing Our Faith* and the series of books and articles related to it, has had broad appeal and a wide reach. The basic definition of Christian practices promoted in that conversation is the following: "*Christian practices are things Christian people do together over time in response to and in the light of God's active presence for the life of the world* [in Jesus Christ]."[12] More specifically, Dorothy Bass and Miroslav Volf explain that a Christian practice is "a sustained, cooperative pattern of human activity that is big enough, right enough, and complex enough to address some fundamental feature of human existence."[13] Concisely, practices make up a way of life in the world, put us in a position to perceive and proclaim God's redemptive presence for the world, are "arenas" where knowledge of God is palpably felt and tested, and are concrete ways in which congregations serve as a sign, instrument, and foretaste of the Kingdom of God. Practices are the means by which the body of Christ embodies its witness to the reality of the reign and rule of God.[14]

Christian practices include ecclesial practices, like baptism and the Lord's Supper, and core devotional practices like prayer and reading scripture that are fundamental, in some form, and provide touch points and meaning for all other practices. These other practices, everyday practices like honoring the body, hospitality, testimony, discernment, healing, singing, shaping communities, dying well, and others, push our ecclesial and devotional practices into the ordinary routines, the banalities, and the exigencies of everyday life.[15] They help us to establish ways of living that lead to flourishing (both ours and others) and they provide an embodied theological perspective for connecting our activity at work, home, and play within the larger society to the redemptive work of God in the world. A missional theology of Christian practices looks through and beyond the ecclesial and devotional practices to acknowledge the fact that God is at work outside the church for the sake of the world. To limit one's notion of church and Christian practices to an imagined life inside the church, embodied primarily in a distinctive ecclesial tradition and practices, is to put oneself in danger of failing to discern the activity of the Holy Spirit outside of the observable church.

The Christian practices that are of interest to Dykstra, Bass, Volf, and others are those that address fundamental human needs in the light of God's redemptive activity in the world and are enacted through the ordinary activities of everyday life. These common practices, which will appear in different forms according to sociocultural context, are recruited and reoriented, or in Guder's parlance "continually converted" in response to God's active presence in the world.[16] Importantly, Christian practices are not techniques applied in an effort to manipulate human action and social dynamics with the goal of controlling God's grace, nor are they an attempt by the church to revitalize itself in the struggle to regain lost cultural significance in the wake of mainline decline.[17] While Christian practices do not create a Christian culture that is somehow separated from the world, a common critique of the practices discourse, Christian social practices do embody convictions and shape people by developing within them certain habits and perspectives. They are, primarily, "habitations of the Spirit,"[18] "arenas,"[19] or means of grace in which the Holy Spirit transforms people in ways that are unpredictable but are oriented toward our witness in the world. Practices are arenas of missional formation. And while God's redemptive work in the world is not contingent upon the church successfully proclaiming the Gospel through them,[20] "the practices of the empirical church are not inconsequential to the proclamation of the gospel," explains John Swinton, "and as such, should not be substituted for a dissociated, ideal ecclesiology. The Christian's task, in the power of the Holy Spirit, is to *bear witness*."[21]

At this point, Kathryn Tanner's reflections about what makes Christian practices *Christian* are extremely helpful for clarifying what practices can and cannot do. She argues Christian communities are neither self-contained nor self-sufficient, which is to say, there can be no "Christian" culture. There are some fairly isolated social activities (ecclesial practices), but Christians have social roles in other spheres such that the perceived boundaries between any Christian and non-Christian way of life are permeable. What Christians have in common among themselves is not their distinctive practices,[22] and certainly "nothing internal to the practices themselves" that unites them as Christian. As Tanner explains, "What unites them is concern for true discipleship, proper reflection in human words and deeds of an object of worship that always exceeds by its greatness human efforts to do so. What Christians are all trying to be true to is not some element within or characteristic of Christian practices themselves."[23] The contemporary practices discussion, particularly those persons involved in that strand that calls upon the work of Alasdair MacIntyre to develop their concept of practices, does refer to "the goods internal to a practice." This language, borrowed from the ethicist, when applied to Christian practices, is a way of acknowledging the fact that experiential knowledge is available through participating in Christian practices that is unavailable any other way. There are no books or seminars available to communicate the knowledge involved in offering or receiving forgiveness—one must forgive and live a life patterned on the forgiveness granted to us in Christ in order to truly know forgiveness. There is no way to know the joy of receiving Christ in the other through practice of hospitality beyond welcoming the other. And, there is no way to experience the reality of God's truthful self-testimony in Christ other than through bearing witness to it. Nonetheless, to Tanner's point, there is "nothing internal to the practices themselves" that unites them as Christian. Instead, I argue, what unites Christian practices is that they are Spirit-enabled means through which congregations participate in the life of God, which is missional.

Along with the problem of permeable boundaries between Christian and non-Christian practices, there is also the issue of ambiguity related to the shape and content of Christian practices. Nicholas Healy, using the example of hospitality, suggests that since hospitable actions take such diverse expressions and are so loosely structured, it can be questioned whether or not hospitality is even a practice.[24] Similarly, Bonnie Miller-McLemore observes that what people say and what they believe infrequently corresponds with their actions, a phenomenon she terms a "religious congruence fallacy."[25] So what is it that makes a practice a Christian practice if not the form of the practice, agreement on the meaning of the practices, or explicit beliefs that inhere in the practice?

Tanner concludes that what holds practices together as Christian practices is "their common reference to the God to whom they all hope effectively to witness."[26] From the standpoint of human response to the Spirit, in various ways and in forms appropriate to a specific context, it is the desire to bear witness to Jesus that makes Christian practices Christian. In the process of yearning for a more faithful witness, Christians become willing to relativize their own practices in both form and understanding and to destigmatize and become open to learning from other expressions of Christian practices.[27] These shared practices must be continually converted so that they may more faithfully shape local congregations for witness and so their embodied witness is more congruent with the announcement they bear. In Tanner's words:

> Through engagement with Christian practices in this critical, reflective fashion, we are called to be active witnesses to what God has done for us in Christ and active disciples of the way of living that Christ himself struggled against the forces of sin and death to bring into existence. Being witnesses and disci-

ples means establishing through effort-filled deliberative processes what Christianity stands for in our own lives for our own time and circumstances. To do so is not a matter of passive reception, of simple immersion in established practices—it cannot be given the messy facts of our existence.[28]

It is fair to represent Guder as agreeing with the statement that Christian practices are at the heart of missional discipleship and serve to refine the fitness of our witness, to help us to "walk worthily." At the same time, Guder would agree Christian practices are ways that we practice witness; they are, in Lesslie Newbigin's language, a "hermeneutic of the gospel,"[29] or in Tanner's terms, a "commentary" on the broader field of cultural life.[30] Christian practices shape and embody our witness in the world.

FOR THE FITNESS OF OUR WITNESS

Despite the lack of an explicit theology of Christian practices in Guder's writings, it is still possible to discern some of his assumptions about Christian practices as they relate to discipleship, that is to say, the concrete following of Jesus Christ. In the following section I will refer to Guder's "theology of practices," but what I am actually referring to is his theology of practices as I have constructed it out of his body of work in a way that is consistent with his theology.

Given the Barthian shape of much of Guder's theology, Karl Barth's reflections on discipleship could provide an accommodating point for developing and articulating Guder's conception of practices. First, in Guder's theological project, following Barth, the doctrines of justification and sanctification do not stand alone, but together provide the basis for Christian vocation in a way that pulls both doctrines forward into the world and makes them dynamic. Vocation keeps the calling related to justification and the upbuilding associated with sanctification from being malnourished and focusing inward on the benefits of salvation. Vocation directs our discipleship to move beyond the community of faith and into neighborhoods, homes, workplaces and other social sectors. The call to discipleship is always related to our participation as Christ's witnesses—we participate, through the Spirit, as witnesses in the prophetic activity of Christ who is the True Witness as we are sent into the world in his name and power. Summarizing, using Barth's words, and highlighting the relationship between justification, sanctification, and vocation: "The call to discipleship is the particular form of the summons by which Jesus discloses and reveals himself to individuals in order to claim [justification] and sanctify [sanctification] them as his own, and as his witness [vocation] in the world."[31]

Guder has also identified Lesslie Newbigin, along with Karl Barth, as a progenitor of his missional theology. Newbigin has stressed that any participation or fellowship (*koinonia*) with Christ is also a participation in his ongoing redemptive mission in the world.[32] Therefore, discipleship is fundamentally missional; a kind of following in the power of the Spirit that is oriented toward the ends of the earth (to which the church bears the witness of Christ) and the end of time (when God gathers people of every tribe and nation together before the throne of God).[33]

Christian practices, as a way that the church embodies discipleship, are tangible expressions of Christian witness that are specific and concrete. For Guder, practices provide an avenue for speaking about discipleship in a way that critiques (an allegedly) Reformed reductionism of witness to the oral proclamation of the Gospel. Practices are a way to emphasize the embodied message of the Gospel and the many other communicative modalities beyond speaking words through which we bear witness. "The spirit-empowered witness is far more than particular oral messages," Guder explains, "It is the demonstration in the life and activity of God's people of the tangible fact that God's rule is breaking in among the disciples of Jesus Christ."[34]

According to Guder's theology, Christian practices bear witness to a universal truth, the Gospel, but they are also "contextually distinctive" concrete responses to specific circumstances. They are congregational activities that bear witness to the universal truth of God's rule with perspectival "confessional authenticity."[35] While practices are authentic in their expression of witness, they are not normative for all times and places—they shape the congregation for faithful witness and are a way that the congregation practices witness together in one place. Therefore, congregations have the freedom to draw upon the rich tradition of Christian practices and shape those inherited practices in a way that is reflective of the community's gifts and circumstances. That diversity, the different expressions of a particular practice, does not delegitimize the value of the concept of practice as Healy suggested, but instead is the necessary diversity required to express a fuller common witness. Guder explains,

> The freedom modeled on Christ will shape practices that, in their diversity, express the common witness of the church. In infinitely varying ways, the common core of practices that distinguish the company of Jesus' followers and apostolic witnesses will become a more and more profound focus of cross-cultural witness and a source of encouragement for the Christian movement. These practices, while culturally distinctive, will demonstrate their catholicity as the worship of the triune God, sacramental celebration, prayer in the name of Jesus Christ, gospel proclamation, scriptural formation of the community, hospitality as the overcoming of human boundaries, invitation to discipleship, concrete acts of mercy, grace and healing, discernment of God's work in human history, and prophetic witness over against the powers that hurt, divide, and demean.[36]

Because practices are responsive to context, and because they are primarily "habitations of the Spirit" rather than methods for accomplishing change, practices cannot be applied in the way that "best practices" are, as methods or techniques that produce results.[37]

When congregations depend upon technique to form Christians then congregations shape people toward whatever end or *telos* they determine is appropriate. The practices remain static and unchangeable, socially determinative instruments of human manipulation oriented toward certain behavioral outcomes. When congregations participate in Christian practices, as Guder understands them, they are participating in a social reality in which the Holy Spirit is the agent of change, the shaper of people and communities. Practices are places of encounter with the Spirit that evoke responses. Healy is certainly correct in his assessment of practices that, "[r]epeated performance of behavior patterns does not, of itself, issue in the right formation of church members nor the acquisition of Christian virtues." But if practices are "habitations of the Spirit," as Dykstra and others have suggested, then we have moved the discussion beyond issues of social determinism. Interestingly, after Healy's strong statement about the deficiency of rote practices, he adds, "[c]haracter is indeed formed through practices, but only as they are performed with appropriate intentions and construals,"[38] which brings us back to the problem of human control over the formative quality of practices.[39] And, he opens up another discussion about the value of Christian practices, and the ability for people with intellectual disabilities to participate in them, which I will explore below. If people with intellectual disabilities are unable to maintain "appropriate intentions and construals" as Healy insists, or cannot participate in the "effort-filled deliberative process" that Tanner suggests is a requirement for being a disciple or witness, are they then disqualified from practicing witness? I will argue below that all people are "enabled" to participate in practicing witness by the Holy Spirit.

To further complexify this discussion of practices, I have argued that practices are not "best practices" or technique, but neither can practices be distilled into simply doing what Jesus or his disciples did. Discipleship cannot be reduced to either a technical or a normative rule for accomplishing ends and it cannot be reduced to simply imitating Jesus Christ. As Barth reminds us, "we might try to copy everything that Jesus demanded and that [his disciples] did, and yet completely fail to be disciples, because we do not do it, as they did, at his particular call and command to us."[40]

Although imitation of Christ is not the goal of Christian practices, Guder can and does speak of the Christological formation that occurs through Christian practices for the sake of mission. While he echoes Barth in suggesting that discipleship is not equivalent to imitation of Christ, he recognizes that we follow Christ in spontaneous and formalized ways (practices) in a process through which we become more Christ-like. For Guder, "[t]his is

Christological formation for missional practice rooted in the transformation of the 'thinking, acting, and feeling' of the witness community, which comes by following Jesus and imitating Jesus."[41] Through the Spirit-enabled process of sanctification, Christian practices must become congruent with the message they are representing.[42] For example, practices that represent the Gospel of peace ought not be performed in a manner that is divisive or judgmental. Practices of hospitality ought not be carried out in ways that fail to demonstrate concern for the outsider. In line with Guder's instincts, Kathryn Tanner asks:

> Is the practice of welcome primarily a means to increase church membership and therefore a way of sustaining the church in troubled times? If so, it would make little sense to welcome into church the very people (the homeless, the mentally ill, gay people, those of radically different ethnic or racial classification from present members) who would prompt current members to leave. The same outcome would not be especially problematic where the practice of welcome is thought to be part of the church's mission to reflect Jesus' own concern for the outsider even at the severest cost to himself.[43]

When Guder speaks about imitation of Christ, he is speaking of the issue of congruence between the concerns of Jesus and the concerns of the church as embodied in the congregation's practices. He also calls this incarnational witness, which is, of course, not possible without embodiment. In our incarnational witness, "holiness" is a way of talking about "the way in which God's Spirit equips the church to practice its vocation so that witness can be credibly made in the world."[44]

If the transformation of the community of disciples for the sake of a more faithful witness is one aspect of the missional nature of Christian practices for Guder, the other is that the practices are themselves a way in which congregations *bear the witness* of the Spirit. Practices don't simply shape congregants by the Spirit transforming their habits and dispositions, forming their "fitness for service" and "useableness for God's mission."[45] Christian practices are missional and are themselves a "credible demonstration" of the Gospel, a "different way of living" that "invites all into friendship and the service of [God's] healing purposes."[46] At the same time, as the Gospel message is embodied in the witness of Christian practices, the congregations will be confronted by the Gospel "as it is translated heard, and responded to" and will experience a continuing conversion while embodying this witness.[47] In order to avoid a kind of morphological fundamentalism that conceives of practices as fixed in form, Christian practices are responsive to God's work in and out the church through the Spirit and are reshaped in ways that avoid normative claims about shape and structure while emphasizing common witness.

AN EMBODIED AND ENABLED WITNESS

To this point, I have made the case that Guder's concept of incarnational witness and his emphasis on forming a community to "walk worthily" in mission are best expressed in the language of missional Christian practices. Through Christian practices congregations practice witness, and the congruence between the Gospel and that proclamation is a matter of the fitness of our witness. Now I want to advance the discussion of Christian practices to consider how people with intellectual disabilities are indispensable to practicing witness.[48]

Do practices have formative value for people who are unable to perform them with "appropriate intentions and construals" or as part of an "effort-filled deliberative process"? I will approach this dilemma from two sides. First, if we understand humans as primarily embodied actors rather than thinking things, as James K. A. Smith suggests, then we need to consider more fully non-linguistic, intuitive, and corporeal ways of knowing. Second, if the power of witness, and the formative power of practices, is not found in technique or in anything "internal to the practices themselves" then we must acknowledge that it comes from elsewhere. I argue that the power of Christian witness is found in God's enabling power to bear witness and not in the intellect, capacities, or abilities of the witness herself.[49]

Smith sets the stage for a practice-centered conception of Christian witness. He argues that human persons are primarily embodied actors rather than thinking things. Consequently, as his interests intersect with the aim of this chapter to address how practices shape and embody the fitness of our witness, he prioritizes formative Christian practices over ideas and worldviews as the site of challenge to malformative cultural practices—practices that form us in ways that are not consistent with life under the reign and rule of God. Much of what Smith proposes I learned through the experience of ministering to and with adolescents with intellectual and developmental disabilities. Specifically, he maintains that Christian formation does not traffic in abstract, disembodied ideas, but is, instead, a holistic endeavor that involves the entire person, "including our bodies, in a process of formation that aims our desires, primes our imagination, and orients us to the world."[50] Somatic, spatial, kinesthetic, aesthetic, inter- and intrapersonal intelligences yield knowledge beyond the critical rational intellect. And, when we are attentive to the different ways that people learn and know, we will be more open to the many different modalities of Christian witness. As Guder has suggested, "our theology of the church, summarized under the imperative 'Be my witnesses,' must be open to the enormous diversity of Christian modes of expression and thought."[51]

Practices address our witness and the ecclesiology that bears it "as if bodies mattered."[52] Mary McClintock Fulkerson explains, "When the only kind of communication theologians recognize is linguistic, then most of the people with intellectual disabilities from group homes become nonpersons, or, at best, objects of pity. However, much of their behavior previously thought to be disruptive—especially that of folks without language—is now recognized by educators as communication."[53] Non-linguistic, intuitive, and corporeal ways of knowing and communicating are an essential aspect of our witness. "[W]e are formed," explains Smith, "by the practices in which we participate, and not merely by the ideas we exchange."[54] Rational discourse and deliberation on concepts and ideas is not the primary shaper of the community of witness. In fact, the presence of people with intellectual disabilities will transgress "the habituations into the proprieties of the dominant group" (linguistic centered rational discourse) and open congregations to a way of practicing witness that leads to a more complete communication of the Gospel.[55]

Finally, and importantly, the Spirit enables all Christian witness. Pentecost was the "unique event of enabling that called forth the church as the 'witnessing community' and sent it out on its pilgrimage."[56] There are no prior qualifications or capacities required to participate in the community of witness. The Spirit enables the communication of the witness and enables the response of faith to that witness. As I have written elsewhere, people with intellectual disabilities "have a Spirit-filled witness—they have the capacity, grounded extrinsically (as it is for all of us), to be signs, instruments and foretastes of the kingdom. Our participation in the prophetic activity of Jesus Christ does not require the capacity for self-determination. My point is that those labeled the disabled do have a capacity. They point differently, taste differently, sound and image differently, but the Spirit whose witness they bear and the kingdom and Lord to whom they bear witness is the same."[57]

NOTES

1. Darrell L. Guder, *The Incarnation and the Church's Witness* (Harrisburg, PA: Trinity Press International, 1999), 6.

2. Though Guder has used the term "practices" on occasion to refer to social activities like worship, sacraments, prayer, and proclamation, he uses the term without precision and does not connect it to the longer "practices" conversation. To connect Guder's embedded understanding of a Christian practice with the broader conversation is one aim of this chapter.

3. Alan J. Roxburgh, "The Missional Church," *Theology Matters* 10, no. 4 (2004): 4–5. See also, Alan J. Roxburgh and M. Scott Boren, *Introducing the Missional Church: What It Is, Why It Matters, How to Become One* (Grand Rapids, MI: Baker Books, 2009), 10.

4. Lois Barrett, ed., *Treasure in Clay Jars: Patterns in Missional Faithfulness* (Grand Rapids, MI: Eerdmans, 2004).

5. Dale Ziemer offers a helpful, though thin, orienting discussion of Christian practices in his chapter, "Practices That Demonstrate God's Intent for the World." In his words, "Our visits uncovered certain patterns of redemptive relationships in community. These patterns, or Christian practices, are communal or social in nature. . . . They contribute essentially to the missional character of the congregation, for they are rooted in the gospel and offer a redemptive contrast

to the social patterns of the dominant North American culture." Barrett, *Treasure in Clay Jars*, 85. Earlier, Inagrace Dietterich used the concept of Christian practices to consider how missional communities are cultivated. "Through the power of the Holy Spirit a 'people sent' are cultivated through the practices by which they are formed, trained, equipped, and motivated as missional communities." Inagrace Dietterich, "Missional Community: Cultivating Communities of the Holy Spirit," in *Missional Church: A Vision for the Sending of the Church in North America*, ed. Darrell L. Guder (Grand Rapids, MI: Eerdmans, 1998), 142–82, here 142.

6. Nicholas M. Healy, "Practices and the New Ecclesiology: Misplaced Concreteness?" *International Journal of Systematic Theology* 5, no. 3 (2003): 287–308.

7. Series with Wm. B. Eerdmans, edited by Pete Ward, Christian Scharen, Paul Fiddes, John Swinton, and James Nieman. "The series has grown out of a convergence around the attempt to rethink the customary divide between empirical and theological analysis of the Church."

8. Clare Watkins, "Practical Ecclesiology: What Counts as Theology in Studying the Church?" in *Perspectives on Ecclesiology and Ethnography*, ed. Pete Ward (Grand Rapids, MI: Eerdmans, 2012), 168.

9. Serene Jones, "Graced Practices: Excellence and Freedom in the Christian Faith," in *Practicing Theology: Beliefs and Practices in Christian Life*, eds. Miroslav Volf and Dorothy Bass (Grand Rapids, MI: Eerdmans, 2002), 57.

10. Darrell L. Guder, *Be My Witnesses: The Church's Mission, Message, and Messengers* (Grand Rapids, MI: Eerdmans, 1985), 105–11, 204–25.

11. J. Todd Billings, *Union with Christ: Reframing Theology and Ministry for the Church* (Grand Rapids, MI: Baker Academic, 2011), 130–32.

12. Dorothy C. Bass, ed., *Practicing Our Faith: A Guide for Conversation, Learning, and Growth* (San Francisco, CA: Jossey-Bass, 1997), 5. Italics in the original. The authors suggest in a footnote in *Practicing Theology* that the parenthetical words "in Jesus Christ," absent from the original *Practicing Our Faith* definition, "would clarify the character and content of the active divine presence that is so central to our understanding of practices." Miroslav Volf and Dorothy C. Bass, eds., *Practicing Theology: Beliefs and Practices in Christian Life* (Grand Rapids, MI: Eerdmans, 2001), 18.

13. Volf and Bass, *Practicing Theology*, 22.

14. Benjamin T. Conner, *Practicing Witness: A Missional Vision of Christian Practices* (Grand Rapids, MI: Eerdmans, 2011), 99.

15. See the wide variety of practices developed in Bass, *Practicing Our Faith*.

16. Bass, 5, 8–9.

17. "The other version seeks to recover and promote traditional ecclesial practices in order to help the church face the unusual challenges brought on by the dominance of secularism and the decline of orthodox Christian identity and church life." Nicholas M. Healy, "Practices and the New Ecclesiology: Misplaced Concreteness?," *International Journal of Systematic Theology* 5, no. 3 (2003): 291. See my discussion in Conner, *Practicing Witness*, 44–45.

18. Craig Dykstra, *Growing in the Life of Faith: Education and Christian Practices* (Louisville, KY: Westminster John Knox Press, 2005), 66, see further, xv, 64, and 78.

19. Dykstra, 56. And again: "I have been arguing that the practices of the life of faith have power to place us where we can receive a sense of the presence of God." Dykstra, 63.

20. Nicholas M. Healy, "Ecclesiology, Ethnography, and God: An Interplay of Reality Descriptions," in *Perspectives on Ecclesiology and Ethnography*, ed. Peter Ward (Grand Rapids, MI: Eerdmans, 2012), 198.

21. John Swinton, "'Where Is Your Church?' Moving toward a Hospitable and Sanctified Ethnography," in *Perspectives on Ecclesiology and Ethnography*, ed. Peter Ward (Grand Rapids, MI: Eerdmans, 2012), 72.

22. Missiologist Andrew Walls does speak about signs of continuity across traditions and cultures, family resemblances among Christian communities that include: "The worship of the God of Israel"; "The ultimate significance of Jesus of Nazareth"; the idea that "God is active where believers are"; "That believers constitute a people of God transcending time and space"; and that believers share common Scriptures and enact rituals that use bread, wine, and water. However, Walls admits a wide variety in the way these beliefs and practices, or "signs of

historic Christianity" are expressed in line with the "infinite translatability of the Christian faith." Andrew F. Walls, *The Missionary Movement in Christian History: Studies in the Transmission of Faith* (Maryknoll, NY: Orbis Books, 1996), 6–7, 22–24.

23. Kathryn Tanner, *Theories of Culture: A New Agenda for Theology* (Minneapolis, MN: Fortress Press, 1997), 152.

24. Healy, "Practices and the New Ecclesiology," 291. However, the fact that Healy can point to instances of hospitality and recognize these actions as participating in some larger practice he can name "hospitality" suggests that there is such a practice. Differences across time and space and even variety among local expressions are part of a larger practice that is grounded in God's hospitality toward humans.

25. Bonnie J. Miller-McLemore, "Five Misunderstandings about Practical Theology," *International Journal of Practical Theology* 16, no. 1 (2012): 5–26, here 21–23.

26. Tanner, *Theories of Culture*, 136.

27. "United in the expectation that a purer witness and discipleship will come of such efforts to work through their disagreements, participants must show a willingness to listen to and be corrected if necessary by all others similarly concerned about the true nature of Christian discipleship." Tanner, *Theories of Culture*, 125.

28. Kathryn Tanner, "Theological Reflection and Christian Practices," in *Practicing Theology: Beliefs and Practices in Christian Life*, ed. Miroslav Volf and Dorothy C. Bass (Grand Rapids, MI: Eerdmans, 2001), 228–42, here 233. I will critique Tanner's insistence on an "effort-filled deliberative process" as a requirement for being a disciple or witness below.

29. See John G. Flett's excellent exposition of Newbigin's phrase in "What Does It Mean for a Congregation to Be a Hermeneutic?," in *The Gospel and Pluralism Today: Reassessing Lesslie Newbigin in the 21st Century*, ed. Scott W. Sunquist and Amos Yong (Downers Grove, IL: IVP Academic, 2015), 195–213. See especially his conclusion: "By describing the congregation as the only hermeneutic of the gospel, Newbigin reminds us that the gospel can only take bodily form. The gospel is no free-floating message, no individual belief system. It creates, shapes and sustains a people, a body. This congregation is a visible entity in history. More than this and as idealistic as it may sound, Newbigin expects the congregations local and mundane, filled with the everyday stumbling Christian, to be a sign of the kingdom—not just called to be so, but given all the necessary gifts in the power of the Spirit." Flett, "What Does It Mean for a Congregation to Be a Hermeneutic?," 213.

30. Tanner, *Theories of Culture*, 152.

31. Karl Barth, *Call to Discipleship* (Minneapolis, MN: Fortress Press, 2003), 7. See further Karl Barth, *The Doctrine of Reconciliation* IV/2 (Edinburgh: T&T Clark, 1958), 534.

32. "[P]articipation in Christ Means Participation in His Mission to the World." J. E. Lesslie Newbigin, *The Household of God: Lectures on the Nature of the Church* (New York: Friendship Press, 1954), 146. And further, "[t]here is no participation in Christ without participation in his mission in the world." Norman Goodall, *Missions under the Cross: Addresses Delivered at the Enlarged Meeting of the Committee of the International Missionary Council at Willingen, in Germany, 1952* (London: Edinburgh House Press, 1953), 190.

33. "[T]he Church's existence is in the act of being the bearer of that salvation to the whole world. 'The Church exists by mission as fire exists by burning.' It has its being, so to say, in the magnetic field between Christ and the world. Its *koinonia* in Him is a participation in His apostolate to the world. Each Christian congregation is the earnest and foretaste, the *arrabon* of the gathering together of all men of every tribe and tongue around the throne of God and of the Lamb. It is true to its own essential nature only when it takes this fact seriously and therefore treats the world-wide mission of the Church as something which belongs to the very core of its existence as a corporate body." Newbigin, *The Household of God*, 142–43.

34. Darrell L. Guder, *The Continuing Conversion of the Church* (Grand Rapids, MI: Eerdmans, 2000), 62.

35. Darrell L. Guder, "The *missio Dei*: A Mission Theology for After Christendom," in *Called to Witness: Doing Missional Theology* (Grand Rapids, MI: Eerdmans, 2015), 20–43, here 36, 43.

36. Guder, 36–37.

37. Along this same line of reasoning, "Christian practices, and their pedagogical analogues, are to be understood neither as theoretical principles to be clinically applied nor as efficient techniques practiced upon students; they depend upon the building of a shared imagination in which students acquire new ways of seeing and understanding their own learning as well as new rhythms commensurate with this renewed imagination." David I. Smith and James K. A. Smith, "Introduction: Practices, Faith, and Pedagogy," in *Teaching and Christian Practices: Reshaping Faith and Learning*, ed. David I. Smith and James K. A. Smith (Grand Rapids, MI: Eerdmans, 2011), 1–23, here 23.

38. Healy, "Practices and the New Ecclesiology," 295.

39. Tanner, while helpfully and explicitly connecting the practices discussion to the concept of witness, also falls into this trap.

40. Barth, *Call to Discipleship*, 70.

41. Darrell L. Guder, "The Christological Formation of Missional Practice," in *Called to Witness: Doing Missional Theology* (Grand Rapids, MI: Eerdmans, 2015), 61.

42. Guder, *The Incarnation and the Church's Witness*, 9.

43. Tanner, "Theological Reflection and Christian Practices," 236.

44. Guder, "The Nicene Marks in a Post-Christendom Church," 87.

45. Guder, 87.

46. Guder, "The *missio Dei*," 43.

47. Guder, *The Continuing Conversion of the Church*, 69.

48. For a full treatment on my thoughts on this matter see, Benjamin T. Conner, *Amplifying Our Witness: Giving Voice to Adolescents with Developmental Disabilities* (Grand Rapids, MI: Eerdmans, 2012).

49. I argue this in *Disabling Mission, Enabling Witness: Exploring Missiology through the Lens of Disability Studies* (Downers Grove, IL: IVP Academic, 2018).

50. James K. A. Smith, *Desiring the Kingdom: Worship, Worldview, and Cultural Formation* (Grand Rapids, MI: Baker Academic, 2009), 39. See also Serene Jones's observation: "It is often through practices that the self is structured into ways reaching beyond the ideational character of beliefs. Practices play a role in writing the unconscious and in ordering the non-conscious ways in which the body 'knows'; and these, in turn, directly inform how we imagine the specifics of the doctrinal landscapes we occupy." Serene Jones, "Graced Practices: Excellence and Freedom in the Christian Faith," in *Practicing Theology: Beliefs and Practices in Christian Life*, ed. Miroslav Volf, and Dorothy C. Bass (Grand Rapids, MI: Eerdmans, 2001), 51–77, here 76.

51. Guder, *Be My Witnesses*, 89–90.

52. Mary McClintock Fulkerson, "A Place to Appear: Ecclesiology as if Bodies Mattered," *Theology Today* 64, no. 2 (2007): 159–71.

53. Mary McClintock Fulkerson, "Interpreting Situations: When is 'Empirical' also 'Theological'?," in *Perspectives on Ecclesiology and Ethnography*, ed. Peter Ward (Grand Rapids, MI: Eerdmans, 2012), 124–144, here 132.

54. Smith, and Smith, "Introduction: Practices, Faith, and Pedagogy," 6.

55. Fulkerson, "A Place to Appear," 171.

56. Guder, *Be My Witnesses*, 44.

57. Conner, *Practicing Witness*, 113.

BIBLIOGRAPHY

Barrett, Lois, ed. *Treasure in Clay Jars: Patterns in Missional Faithfulness*. Grand Rapids, MI: Eerdmans, 2004.

Barth, Karl. *Call to Discipleship*. Minneapolis, MN: Fortress Press, 2003.

———. *The Doctrine of Reconciliation IV/2*. Edinburgh: T&T Clark, 1958.

Bass, Dorothy C., ed. *Practicing Our Faith: A Guide for Conversation Learning Growth*. San Francisco, CA: Jossey-Bass, 1997.

Conner, Benjamin T. *Practicing Witness: A Missional Vision of Christian Practices*. Grand Rapids, MI: Eerdmans, 2011.

Dietterich, Inagrace. "Missional Community: Cultivating Communities of the Holy Spirit," in *Missional Church: A Vision for the Sending of the Church in North America*, edited by Darrell L. Guder, 142–82. Grand Rapids, MI: Eerdmans, 1998.

Dykstra, Craig. *Growing in the Life of Faith: Education and Christian Practices*. Louisville, KY: Westminster John Knox Press, 2005.

Flett, John G. "What Does It Mean for a Congregation to Be a Hermeneutic?," in *The Gospel and Pluralism Today: Reassessing Lesslie Newbigin in the 21st Century*, edited by Scott W. Sunquist and Amos Yong, 195–214. Downers Grove, IL: IVP Academic, 2015.

Fulkerson, Mary Mcclintock. "Interpreting Situations: When Is 'Empirical' also 'Theological'?," in *Perspectives on Ecclesiology and Ethnography*, edited by Peter Ward, 124–44. Grand Rapids, MI: Eerdmans, 2012.

———. "A Place to Appear: Ecclesiology as If Bodies Mattered." *Theology Today* 64, no. 2 (2007): 159–71.

Goodall, Norman. *Missions under the Cross: Addresses Delivered at the Enlarged Meeting of the Committee of the International Missionary Council at Willingen, in Germany, 1952*. London: Edinburgh House Press, 1953.

Guder, Darrell L. *Be My Witnesses: The Church's Mission, Message, and Messengers*. Grand Rapids, MI: Eerdmans, 1985.

———. *Called to Witness: Doing Missional Theology*. Grand Rapids, MI: Eerdmans, 2015.

———. *The Continuing Conversion of the Church*. Grand Rapids, MI: Eerdmans, 2000.

———. *The Incarnation and the Church's Witness*. Harrisburg, PA: Trinity Press International, 1999.

Healy, Nicholas M. "Ecclesiology, Ethnography, and God: An Interplay of Reality Descriptions," in *Perspectives on Ecclesiology and Ethnography*, edited by Peter Ward, 182–99. Grand Rapids, MI: Eerdmans, 2012.

———. "Practices and the New Ecclesiology: Misplaced Concreteness?" *International Journal of Systematic Theology* 5, no. 3 (2003): 287–308.

Jones, Serene. "Graced Practices: Excellence and Freedom in the Christian Faith," in *Practicing Theology: Beliefs and Practices in Christian Life*, edited by Miroslav Volf and Dorothy C. Bass, 51–77. Grand Rapids, MI: Eerdmans, 2001.

Miller-McLemore, Bonnie J. "Five Misunderstandings about Practical Theology." *International Journal of Practical Theology* 16, no. 1 (2012): 5–26.

Newbigin, J. E. Lesslie. *The Household of God: Lectures on the Nature of the Church*. New York: Friendship Press, 1954.

Roxburgh, Alan J. "The Missional Church." *Theology Matters* 10, no. 4 (2004): 4–5.

Roxburgh, Alan J., and M. Scott Boren. *Introducing the Missional Church: What It Is, Why It Matters, How to Become One*. Baker Books, 2009.

Smith, David I., and James K. A. Smith. "Introduction: Practices, Faith, and Pedagogy," in *Teaching and Christian Practices: Reshaping Faith and Learning*, edited by David I. Smith and James K. A. Smith, 1–23. Grand Rapids, MI: Eerdmans, 2011.

Smith, James K. A. *Desiring the Kingdom: Worship, Worldview, and Cultural Formation*. Grand Rapids, MI: Baker Academic, 2009.

Swinton, John. "Theological Reflection and Christian Practices," in *Practicing Theology: Beliefs and Practices in Christian Life*, edited by Miroslav Volf and Dorothy C. Bass, 228–42. Grand Rapids, MI: Eerdmans, 2001.

———. "'Where Is Your Church?' Moving toward a Hospitable and Sanctified Ethnography," in *Perspectives on Ecclesiology and Ethnography*, edited by Peter Ward, 71–94. Grand Rapids, MI: Eerdmans, 2012.

Tanner, Kathryn. *Theories of Culture: A New Agenda for Theology*. Minneapolis, MN: Fortress Press, 1997.

Volf, Miroslav, and Dorothy C. Bass, eds. *Practicing Theology: Beliefs and Practices in Christian Life*. Grand Rapids, MI: Eerdmans, 2001.

Walls, Andrew F. *The Missionary Movement in Christian History: Studies in the Transmission of Faith*. Maryknoll, NY: Orbis Books, 1996.

Chapter Nine

Missional Ecclesiology

Proposing Some Friendly Kuyperian Amendments

Richard J. Mouw

The churches in the West are in a missionary context. We can no longer maintain the illusion—long reinforced by the remnants of "Christendom" thought and practice—of being embedded in a "Christian culture." We now face the challenge of rethinking our traditional ecclesiological perspectives in the light of a robust missiology.

I wholeheartedly endorse those sentences I have just written. My understanding of what they affirm has been greatly shaped and enhanced by studying the "missional church" writings of Lesslie Newbigin, George Hunsberger, Craig Van Gelder, and others. And, of course, the work of Darrell Guder, whose pioneering explorations in this area I am pleased to join others in celebrating in these pages.

The issues I point to in those opening sentences are crucial for an obedient commitment to the cause of the Gospel in the twenty-first century. Unfortunately, though—as Darrell Guder has frequently pointed out in some of his recent writings—the term "missional" is open these days to a variety of meanings. Even folks who would offer their enthusiastic endorsement to themes associated with missional church thinking often operate with different interpretations from those set forth by Darrell and his closest allies in the cause.

While I basically side with Darrell and his allies on these matters, I do have some questions about the present state of the discussion of missional church. I am a "neo-Calvinist" of the strand of Dutch Reformed thought that draws inspiration from the nineteenth-century writings of Abraham Kuyper and Herman Bavinck. I am firmly convinced that they would strongly endorse the basic themes of the missional church theological project. I am

139

also convinced, however, that they would want to offer some nuances on those themes in the light of their own version of Reformed orthodoxy. I will not give much attention in my reflections here to expositing their views. Rather, representing what I take to be the basic spirit of their thinking on issues of theology and culture, I will suggest, as a twenty-first-century advocate for their perspective, some neo-Calvinist nuances for missional church theology. I want to stress the fact, though, that I do so as one who has been deeply appreciative of—and significantly influenced by—the marvelous contributions of those who have pioneered in recent decades in formulating a vibrant theology of and for the missional church. My comments in what follows are not so much criticisms as they are friendly amendments.

EXISTING NUANCES: AN ASIDE

In talking about my concern to introduce some nuances I do not mean to suggest that Darrell and his allies have been unnuanced in setting out their views. Indeed, I find these thinkers refreshingly complex in dealing with some key themes in their perspective that are often expressed with over-wrought rhetoric by others who pick up on these themes.

A case in point is the depiction of the historical realities associated these days with the terms "Christendom" and "Constantinianism." I have no serious disagreements with the contention that these labels signify patterns of relationships between the church and culture that have seriously weakened the church's efforts to be faithful to the Gospel. But I do worry about confusions often associated with the "post-Christendom" rhetoric. I often find that the issues are not really about whether we should be "post-Constantinian" as such but, rather, about continuing differences—ones that I consider to be highly significant—between the Reformed and Anabaptist theological perspectives.

In any event, I find the treatment of these matters by both Newbigin and Guder to be admirably balanced. Here is Newbigin on the subject: "Much has been written," he observed, "about the harm done to the cause of the gospel when Constantine accepted baptism, and it is not difficult to expatiate on this theme." He immediately goes to ask, however: "But could any other choice have been made?" There was, during Constantine's reign, a serious spiritual crisis in the larger culture, and people "turned to the church as the one society that could hold a disintegrating world together." What should the church have said in response? asked Newbigin. Should it simply "have refused the appeal and washed its hands of responsibility for the political order?"

In acknowledging these conditions, Newbigin is not retracting his own criticisms of the Constantinian arrangement. It would be a serious error, he says, to ignore the ways in which Christians "fell into the temptation of worldly power." But, he asks, do we really think that the cause of the Gospel would have been better served "if the church had refused all political responsibility, if there had never been a 'Christian' Europe?" His straightforward answer: "I find it hard to think so."[1]

And while Darrell also consistently warns against various dangerous reductionisms associated with the Christendom pattern, he likewise rejects what he acknowledges is a widespread "reckless 'Christendom-bashing' going on" these days. We should not give the impression, he says, "that the Holy Spirit left the earth around the fourth century, when Constantine came to power, only to reappear in the modern group or movement with which we may now be affiliated." We must be open to acknowledging the ways that "God has been present and at work through this very ambiguous history that we call Christendom."[2]

THE RANGE OF "ECCLESIAL"

Missional church thinking at its best—and I have already identified authors whose work I refer to here—has performed an important theological service by combatting various reductionisms that have long plagued the life and mission of the church. Christ's redemptive mission is not only, or even primarily, about individual salvation. Nor should our thinking about the Gospel be restricted to the dominant cultural embodiments of Western Christianity. The church's calling must be defined with a central emphasis on our calling to participate in the *missio Dei* in the larger world.

All of that, I say, comprises a significant contribution to our understanding of what it means to be an obedient Christian community in contemporary life. In the spirit of that contribution I want to push the anti-reductionism project a little further by pointing to two areas where I do not find enough—or even much—being said by my favorite missional theologians about what kinds of entities we are willing to include in our understanding of "church," and I will illustrate my concern with an account of a personal experience.

While undertaking graduate study in philosophy in the 1960s at the University of Alberta in Edmonton, Canada, I saw a notice in a church bulletin that the Christian Farmers Federation of Alberta was going to hold a discussion on the topic of raising chickens. This was an organization of farmers, mostly Dutch Reformed along with a few Mennonites, who were deeply serious about relating their faith to farming practices. I decided to attend to hear what they had to say about chicken farming.

Much of their discussion that evening was about the use of land and other resources, with attention also to possible ways in which their efforts could be connected to meeting the needs of hungry people, both locally and internationally. Toward the end of the meeting, though, one older farmer stood to speak in a very specific way about what it could mean for a Christian to raise chickens.

He spoke with a heavy Dutch accent, and his face was heavily tanned from spending many hours working out-of-doors. And while he apparently had not received any advanced formal education, he was in his own way quite eloquent as he spoke about how we are to view chickens from a biblical perspective. "Colonel Sanders wants us to think of chickens," he said, "only in terms of dollars and cents. For him they are nothing but little pieces of meat to be bought and sold for food. And so we're supposed to crowd them together in small spaces and get them fat enough to be killed." And then he moved toward his theological lesson: "But that's wrong! The Bible says that God created every animal 'after its own kind.' Chickens aren't people, but neither are they nothing but hunks of meat. Chickens are *chickens* and they deserve to be treated like chickens! This means that we have to give each chicken the space to strut its stuff in front of other chickens."

I have told that story many times, typically as what I see as a delightful example of practical Christian thinking about "creation care."[3] Here, however, I want to use it in raising a question about what we might think of as "ecclesial ontology": what kinds of modes of organization are properly to be included with the scope of "church"?

Those familiar with Kuyper's thought will see that I am pushing here for a recognition of his distinction between "the church as an institution" and "the church as an organism."[4] By the first term, the Dutch neo-Calvinists understand the body of Christian believers as it is organized for very specific purposes—purposes often described in the Reformed tradition as the church's "three marks," namely, the preaching of the Word, the conducting of the community's sacramental life, and the exercise of church discipline. Many of us would want to be sure that this understanding of the proper purposes of the institutional church also explicitly includes *catechesis*: a robust teaching ministry.

While the formulation given here highlights the life and mission of the local congregation, the institutional church is also characterized by what we Presbyterians like to refer to as "connectionalism." The local congregation must recognize bonds with other congregations, thus requiring broader ecclesial entities—presbyteries, general assemblies, synods—associated with membership in a denomination.

The neo-Calvinists introduced the second term, "church as organism," to account for a broader set of entities that typically have only an informal relationship to the institutional church. This includes some Christian educational institutions, groups with a vocational focus, and other such voluntary religious organizations. The church as an organism, in this sense, encompasses the ways in which Christians seek, or ought to seek, to live out their lives as Christians in the world.

The Christian Farmers Federation is an example of church as organism. The group is not associated with the institutional church. Members belong to diverse local congregations. They are united, not by shared confessional commitments, but by a mutual interest in seeking divine guidance for their farming practices. Other examples of entities that fall under this rubric would be Christians in the Visual Arts, the Fellowship of Christian Athletes, and the Christian Legal Society.

Here is how I see the ecclesial "mapping" of such groups, using the farming discussion as a case in point. The chicken farmer is an active member of a local congregation and he regularly hears things in the life of the worshiping and catechizing community that strike him as having a direct bearing on his or her daily work. God cares about the whole creation: plants, water supply, soil, animals. Christians are to be good stewards of the creation. The fact that our "chief end" as humans "is to glorify God and enjoy God forever" means that our engagement with the larger world, human and non-human reality alike, must honor God's creating and redeeming purposes.

The farmer takes all of that very seriously, but he or she does have important questions about how to apply these general concerns to specifics. This is not an area where the pastor, or the congregational elders, should be expected to have any expertise. The natural strategy, then, is for the farmer to get together with other farmers for more in-depth discussion of how biblical teaching can inform agricultural practices.

Now, could this be a function of the local church? Of course, particularly in a setting where farming is the dominant occupation. But even in such a context we should not assume a congregation-based group would bring the right people together. Consider, for example, a large congregation in a city where there are advanced medical facilities. The Christian Medical Society brings health-care specialists together for discussions of health care as a vocation wherein issues of discipleship are important to discuss. It is important in this kind of vocational context for, say, surgeons to spend time talking with other surgeons. This means that such conversations will of necessity have an ecumenical scope, with Reformed, Pentecostal, Catholic, and persons from other communities sharing common concerns and challenges. For such interactions, operating by insisting on a "parish" framework would be arbitrarily restrictive.

The picture that Darrell Guder portrays in his writing strikes me as unnecessarily restrictive in this regard. He certainly raises the right question in this important area. "How do we equip each other," he asks, "to be worthy of our calling in the personal apostolates into which God sends us every time we make the transition from gathered to scattered community?"[5] And he goes on to insist that, if we are going to "learn how to translate the Gospel into these various contexts, we will need to foster the kind of discipling [that] must, very concretely and practically, take account of the challenges that we meet in our apostolates." Darrell even gets appropriately specific on this point:

> How shall the Christian teacher in the public school system carry out her apostolate in a context where conversation about the faith is virtually prohibited? How should the Christian businessperson carry out his or her apostolic vocation when the neighbor you are to love is your competitor? How should the Christian accountant advise his or her clients with integrity when the normative conduct of the prevailing culture is to manipulate the financial data for personal gain and reduced taxes?[6]

These are wonderful questions that warm the heart of the Kuyperian. But the heart cools quickly when Darrell offers his counsel. The leadership of the local church, he proposes, "will have to practice a collegiality of shared experience and expertise." Furthermore, we cannot expect the pastoral leadership to be able to address these matters effectively. The solution, then? "There are likely to be more qualified equippers of the saints among the ruling elders who live in that Monday-to-Saturday world than among the teaching elders."[7]

There are both practical and ecclesiological questions that can be raised here. The practical concern is whether the kind of context-specific equipping that is at stake here should fall within the task of ruling elders. Is a local congregation failing in its duties if it does not have among its congregational leaders persons who can help the accountant deal with specific faith challenges that emerge in her daily work? To insist that this kind of expertise be taken into account when choosing leaders for the local church strikes me as requiring an extensive rethinking of issues regarding church order.

The polity issue leads to the larger theological question. What prohibits us from affirming, as Darrell does, that it is an obligation of the church to assist in rather detailed ways to translate the claims of the Gospel into the details of concrete apostolic vocations, and then affirming that the vocation-specific gatherings beyond the boundaries of the local congregation are genuine manifestations of "church"?

It may be enough simply to agree to disagree on this. We Kuyperians can draw on the strength of a missional understanding of the institutional church, while including other entities with the scope of our ecclesial ontology, with others drawing more restrictive ecclesiological boundaries. But I do think that the questions we Kuyperians raised about how, if at all, organizations like the Christian Farmers Federation fall legitimately within the broader boundaries of church—performing equipping functions that should not be required of local congregations—need to be addressed more clearly by those who have done so much to clarify the overall missional character of the gathered people of God.

THE STATUS OF "ORDERS"

Since it may seem strange that I would lodge what appears to be a serious complaint about Darrell Guder's ecclesiology in a contribution to a volume honoring his contribution to missional church thought, I want to explain my intentions on this matter with two clarifying comments here.

One is that my real purpose is to make Darrell's important work in missional ecclesiology more accessible to those working within the neo-Calvinist tradition. I am convinced that Kuyper's institute-organism distinction has been responsible for some serious ecclesiological distortions among his followers—even though I am also convinced that Kuyper did not intend to promote these distortions. The tendency among many neo-Calvinists is to treat the institutional church as simply one of many manifestations of "church." The farmers' gatherings are the church gathered for agricultural discussion. The medical association is the church gathered for explorations of issues in health care. The conferences of Christian visual artists are the church gathered for exchanges regarding aesthetic norms. And the local congregation—well, that is simply the church gathered for worship and catechesis. I have heard that word "simply" used many times by my fellow Kuyperians, as they warn against elevating the institutional church to a "privileged" status, and thus falling into "the trap of ecclesiasticism."

The truth is, as I see things, that the congregation does indeed have a privileged status in understanding the nature of "church." And missional ecclesiology is clear about this. The local congregation is a "sending" entity. It gathers God's people for worship in order to equip and inspire Christians to go forth as agents of the *missio Dei* in the larger world. And it is only after being clear about this that a healthy neo-Calvinism will go on to argue for forming other modes of Christian association, entities that stand between the worshiping community and individual vocational pursuits, spaces where Christians can wrestle together with serious questions about how to take the general mandate issued by the institutional church into specific areas of Christian service.

A second clarification has to do with the fact that, while Darrell does not attend to these "between" entities in his recent writing about missional ecclesiology, he was actually the one who helped me to think more clearly about how these entities might fit into a robust ecclesiology. In one of my first conversations with Darrell, in the early 1980s when we were both together at the Young Life Institute in Colorado Springs, he described a project in which he was engaged, aimed at clarifying the ecclesial status of Young Life as a ministry not directly sponsored by, or officially accountable to, the institutional church.

The question was: How do we understand the ecclesial nature of a Young Life "club" at a local high school? Christian students, drawn from a diversity of local congregations, gather during the week to encourage each other in the faith for prayer, Bible study, and discussions focused on their unique life challenges and opportunities as teenagers. Darrell said that he was exploring the idea that this kind of entity should be understood ecclesiologically as having some parallels to a "religious order" in Catholicism. To be sure, a Franciscan community has a sacramental life, which makes it "church" in a rather straightforward sense. But—and here I am likely going beyond what clear memoires of my conversation with Darrell would support—there is a parallel between the Young Life club and the Franciscan community in the fact that in each case the gathering is bound together by "special vows"— commitments that are not required of all members of a local parish, but which grow out of a desire to pursue the focus linked to a particular vocation.

To think, then, of a Young Life club as a social space where young people share a common goal of faithful discipleship in a public high school is to see the group's purpose in terms of a legitimate desire to apply the church's call to serve the Kingdom in their unique context. And the same could be said for the Christian Farmers Federation and the Fellowship of Christian Athletes.

Whether I have remembered Darrell's point correctly on the relevant dimensions of this subject, I do credit him with helping me to explore a topic that I believe deserves serious ecclesiological attention. It is not enough, for example, simply to classify Young Life and the Christian Farmers Federation as "para-church." Without additional nuancing, we could also classify local citizens groups—organizations that meet to discuss and act on behalf of issues of racial justice and environmental stewardship—as "para-church." They exist in specific communities "alongside of" local congregations, and church members participate in their activities as a response to being sent out into the world as agents of the Kingdom. But they are not, as such, faith communities, even though they serve purposes to which people of faith are committed.

The Young Life club and the Christian Farmers Federation, however, have a different relationship to the church than those "secular" organizations. They are established as social spaces that are intended to be the next venue— after the worship gatherings of the local church—for explicit Christian explo- ration of vocationally-specific applications of the church's mandate to serve as disciples of Christ in the world.

I am aware, of course, of a likely objection to the Young Life example. Why cannot these kinds of discussions among high school students take place within the life of the local church? Is that not why we have youth ministry programs in our congregations? That is a legitimate concern that needs to be addressed. And there may indeed be local contexts in which the "para-church" youth organization and a ministry of the local congregation compete with each other in unhealthy ways.

It is important to note that this kind of competition has also occurred in contexts where a Catholic order exists alongside of a local parish. I once read an account of a medieval dispute somewhere in the European Low Countries, between a bishop and the abbot of a monastery. The abbot had a talent for sponsoring events that would draw parishioners away from the local parishes for a variety of special occasions. And the attraction to the monastery was reinforced by regular reports of healings and other manifestations of divine mercy occasioned by those visits.

The actual dynamics of church life can require us to live with some messiness in our ecclesiology. My own sense, though, is that the messiness should push us in the direction of an expansive, rather than a restrictive, ecclesiology. The different status between, say, a skid row "rescue mission" and a community sponsored homeless shelter deserves to be addressed theologically. The latter is a service that those outside the church offer to Christians as an opportunity for support and service. The former is—in an important sense, I believe—the church reaching into the larger community *as church*, even though it may not be "officially" connected to the institutional church.

THE LEARNING DIMENSION

My second anti-reductionism concern is about the spirit or posture of what the people of God do as they "scatter" into the world of diverse daily vocations. Here I suspect I am merely wanting to place an emphasis on something that I would like to see spelled out more in a robust missional theology.

I can illustrate my concern here by looking briefly at how Lesslie Newbigin sets forth the agenda for the Christian mission in public life. In his stimulating book, *Truth to Tell: The Gospel as Public Truth*, Newbigin rightly places a strong emphasis on the proclamation of the Gospel, both to individuals as well as in the larger arenas of human culture:

> We have a gospel to proclaim. We have to proclaim it not merely to individuals. . . . We certainly have to do that. But we have to proclaim it as part of the continuing conversation that shapes public doctrine. It must be heard in the conversation of economists, psychiatrists, educators, scientists and politicians.[8]

While I appreciate by Newbigin's insistence here on the Gospel's application, not only to the lives of individuals, but also to the larger patterns of life in the public square, I worry a bit about his putting the case in terms of proclamation. To be sure, the emphasis on proclaiming the Gospel has often been underplayed in liberal Protestantism. Martin Copenhaver made this point nicely in his account of how he had been originally trained to preach as "a child of American liberal Protestantism." An atheist friend, he reported, captured the liberal style of preaching well in this characterization: "You hear what the psychologist says, what the historian says, what the *New York Times* editorial writer says, and then the sermon concludes with, 'And perhaps Jesus said it best . . .'" There came a point in his own ministry, Copenhaver testified, when he realized that he had to preach a message that stands over against the "accumulated wisdom of humankind." Instead of "perhaps Jesus said it best" he senses an obligation to proclaim, "You have heard it said . . . but Jesus says to you . . ."[9]

Proclamation is a mandate in the church's preaching and evangelistic ministry. But I do think that the proclamatory mode is less appropriate as we enter into discussions of how we bring the Gospel to bear on the challenges of our daily lives. I do not know, for example, how much proclamation should take place among high school students meeting in Young Life clubs, or in the explorations of farming concerns in gatherings of the Christian Farmers Federation.

Nor do we turn to the proclamatory mode when we begin to address non-Christians in specific vocational contexts. For this reason I am uneasy about the language Newbigin uses when describing those encounters. When we "bring the faith into the public arena," he says, we are required "to publish it, to put it at risk in the encounter with other faiths and ideologies in open debate and argument."[10] I am not denying that there will be times when, in bringing our faith into public life, we will "proclaim," "publish," and engage in "open debate and argument" with persons representing non-Christian perspectives. But to describe the basic approach to public discipleship in these terms is, I fear, to promote a confrontational spirit that has too often—and this is especially the case in the evangelical world where I make my way theologically—featured an "over against" spirit.

Newbigin does say some things that call for a less confrontational mode of address in the public arena. He tells us that to bring the Gospel into public life is to be engaged "in the risky business of discovering what Christian obedience means in radically new circumstances and in radically different human cultures."[11] And since "we do not yet know all that it means to say that Jesus is Lord," we must see ourselves as "learners, only beginners." Our mission is "not a one-way promotion but a two way encounter in which we learn more of what the Gospel means. We are learning as we go."[12]

That insistence on a learning posture is exactly right. However, to couple this with a portrayal of ourselves as "only beginners" could give the impression that we are mainly learning from our mistakes—like a young violinist who must keep practicing in order to get to a level of skillful performance. This is where those of us in the Kuyperian tradition will want to be very explicit about the need to see ourselves in an ongoing process of learning from those who are outside of the circle of Christian faith. We get this from

Calvin himself, who continued after his conversion to draw on the ancient Roman thinkers whom he had read in his law studies—Seneca was a favorite. Pagan writers, he says in the *Institutes*, often display a "peculiar grace of God," by offering us thoughts that are "clothed and ornamented with God's excellent gifts." This means, then, that "[i]f we regard the Spirit of God as the sole fountain of truth, we shall neither reject the truth itself, nor despise it where it shall appear, unless we wish to dishonor the Spirit of God."[13]

Herman Bavinck echoes Calvin's theme of the extra-ecclesial workings of the Spirit, but with an expanded Trinitarian formulation. The Christian community has much to learn from other religious perspectives, referring particularly to "founders of religions, like Mohommed" in making his point: "Also among pagans, says Scripture, there is a revelation of God, an illumination by the Logos, a working of God's Spirit."[14] And Kuyper similarly sees a divine grace—although non-salvific in its nature—at work in the "interior" lives of unbelievers, "wherever civic virtue, a sense of domesticity, natural love, the practice of human virtue, the improvement of the public conscience, integrity, mutual loyalty among people, and a feeling for piety leaven life."[15]

Again, the posture of learning being suggested here goes beyond the kinds of efforts appropriate for "beginners" who have not yet mastered the necessary skills of conversation with those with whom they disagree. It is a genuine willingness to learn from others, even on the part of seasoned participants in the patterns of life and thought in the public square.

AMENDING, NOT CORRECTING

I used the phrase "friendly amendments" in the title of this chapter. I hope the intended friendly tone has been obvious. And "amendments" is employed here in the spirit of support for a shared project. Sometimes an amendment can be offered as a corrective to something that has been proposed. But often—and that is what I have meant to be doing here—an amendment is proposed for promoting further clarity in what was originally set forth for consideration. My efforts at clarity here flow from a deep appreciation for those who have pioneered in impressing upon all of us that the people of God are called to participate actively and faithfully in God's mission in the world.

NOTES

1. J. E. Lesslie Newbigin, *Foolishness to the Greeks: The Gospel and Western Culture* (Grand Rapids, MI: Eerdmans, 1986), 100–1.

2. Darrell L. Guder, *Called to Witness: Doing Missional Theology* (Grand Rapids, MI: Eerdmans, 2015), 80–81.

3. The use to which I put the story in Richard J. Mouw, *Praying at Burger King* (Grand Rapids, MI: Eerdmans, 2007), 51–53.

4. For a thorough study of the development of Kuyper's ecclesiology over several decades, see John Halsey Wood Jr., *Going Dutch in the Modern Age: Abraham Kuyper's Struggle for a Free Church in the Netherlands* (London: Oxford University Press, 2013). For Wood's account of Kuyper's "Institute" and "Organism" distinction, as I am using the terms here, see 172–75.

5. Guder, *Called to Witness*, 159.

6. Guder, 162.

7. Guder, 162.

8. J. E. Lesslie Newbigin, *Truth to Tell: The Gospel as Public Truth* (Grand Rapids, MI: Eerdmans, 1991), 64.

9. Martin B. Copenhaver, Anthony B. Robinson, and William H. Willimon, *Good News in Exile: Three Pastors Offer a Hopeful Vision for the Church* (Grand Rapids, MI: Eerdmans, 1998), 9–11.

10. Newbigin, *Truth to Tell*, 60.

11. Newbigin, 60.

12. Newbigin, 34.

13. John Calvin, *Institutes of the Christian Religion*, trans. Ford Lewis Battles (Philadelphia: Westminster Press, 1960), II.2.15, 273–275.

14. Herman Bavinck, *Reformed Dogmatics, Vol. 1: Prolegomena*, trans. John Vriend (Grand Rapids, MI: Baker Academic, 2003), 318.

15. Abraham Kuyper, "Common Grace," in *Abraham Kuyper: A Centennial Reader*, ed. James D. Bratt (Grand Rapids, MI: Eerdmans, 1998), 181.

BIBLIOGRAPHY

Bavinck, Herman. *Reformed Dogmatics, Vol. 1: Prolegomena*. Translated by John Vriend. Grand Rapids, MI: Baker Academic, 2003.

Calvin, John. *Institutes of the Christian Religion*. Translated by Ford Lewis Battles. Philadelphia: Westminster Press, 1960.

Copenhaver, Martin B., Anthony B. Robinson, and William H. Willimon. *Good News in Exile: Three Pastors Offer a Hopeful Vision for the Church*. Grand Rapids, MI: Eerdmans, 1998.

Guder, Darrell L. *Called to Witness: Doing Missional Theology*. Grand Rapids, MI: Eerdmans, 2015.

Kuyper, Abraham. "Common Grace," in *Abraham Kuyper: A Centennial Reader*, edited by James D. Bratt, 165–204. Grand Rapids, MI: Eerdmans, 1998.

Mouw, Richard J. *Praying at Burger King*. Grand Rapids, MI: Eerdmans, 2007.

Newbigin, J. E. Lesslie. *Foolishness to the Greeks: The Gospel and Western Culture*. Grand Rapids, MI: Eerdmans, 1986.

Newbigin, J. E. Lesslie. *Truth to Tell: The Gospel as Public Truth*. Grand Rapids, MI: Eerdmans, 1991.

Wood Jr., John Halsey. *Going Dutch in the Modern Age: Abraham Kuyper's Struggle for a Free Church in the Netherlands*. London: Oxford University Press, 2013.

Chapter Ten

Church Spawning

Reimagining New Church Development

George R. Hunsberger

A few years ago, I taught a seminary course entitled "Foundations for Church Planting" for the first time. Teaching the course became an occasion to interact more fully with this theme, which has increasingly impacted the way churches construe their mission. As the course unfolded, I found myself playing back old memories: of my experience as a pastor (in reality, a Continuation Planter) of a small and newly formed congregation in the 1970s; of the formative effect of key theological-missional voices I was listening to in my early ministry years; of the fruit of doctoral research in mission and ecumenics that focused on the work of Lesslie Newbigin; of the stimulus of collaboration with numerous academic and practitioner colleagues in the context of the Gospel and Our Culture Network; and of conversations all along the way with numerous people who were, or had been, or anticipated becoming church planters.

While I had not previously focused my missiological attention or teaching on this avenue of mission expression, I was discovering that it had always been there around the edges of the missional issues I was engaging. As I was busy seeking to clarify a missional ecclesiology for our contemporary North American moment, I found it impossible to avoid the ways in which that project implicates, and is implicated by, attempts to plant, start, or initiate new congregations. Taking notice of such efforts had often stirred my imagination for the kind of missional recovery I believed was essential for all churches. New ground was being tilled, and new experiments in mission were being explored. Conversely, as I noticed the broad landscape of fascination with starting new congregations, counter models were also evident. The approaches at both denominational and local levels seemed too easily to further entrench the consumer logic that has such a commanding hold on North American church life.[1]

I found the experience of teaching a course on church planting to be a wonderful caldron in which to watch practicality and theology mix and swirl together. Nowhere did I find more help to portray and interpret that dance (to shift the metaphor) than in a pair of books by Stuart Murray, whose perspectives in this field I quickly grew to appreciate for their theological texture, missiological focus, and research-based pragmatic usefulness.[2] As required texts, this pair of books leaned structure as well as substance to the course.

In the titles of his books and throughout them, Murray, uses the phrases "church planting" or "planting churches" generously and fully, but not uncritically. In the latter of the two books (*Planting Churches in the 21st Century*), he raises questions about the phrase itself. To me, this came as no surprise, because all along, the vision he espoused had superseded, if not overturned, the meanings inherent in that language as it is popularly used today. He asks:

> Is the language of "church planting" worth retaining? Can it be detached from various assumptions, expectations, strategies, priorities, and other baggage that are now regarded with understandable suspicion, and redeemed for use in a different context and a different ethos? . . . I recognize that there are serious problems with the way the language has been used and that a period of rehabilitation will be necessary if "church planting" is again to convey images of adventure, exploration, provisionality, creativity, gentleness, and humility rather than imperialism, imposition, colonization, insensitivity, and marketing.[3]

Murray indicates he is sensitive to the "significant concerns" many have with the language. Some see the notion of planting to be "inherently imperialistic," coming as it often does as "a predetermined model of church imported and imposed on a community." (It is worth noting that this can happen as easily with new, contemporary models as with older, historic ones.) For some others, Murray notes, the idea of church planting "reinforces an ecclesiocentric approach to mission," minimizing other dimensions of mission. Others believe it "discourages reflection on what it means to be church today," missing the opportunity to check the "cloning" character of uncritically presumed models or "well-marketed" alternatives. Still others are concerned that "the language of 'church planting' encourages pioneers to establish new congregations rather than missional communities."[4]

Yet Murray is not ready to abandon the language, for which he offers several reasons.[5]

"[T]he language of 'church planting' has been used for many centuries." The longevity of its use, however, is less direct and more ambiguous than Murray acknowledges. Current understandings and practices, Stefan Paas has recently argued, have collapsed the phrase's classic, historic meaning. Based on what he sees in contemporary evangelical church planting initiatives in the European context, he concludes that evangelicals have collapsed the multilayered process of classic church planting (evangelizing, forming communities, and planting a church) into the single act of church planting . . . reducing the church to its most transportable, replicable core. And this usually would mean that a public worship service had to be set up as soon as possible.[6]

"[T]he imagery of 'church planting' has deep biblical roots," says Murray. He points to what is generally considered the classic text in this regard, 1 Corinthians 3:6–9, "in which Paul tells the church in Corinth that he planted the seed and Apollos watered it, but God made it grow." Murray's summary of the text quite naturally inserts the word "seed" in his paraphrase, which is not in the text itself. That he does so, however, highlights the fact that neither does the word "church" appear as the direct object of the planting. Murray acknowledges that in light of the passage "we may prefer to talk of planting seeds and trusting God for what grows rather than planting churches, if the latter phrase conveys imposition and franchising." I would suggest that, in fact, the logic of the phrase does already convey imposition and franchising. So when in the end Murray says he is "loathe to move too far away from this biblical imagery," he is doing just that. Allowing the imagery to justify using "planting churches" language does not stay close *enough* to the biblical imagery.

Further, "alternative terms have their own limitations." The alternative terms Murray finds too limiting ("fresh expressions" and "emerging church") may in fact be so. If these are the only alternative possibilities, perhaps we are left without options. But it will be the argument of this chapter that it is important to find other possibilities.

Finally, Murray argues, "abandoning 'church planting' may hinder those involved in emerging churches, fresh expressions, and other mission initiatives from drawing on the hard-won experience of church planters." There is need, Murray says, for "recent and historic forms of church planting" to be in constructive conversation with each other. True enough. But if true, such a conversation needs to engage not only the wisdom of the past but questionable baggage that has come with it.

It does not seem to me that the reasons Murray offers for continuing to use the language of "church planting" are of sufficient weight to overcome the problems he acknowledges. What he indicates to be the "serious problems" with the language, I would argue, are a set of mental habits very deeply ingrained in the conversation (and in wide swaths of modern Western Christianity) and the phrase itself plays a role in perpetuating them. If there is to be a "period of rehabilitation" of the language (which Murray has said is "necessary") and of the field of missional engagement it seeks to describe, it

will need to start with a more thorough critique of the mental models operative in the language and then seek an alternate imagination of what we are
talking about and what we think we are doing.

THE ANATOMY OF A SLOGAN

By what rationale, and with what logic, does *church planting* imagination
function? Several key questions may help us interpret that imagination.

Is Church Planting a Means of Evangelism?

It is typical these days for a book on church planting to begin by articulating
what is believed to be a biblical, theological rationale for making the planting
of new churches a priority. Invariably, it seems, the case will include repeating the assertion by Peter Wagner in his 1990 book, *Planting Churches for a
Greater Harvest*: "the single most effective evangelistic methodology under
heaven is planting new churches."[7] The assertion is made in the first paragraph of the first chapter, and it presents itself as the thesis of the book. He
echoes and amplifies it a few pages later: "there is no more practical or cost
effective way of bringing unbelievers to Christ in a given geographic area
than planting new churches."[8] The ubiquity of the assertion in church planting literature and the geographic and historical scope of its claim ("under
heaven") begs more than a few questions. On what ground is the assertion
made, and is church planting a means of evangelism as it presumes?

When I read Peter Wagner's book at the time it was first published, I was
struck by the fact that having made such an assertion at the outset, the rest of
the book scarcely mentioned evangelizing. It neither defined it (unless by
implication its object is simply to increase the number of members in
churches) nor did it attempt to say exactly *how* planting churches evangelizes
anyone, how it may be "bringing unbelievers to Christ." I am open to the
possibility, even the likelihood, that in church planting initiatives there is
genuine evangelizing going on. But that's a far cry from claiming that church
planting itself is an "evangelistic methodology," a means of evangelizing, let
alone the most effective means.

Murray poses similar questions about Wagner's assertion. In *Planting
Churches in the 21st Century*, he laments that "it seems church planting in
the 1990s [in the UK] was very narrowly focused and that the theological
foundation of *missio Dei* was often not in place. . . . The limited scope of
church planting was evident from the popularity of its accolade: 'the most
effective means of evangelism under heaven.'" (This of course was drawn
from Peter Wagner.) Murray continues: "Not only was this claim untested by
comparative research into other evangelistic activities, but few questioned
the assumption that church planting was essentially a means of evangelism."[9]

Murray affirms as a better way to understand the relationship between church planting and evangelism the definition given in the Anglican report, *Mission-shaped Church.*

> Church planting is the process by which a seed of the life and message of Jesus embodied by a community of Christians is immersed for mission reasons in a particular cultural or geographic context. The intended consequence is that it roots there, coming to life as a new indigenous body of Christian disciples well suited to continue in mission.[10]

Far from being a means of evangelism, the planting of a church is the fruit of evangelism, the expected consequence!

Does Jesus Commission Us to Plant Churches?

The same presumption at work in Wagner's assertion—that church planting and evangelizing are easily conflatable—is evident in the way many advocates of church planting extend the rationale by appealing to what we have called the Great Commission, particularly Matthew's account of it (Matt. 28:18–20). Ed Stetzer, for example, argues this way: "The early church fulfilled the Great Commission by planting churches. The first believers heard the commission, left their homes, and went out to plant. When we hear the Great Commission, we should also be motivated to go out and plant new congregations."[11] The text in Matthew says to disciple the nations, baptizing and teaching, and Stetzer claims that going out to plant churches fulfills that. He presumes far too much. Why and how would the plain sense of all of Jesus's commissioning statements about being sent to be witnesses, to announce the Gospel, to disciple the nations, so quickly and easily turn into going around planting new congregations everywhere? In fact, it didn't. The earliest Christians, we are told, "went from place to place, proclaiming the word" (Acts 8:4), not trying to start congregations.

Did Paul (Or Other Apostles) Set Out to Plant Churches?

Paul, it is normally claimed, is the archetype of church planters. He gives the pattern and sets the priority and the agenda. He is portrayed as having gone out on his several missionary journeys to plant churches, and was fruitful in doing so.

It is true enough, as Roland Allen has pointed out so forcefully, that "in little more than ten years St Paul established the Church in four provinces of the Empire, Galatia, Macedonia, Achaia and Asia. Before AD 47 there were no churches in these provinces; in AD 57 St Paul could speak as if his work there was done."[12] Paul valued and cared for these "churches" and certainly celebrated the work of God that had brought them about. They were the objects of his pastoral nurture. He knew and expected the Gospel to bear such fruit.

But, nonetheless, it is one thing to affirm the existence of churches as the fruit of his work, and it is something quite different to claim that he had set out in order to establish churches. It is my thesis that in fact, *Paul never set out for the purpose of starting new churches*. There is no evidence in the New Testament, I would argue, that suggests otherwise. There is not a whisper in Acts that either he, or his companions, or the churches that sent them, had it as their motivating intention to plant churches. Rather, when he set out, he always did so for the purpose of conveying the Gospel's news among Jewish communities and the general Gentile population. He certainly knew that the Holy Spirit would use that news to bring many to faith in Jesus, and thus the church of that new place would be born. He cared for and nurtured such communities as they came into being. But he never set out to plant churches. Contrary to today's conventional wisdom, Paul did not start new churches as a way to evangelize, he evangelized as the way new churches would be birthed.

To cast Paul as a modern-day church planter and claim that this was his conscious intent is to distort the evidence and do serious injustice to Paul (and the One who called him). In his recent book, Stefan Paas underscores this point. He responds to the logic he sees in much of the church planting literature.

> In other words, out of the New Testament pioneer practice where evangelism usually (but not always) resulted in the planting of a church, it is concluded that church planting rather than evangelism was the first intention of the apostles. I believe that this is a distortion of the biblical material; it amounts to confusing the nature of an activity with its results. [13]

He notes that the New Testament scholar L. J. Lietaert Peerbolte speaks similarly: "Notwithstanding Paul's active part in defining the new, Christian community, he was not interested in the formation of this new group as a goal in itself. It was the proclamation of the gospel, the Christ event, that really mattered to Paul." [14]

In the end, Murray concludes, we need to recognize that "the subject of church planting . . . is peripheral rather than central in the New Testament, whereas the kingdom of God is arguably the central theme of Jesus' teaching and the integrating paradigm for the mission of the church." [15]

What Does It Mean to Plant a Church?

What does it really *mean* after all to *plant* a *church*? More specifically, what do we think we are planting when we say we are planting churches? A quick Google search for images of "church planting" on the web yields an interesting result. Most of the images follow this pattern: a pair of cupped hands holding some soil and a seedling, lowering it to the ground. Either with the seedling, or in place of it, most images of church planting have a small replica of a classic little church building. Architecture intrudes onto a biological image.

Planting a physical structure does in fact have a way of dominating some imaginations of church planting. At least, this was very much the case with denominational efforts in the mid-twentieth century. Buy a piece of property, put up a small first building (or in the case of the church for which I was pastor, park a triple-wide trailer!), and open the doors on a Sunday morning. This model was rightly called in those days "church extension." Extend what we know elsewhere to be churches to this new spot.

Even when the notion is not so facility oriented, what is conceived as the "church" being planted is easily (and I think normally) a set of organizational activities, customs, roles, and practices, the forms of life we expect any church to have—a meeting space, a set time, a main event (usually on a Sunday morning), some religious programs, and some staff person or people to organize and offer them. So church planting means we are planting the organizational structures of a church in a new place and seeking to fill them with people looking for the opportunities and services they provide. (As noted earlier, this can be the default setting for new and innovative forms as well as classically traditional ones.) When church is thus conceived as easily "transportable and replicable," as Paas suggests, it represents a collapsed ecclesiology.

But what if the word *church* in the phrase *church planting* is people? The biblical language of "church" designates a body of people! They may have developed certain forms of life and activity, but those forms are not the church. The body of people who inhabit them are the church. A congregation is not people being served by something called church, they *are* the church. Reclaiming this would certainly shift the way church planting language works.

In 1991, I was invited to address the Presbytery of Lake Michigan (PCU-SA) on the topic, "A Theological Rationale for New Church Development."[16] I was new to Michigan and had just transferred my membership to that Presbytery. Knowing that I was the newly installed professor of missiology at Western Theological Seminary, the Outreach Committee of the Presbytery suggested that I be invited to give such an address as a way to bolster its efforts to seek support in the Presbytery for developing new churches.

I'm pretty sure the inviters expected me to give a motivational speech to rally the troops, secure commitments for funding, and inject serious motivation to renewed efforts. While I didn't consider myself to be an opponent of church planting by the Presbytery, neither was I of a mind to give automatic endorsement to the idea without regard to the assumptions that seem always to lie just beneath the surface.

The Outreach Committee seemed to like what I said, but for reasons they couldn't figure out. Some of my friends on the Social Witness Committee liked what I said—or so they thought. But they weren't quite sure. (These two committees, of course, were fighting for the same limited resources, and they represented two very different streams of thought in the Presbytery about the church's mission.)

Essentially, what I said was that a theological rationale is not so easy. It depends. Given our denominational decline and the vast societal shifts breaking apart the presumed symbiosis of church and culture, I said, "The question . . . is not *why* we should start them but *how*. The issue is not the *amount* of churches, but the *kind* of churches we begin." I suggested that there would be a compelling theological rationale for starting *certain kinds* of churches and doing so in *certain ways*. I offered a series of five ways of proceeding for which there would be a compelling theological rationale. The first was this:

> *Plant Christian communities that are genuinely "in mission."* There are two parts to this: community and mission. Planting new churches must be a planting of a genuine Christian community, not just setting up the brick and mortar housing for one. But also, newly planted churches should be communities that are missionary about their presence in an area, not just a group that fills up a set of programs established as a kind of religious "service station."[17]

There had been a time, not entirely passed, when the Presbyterian Church (USA) and its predecessor denominations would "plant a church to serve the Presbyterians in the area." I turned that on its head. Instead, I suggested that we "plant Presbyterians who will represent the reign of God there—to serve the gospel in the area." In other words, root the imagination in the "people" meaning of church, in *who* (not *what*) is being planted. And root that planted community in its service and witness to the reign of God in Jesus Christ.

Planting churches ought to mean planting Christian communities; notice, it means planting people, planting a community of people. We might call it a team, we might call it a beginning nucleus, we might call it a lot of things, but essentially, if we're planting the *church* we need to be clear that we're planting a *community of people*, called by God, sent by Christ, in whom the Holy Spirit is living and creating. Plant Christian communities that are genuinely "in mission," which principle has an immediate effect on the next choice: Where should such communities be planted? This is what I went on to propose in my address:

> *Place them where their healing presence is most needed.* This means not just chasing folks to the suburbs, where we end up playing to the religious consumerism. . . . Wouldn't it be more interesting—and more faithful (and costly)—

to base our choices on an area's need for a healthy and healing Christian community in its midst? [18]

In such a place, the appropriate manner and effect of their life is more readily discerned and sustained.

> *Focus them toward being the hermeneutic of the gospel.* New church developments are not automatically "evangelistic." . . . The most pressing evangelistic task in our day is to present by our collective life a credible demonstration that it is a plausible thing to live under the reign of God. [19]

The congregation is "the hermeneutic of the gospel," as Lesslie Newbigin has helped us see. [20] That is, the Christian community is the embodiment of the good news, and thereby it is the interpretive lens by which people will see and experience and come to know what the Gospel is and recognize its relevance at this time, in this place.

TOWARD A *CHURCH SPAWNING* IMAGINATION

Somewhere in the midst of these propositions, I have come to realize, there is a double reference in the way we can, and I believe should, speak about the church when we're talking about church planting. If, as I have argued, the church is not the means of evangelizing but the fruit of it, and if it is also true that evangelizing is something a community does as it represents the Gospel in life, deed, and word, then there is in a real sense a church at the beginning of the process and another at the end of it. In other words, it is essential to plant the church (in the sense of a body of people) who will bear witness to and demonstrate the Gospel, in the hope that as the Holy Spirit brings about the response of faith, a new church (also in the sense of a body of people) is birthed. In this sense, there are two plantings in view. The initial one, planting a Christian community into a place where its witness needs to be born, and the envisioned one—more a birthing than a planting—that arises as the fruit of the witness, by the power of the Spirit.

This has resonance with the definition of church planting in the *Mission-shaped Church* document noted earlier, which bears repeating at this point.

> Church planting is the process by which a seed of the life and message of Jesus embodied by a community of Christians is immersed for mission reasons in a particular cultural or geographic context. The intended consequence is that it roots there, coming to life as a new indigenous body of Christian disciples well suited to continue in mission. [21]

Notice the flow of the key words: a seed, embodied, immersed, in a context, consequence, roots, life, indigenous body, in mission. The awkwardness of speaking about ultimately planting church—as though it is a thing to be placed on the ground somewhere—gives way to a sustained organic imagination. In light of that, and in concert with an increasing number of voices (such as Murray, Paas, and Mary Sue Dehmlow Dreier) seeking to ground our imagination in a better ecclesiology, missiology, and pneumatology, I propose an alternate language yielding an alternate imagination. Instead of continuing to call it "church planting" or "planting churches," I propose the phrase "church spawning" or "spawning churches." I propose that this better names what we are doing when we initiate an effort to have a seed planted and see a new congregation grow from it. The seed planting is the first element in a larger imagination, the hope of seeing a church *spawned* in a new place. I suggest that shifting our language to *church spawning* imagery has some important effects.

It Roots Our Efforts in the Creating Action of the Holy Spirit

Mary Sue Dehmlow Dreier has raised to greater visibility the necessity of a Spirit-oriented approach to new church development with the publication of her edited volume, *Created and Led by the Spirit.* In her own contribution to the conversation, she affirms that "planting missional congregations" rests on the recognition of "the Holy Spirit as the primary church planter." It is in those terms that she seeks "to discern the fourfold reality of the Spirit as a public, reconciling, life-promising, and joyful force who creates new churches to bear those same traits in the world."[22]

It Clarifies the Role of the Team Immersed in the New Place

If the Spirit creates the church, and if that is so specific as to have direct bearing on the emergence of a new church anywhere, then, for Dreier, that recalibrates the role of "human church planters" in the process. They are, she suggests, "missional midwives to that divine creativity." She shows how this unfolds: "Church planters as midwives participate with God by discerning, assisting, and promoting the possibilities and potential of new missional congregations so created and led by the Spirit." This is the vocation of church planters or mission developers.[23]

Dreier's proposal to view planters/developers as midwives makes a bold and essential contribution to a church spawning imagination. "The midwife image reinforces the fact that ours is a vital but secondary role. . . . Even though it is the Holy Spirit giving birth to the church, our task as church-planting midwives is nonetheless crucial and challenging—and ongoing." And at times, she is careful to note, such midwifery is "a precarious walk among spiritual and institutional realities."[24]

Decades ago, Ivan Illich, a mission educator, spoke in similar terms. He viewed mission to be "the spawning of local church from the Universal Church." And he likened mission practice to "midwifery." "The missioner stands where the Universal Church gives birth to a new community in a new world. He is technical assistant."[25]

David Bosch concurred: "Mission, to borrow Illich's metaphor, is not the mother of what is to come, but the midwife—facilitating the birth of something not of its own making, nor created in its own image. It would be utterly foolish for any midwife to expect the newborn infant to bear the stamp of her own features!"[26]

It Keeps Our Focus on Missional Reasons and Practices

After providing an extensive survey identifying and assessing eighteen different reasons people or churches indicate for starting a new church, Murray concludes by marking what he takes to be essential in the end.

> Having said all this, though, it is the missional motives for church planting that we should prioritize if church planting is not to be domesticated or co-opted. Whatever the benefits of church planting for churches, denominations, or church planters, the primary reason for planting new churches is to participate in God's mission within the neighborhoods and networks where the gospel is not at present effectively incarnated.[27]

It comes as no surprise that his view sounds so similar to the language of the statement from the *Mission-shaped Church* document quoted above: "a seed of the life and message of Jesus embodied by a community of Christians is immersed for mission reasons in a particular cultural or geographic context."

A church spawning imagination, recognizing our midwife relationship to what the Spirit is birthing, means that the primary attention will be on the contextually fitting witness rendered, not the form of the ultimate outcome. Paas commends "simple missionary practices."

> So, a necessary way to allow the process of renewal is by adopting simple missionary Christian practices and disciplines. . . . If they are embedded in the fundamental tasks of witnessing and disciple making, and if adequate leadership is present, these practices and disciplines will lead the community into a deeper understanding of the mission of God (*missio Dei*), a deeper commitment to the Kingdom of justice and peace, and a deeper trust in the uniqueness of Jesus Christ as universal Savior.[28]

It Warns Us to Remain Hopeful but Tentative

Because we know the Spirit's passion and power, we have good reason to believe that the seed presented and planted in a neighborhood will not come back empty (cf. Isaiah 55:11). There will be some who believe and become followers of Jesus, and thus a new community is being birthed. But it is always tempting to get ahead of the process and overrun the Spirit by focusing on the form of the outcome, of the new congregation. Paas expresses concern about that tendency and the urges toward control and certainty that may drive it. He counsels caution regarding too concrete a determination of what a future new congregation will be like. Outcomes do not always match strategies, expectations, and hopes. There are a lot of possible eventualities for the way a new forming group may want to cast itself. "Sometimes, a church will emerge out of this after all, but not necessarily so."

It is the "not necessarily so" that is striking in Paas's comment. He encourages a more humble and tentative approach.

> In other words, precisely by not concentrating on the formation of a church too soon, the nature and mission of the church may be taken much more seriously in the end. What "church" is in this particular context may become a journey of discovery rather than an imposed outcome. [29]

It Trusts the Freedom of the Holy Spirit and the Newborn Congregation

"The Spirit is sovereign and free, and the missionary must trust the Holy Spirit to do his own work." This summarizes the ultimate thrust of Roland Allen's work that pressed so thoroughly into Lesslie Newbigin's thinking. The hard work of trusting the Spirit's sovereign freedom is with us in every dimension of mission, including what we have called church planting or spawning. It touches virtually everything. [30]

In the spirit of Allen's wisdom, Newbigin insisted that "mission is not just church extension. It is something more costly and more revolutionary." [31]

> If the church that is the bearer of the gospel has also the right to lay down for new converts the ethical implications of conversion, the mission has become simply church extension. I have insisted that to regard it so is to fail to acknowledge the sovereign freedom of the Holy Spirit. [32]

As with ethical implications, so also with respect to ecclesial forms. A newly spawned congregation "should have its own proper character as distinct from that of the community from which the mission came." [33] True in India. True also, we may add, in America. Newbigin maintains the confidence in the Spirit he commends to us all.

> God is able to raise up something which is not a reproduction of the church from which the missionary came, but a new creation—the first-fruit of a whole new community remade in Christ, a fresh adumbration of the new life in Christ in the idiom of this people. [34]

So, if we plant a (missionary, provisional, radiating, witnessing) Christian community that gives witness to the Gospel, and recognize that from that witness the Spirit may spawn within the neighborhood a new local Christian community, careful consideration will always need to be given to the relationship between the two communities. While there will surely be an inevitable overlapping in relationships, practices, and styles, how will the integrity of the new community be preserved? How will the initial community resist imposing its own preferences to be the form of life and activity the new community must adopt? How will the new community live responsibly in its freedom, led by the Spirit?

Something of this set of issues was in my mind when I gave the Presbytery address I have mentioned above. I added to the principles I was suggesting:

> *Let them find new ways of being the church.* We are caught between a Christendom that is over (and isn't coming back), and a relegation to the private realm of purely personal opinion (while believing that the gospel we hold is for the public life of the whole world). New churches may be the most free to struggle with the dilemma and form new models.[35]

At that time, I had not yet differentiated between the initially planted community and the ultimately envisioned one spawned by the Spirit. I was undoubtedly equating the two. But now I would need to be clearer. This principle should certainly be the case for the planting of the Christian community from the outset. But as a new community is spawned, it becomes especially important that they not be robbed of the same privilege and responsibility to discover and discern "new ways of being the church," forms of church life for this moment, in their particular place. For that the Spirit equips them and leads them.

SEED, SOILS (AND SALT?)

Thus far, the imagination I am commending has been cast primarily in biological terms (spawning, birthing, midwifery). But giving closer attention to horticultural terms (seeds, soils, gardening) can further illumine the mission of church spawning. The horticultural images themselves comprise a parable of church spawning.

We have already noted the seed language with which the *Mission-shaped Church* document speaks: "a seed of the life and message of Jesus embodied by a community of Christians is immersed." This echoes the spirit of Jesus's parable, "The kingdom of God is as if someone would scatter seed on the ground, and would sleep and rise night and day, and the seed would sprout and grow, he does not know how" (Mark 4:26–27). Robert Schreiter notes the pattern in the approach of Vincent Donovan, himself very much influenced by Roland Allen. "Here the method is one of planting the seed of faith and allowing it to interact with the native soil, leading to a new flowering of Christianity, faithful both to the local culture and to the apostolic faith."[36]

Consider the soils in the place into which the seed is being immersed. Some are social soils, others personal. Is this the kind of ground ready to grow something? What will grow here, what will not? What seems hard to grow here, but yet might grow anyway. What surprises might there be? What things are ready to grow beyond what we ever dreamed?

In the midst of the various kinds of soil found in a place—personal, social, cultures, histories—and the particular conditions of the soils, too compacted, too rocky, too weed-laden, good for growing (perhaps previously tended and tilled), a sower comes sowing seed (cf. Mark 4:1–9, 14–20). The seed is variously seen to be the word (Mark 4:14), or the Gospel, or it is the seed of faith, or in the most embracing of terms, the "seed of the life and message of Jesus."

It is not hard to find ourselves in the picture. Like Jesus, we come sowing the word, aware of the kinds of ground we are on. But if the *Mission-shaped Church* document is our guide, it suggests more. We embody the seed—the life and message of Jesus. In a very fundamental sense, then, we are both a sower of the seed and its embodiment. Elsewhere, Jesus pushes the image even further. In Jesus's explanation of another parable about seed and sowers (where wheat and weeds end up growing together), he explains the parable and says, "the good seed are the children of the kingdom" (Matt. 13:38). The seed personified, incarnate. We are the sower, the embodiment, and the very seed itself! A community of Christians who embody and are the seed are sowed upon the ground by Jesus. Slowly, sowing and being sown, sleeping and rising, the sprouts spring up and grow, "and we do not know how" (but the Spirit does!).

There is yet another element in the picture. In addition to being seed-bearers and the seed itself, Jesus says, "You are the salt of the earth" (Matt. 5:13). Here we need to revisit what we may have taken that to mean. The tendency has been to assume that looking at our salt shaker on the dining table provides the clue. Salt makes things tastier. We make life more flavorful. Or, we have remembered pre-refrigeration culture when salt would be pressed into meats in order to preserve them. So, we must be a preservative of sorts for our social environment.

While both of these interpretations may be suggestive, in the end they seem tenuous. The table salt we immediately think about is not the only kind of salt out there. For example, consider the bag of fertilizer you may have bought for your yard or garden. Check out the ingredients. Most of them are salts of one sort or another. They are salts that are used *for* the earth, they are used to fertilize, to enrich the soil, to replenish nutrients that are not sufficiently present in the soil. Agricultural uses of salt have a long history, and were current at the time of Jesus.

In one particular comment by Jesus, we can see this agricultural perspective clearly. He says, "Salt is good; but if salt has lost its taste, how can its saltiness be restored? It is fit neither for the soil nor for the manure pile; they throw it away. Let anyone with ears to hear listen!" (Luke 14:34–35). It is clear that Jesus presumes that if salt still *has* its saltiness, the soil and the manure pile are precisely what the salt *is* "fit" for! In Jesus's mind salt has an agricultural use. Further, we should notice that in Matthew 5, the word translated "earth" is the same Greek word (from which we get words like geography, geology, geothermal) that is translated in the parable of the sower with the English word "soil." It literally means, soil, ground, or earth (in the soil/ground sense of the word, not as a designation of a planet or a synonym of "world"). So Matthew 5:13 could legitimately be translated, "You are the salt for the soil." Jesus is here indicating an additional role in the horticulture of mission: we are fertilizer for the soils where the seed is being sown. Our presence and interactions nourish the soil, helping its ability to receive and grow the seed.[37] Church spawning lives in the interplay of soils and seeds and salts and immersing a Christian community in any place for missional reasons is the way the Holy Spirit has chosen to use us in that interplay. And from the force field of soils, seeds, and salts, the Spirit creates a new local community of Christ. And sometimes in the most unexpected places!

NOTES

1. For further description of what is meant by "consumer logic," see George R. Hunsberger, "Dilemma: A Vendor-Shaped Church," in *The Story That Chooses Us: A Tapestry of Missional Vision* (Grand Rapids, MI: Eerdmans, 2015), 33–42.

2. Stuart Murray, *Church Planting: Laying Foundations* (Scottdale, PA: Herald Press, 2001); Stuart Murray, *Planting Churches in the 21st Century* (Scottdale, PA: Herald Press, 2010).

3. Murray, *Planting Churches in the 21st Century*, 17.

4. Murray, 18.

5. For here, and in what follows, see Murray, 18–19.

6. Stefan Paas, *Church Planting in the Secular West: Learning from the European Experience* (Grand Rapids, MI: Eerdmans, 2016), 221–22. Paas also suggests Murray may be a little naïve when he argues that "Christians in many traditions, Catholic and Orthodox as well as Protestant, are familiar with this term." They are not so homogeneous in what they take "church planting" to mean. See Paas, 218n78.

7. C. Peter Wagner, *Planting Churches for a Greater Harvest* (Ventura, CA: Regal Books, 1990), 11; see also Wagner, 16, 22, 24.

8. Wagner, 21.

9. Wagner, 20.

10. *Mission-Shaped Church: Church Planting and Fresh Expressions of Church in a Changing Context* (London: Church House Publishing, 2004), 32.

11. Ed Stetzer, *Planting New Churches in a Postmodern Age* (Nashville, TN: B&H Academic, 2003), 36.

12. Roland Allen, *Missionary Methods: St. Paul's or Ours?* (Grand Rapids, MI: Eerdmans, 1962), 3.

13. Paas, *Church Planting in the Secular West*, 246.

14. L. J. Lietaert Peerbolte, *Paul the Missionary* (Leuven: Peeters, 2003), 220, as cited in Paas, *Church Planting in the Secular West*, 247.

15. Murray, *Planting Churches in the 21st Century*, 47.

16. An abbreviated form of the address was subsequently published as "Planting New Churches in New Ways" in the Synod of the Covenant newspaper *Communiqué*, February 1992, 4.

17. Hunsberger, "Planting New Churches in New Ways," 4.

18. Hunsberger, 4.

19. Hunsberger, 4.

20. Newbigin, *The Gospel in a Pluralist Society*, 222–33.

21. *Mission-Shaped Church*, 32.

22. Mary Sue Dehmlow Dreier, ed., *Created and Led by the Spirit: Planting Missional Congregations* (Grand Rapids, MI: Eerdmans, 2013), 1–2. Many others likewise affirm that the church is "a creation of the Spirit." See Stephen B. Bevans, "The Church as Creation of the Spirit: Unpacking a Missionary Image," *Missiology* 35, no. 1 (2007): 5–21; Graig Van Gelder, *The Essence of the Church: A Community Created by the Spirit* (Grand Rapids, MI: Baker Books, 2000); Newbigin, *The Household of God*, 94–122; Hans Küng, "The Church as the Creation of the Spirit," in *The Church* (Garden City, NY: Doubleday Image, 1976), 201–66.

23. Dreier, *Created and Led by the Spirit*, 2. See further "Planting Missional Congregations: Imagining Together," in *Created and Led by the Spirit: Planting Missional Congregations*, ed. Mary Sue Dehmlow Dreier (Grand Rapids, MI: Eerdmans, 2013), 10–14.

24. "Planting Missional Congregations," 10–11.

25. Ivan Illich, "Mission and Midwifery. Part II: Selection and Formation of the Missioner," in *Ivian Illich: The Church, Change, and Development*, ed. Fred Eychaner (Chicago, IL: Urban Training Center Press, 1974), 98–111, here 105.

26. David J. Bosch, "Theological Education in Missionary Perspective," *Missiology* 10, no. 1 (1982): 13–34, here 25.

27. Murray, *Planting Churches in the 21st Century*, 51.

28. Paas, *Church Planting in the Secular West*, 223–24.

29. Paas, *Church Planting in the Secular West*, 223.

30. Newbigin, *The Open Secret*, 130. See further Roland Allen, *The Ministry of the Spirit* (Grand Rapids, MI: Eerdmans, 1962).

31. Newbigin, 59.

32. Newbigin, 137.

33. J. E. Lesslie Newbigin, "What is a 'Local Church Truly United'?," *The Ecumenical Review* 29, no. 2 (1977): 115–128, here 123.

34. J. E. Lesslie Newbigin, "From the Editor," *International Review of Missions* 54, no. 1 (1965): 145–50, here 147.

35. Hunsberger, "Planting New Churches in New Ways," 4.

36. Robert J. Schreiter, *Constructing Local Theologies* (Maryknoll, NY: Orbis Books, 1985), 11. See also Vincent J. Donovan, *Christianity Rediscovered* (Chicago, IL: Fides/Claretian Press, 1978). Others who speak in similar terms include David J. Bosch, *Transforming Mission: Paradigm Shifts in Theology of Mission* (Maryknoll, NY: Orbis Books, 1991), 454–55; and "Decree on the Mission Nature of the Church, *Ad Gentes Divinitus* (AG)," §22.

37. For further reference regarding "salt for the soil" see Alan Kreider, "Salty Discipleship: Bringing New Worlds to Life," *The Other Side* March/April (1989), 34–37; and Eugene P. Deatrick, "Salt, Soil, Savior," *The Biblical Archaeologist* 25, no. 2 (1962): 41–48.

BIBLIOGRAPHY

Allen, Roland. *The Ministry of the Spirit*. Grand Rapids, MI: Eerdmans, 1962.
———. *Missionary Methods: St. Paul's or Ours?* Grand Rapids, MI: Eerdmans, 1962.

Bevans, Stephen B. "The Church as Creation of the Spirit: Unpacking a Missionary Image." *Missiology* 35, no. 1 (2007): 5–21.

Bosch, David J. "Theological Education in Missionary Perspective." *Missiology* 10, no. 1 (1982): 13–34.

———. *Transforming Mission: Paradigm Shifts in Theology of Mission*. Maryknoll, NY: Orbis Books, 1991.

Deatrick, Eugene P. "Salt, Soil, Savior." *The Biblical Archaeologist* 25, no. 2 (1962): 41–48.

"Decree on the Mission Nature of the Church, *Ad Gentes Divinitus*," in *Vatican Council II: The Conciliar and Post Conciliar Documents*, edited by Austin Flannery, 813–62. Northport, NY: Costello, 1996.

Donovan, Vincent J. *Christianity Rediscovered*. Chicago, IL: Fides/Claretian Press, 1978.

Dreier, Mary Sue Dehmlow, ed. *Created and Led by the Spirit: Planting Missional Congregations*. Grand Rapids, MI: Eerdmans, 2013.

———, ed. "Planting Missional Congregations: Imagining Together," in *Created and Led by the Spirit: Planting Missional Congregations*, 10–14. Grand Rapids, MI: Eerdmans, 2013.

Hunsberger, George R. "Dilemma: A Vendor-Shaped Church," in *The Story That Chooses Us: A Tapestry of Missional Vision*, 33–42. Grand Rapids, MI: Eerdmans, 2015.

Illich, Ivan. "Mission and Midwifery. Part II: Selection and Formation of the Missioner," in *Ivian Illich: The Church, Change, and Development*, edited by Fred Eychaner, 98–111. Chicago, IL: Urban Training Center Press, 1974.

Kreider, Alan. "Salty Discipleship: Bringing New Worlds to Life." *The Other Side* March/April (1989): 34–37.

Küng, Hans. "The Church as the Creation of the Spirit," in *The Church*, 201–66. Garden City, NY: Doubleday Image, 1976.

Mission-Shaped Church: Church Planting and Fresh Expressions of Church in a Changing Context. London: Church House Publishing, 2004.

Murray, Stuart. *Church Planting: Laying Foundations*. Scottdale, PA: Herald Press, 2001.

———. *Planting Churches in the 21st Century*. Scottdale, PA: Herald Press, 2010.

Newbigin, J. E. Lesslie. "From the Editor." *International Review of Missions* 54, no. 1 (1965): 145–50.

———. *The Gospel in a Pluralist Society*. Geneva: WCC, 1989.

———. *The Household of God: Lectures on the Nature of the Church*. New York: Friendship Press, 1954.

———. *The Open Secret: An Introduction to the Theology of Mission*. Grand Rapids, MI: Eerdmans, 1995.

———. "What is a 'Local Church Truly United'?" *The Ecumenical Review* 29, no. 2 (1977): 115–28.

Paas, Stefan. *Church Planting in the Secular West: Learning from the European Experience*. Grand Rapids, MI: Eerdmans, 2016.

Peerbolte, L. J. Lietaert. *Paul the Missionary*. Leuven: Peeters, 2003.

Schreiter, Robert J. *Constructing Local Theologies*. Maryknoll, NY: Orbis Books, 1985.

Stetzer, Ed. *Planting New Churches in a Postmodern Age*. Nashville, TN: B&H Academic, 2003.

Van Gelder, Graig. *The Essence of the Church: A Community Created by the Spirit*. Grand Rapids, MI: Baker Books, 2000.

Wagner, C. Peter. *Planting Churches for a Greater Harvest*. Ventura, CA: Regal Books, 1990.

Chapter Eleven

Revisiting Newbigin's Ambivalence toward Interreligious Dialogues

*How Can We Reengage in
Interreligious Dialogues in Asia?*

Seong Sik Heo

As a Western missionary sent to South India, it is well-known that Lesslie Newbigin made a concerted effort to engage in interreligious dialogue with Hindus. In his autobiography, *Unfinished Agenda*, he speaks of his reading the Gospel of John, the Upanishad, and the Visishtadvaita of Ramanuja together with his Hindu neighbors.[1] But this is an observation from the time when he was a new missionary. Why did this apparent commitment to interreligious dialogue recede as Newbigin over time became a bishop, ecumenist, missiologist, and pastor?

This alleged neglect of interreligious dialogue in Newbigin's later life calls for some explanation. Bob Robinson, commenting on the recent major works on Newbigin by Tom Foust, George Hunsberger, and Geoffrey Wainwright, points to "a puzzling omission," that is, "a failure to discuss his reluctance during and after his years in India to engage the Hindu world with the degree of vigour and rigour he later displayed in his wide-ranging critique of post-Enlightenment modernity."[2] He then rightly criticizes them for displaying "uncritical deference to and acceptance of Newbigin's comments on Hinduism with little or no discussion of his diminishing level of interest in the Hindu world during his years in India."[3] He notes that "in fact, from about the mid-1960s, there is little or no evidence of N's [*sic*: representing Newbigin] engagement at depth with Hinduism in any of its forms. In his later revisions of material that touches on Hinduism, there is a distinct lack of content that specifically addresses the Hindu world and the illustrations from

169

Hinduism remain few and increasingly dated or even secondary."[4] Robinson is correct in pointing out "a distinct lack" of Newbigin's engagement with Hinduism or Buddhism, something I too discovered in reading his works.

The question remains why Newbigin became so reluctant to carry on his interreligious dialogues with other faiths. One explanation might point to the type of debates that occurred in the United Kingdom during the 1980s. During this period, Newbigin spent more time debating with religious pluralists within Western Christendom than with other religious peoples in the non-Western world, especially in India. It is indeed true, on the one hand, that Christians should debate the question of religious pluralism to help keep their Christian faith from "different gospels." On the other hand, however, the time is ripe for reengaging in interreligious dialogue with other faiths, particularly those in Asia. In so doing, one might also learn what it is like to live as a Christian within a religiously plural context.

NEWBIGIN'S ENGAGEMENT IN
RELIGIOUS PLURALISM DEBATES

Before discussing Newbigin's debates with the religious pluralists, let us consider the threefold typology often mentioned in the context of religious pluralism, that of: exclusivism, inclusivism, and pluralism.[5] First of all, it is noteworthy that Newbigin himself rejected this typology,[6] because its division depends on the question of the salvation of non-Christians—"who is to be saved and who is not"—which he believed was the business of God alone.[7] There have been numerous debates on the problematic nature of this typology, along with attempts to develop alternate typologies to describe the diverse responses of Christians toward other religions in a more modest manner. Paul Knitter, for examples, speaks of four models: replacement, fulfillment, mutuality, and acceptance. According to Knitter's typology, Newbigin might best fit within two models—replacement (specifically, total replacement like Karl Barth and Hendrik Kraemer) and acceptance (like Mark Heim)—though Knitter himself categorizes Newbigin only under the total replacement model.[8]

Pressured by the demand to identify his position on the religions, Newbigin presented his argument in this way:

> The position which I have outlined is *exclusivist* in the sense that it affirms the unique truth of the revelation in Jesus Christ, but it is *not exclusivist* in the sense of denying the possibility of the salvation of the non-Christian. It is *inclusivist* in the sense that it refuses to limit the saving grace of God to the members of the Christian Church, but it *rejects the inclusivism* which regards the non-Christian religions as vehicles of salvation. It is *pluralist* in the sense of acknowledging the gracious work of God in the lives of all human beings,

but it *rejects a pluralism* which denies the uniqueness and decisiveness of what God has done in Jesus Christ.[9]

Newbigin's own exegesis of typology demonstrates his suspicion that it was used more to criticize certain positions than to enlighten the discussion.[10] Harold Netland observes, regarding the term "exclusivism" that "[i]t is a pejorative term with unflattering connotations: exclusivists are typically branded as dogmatic, narrow-minded, intolerant, ignorant, arrogant and so on, and those rejecting exclusivism for more accommodating perspectives are regarded as exemplifying the virtues believed deficient in exclusivists." In place of exclusivism, Netland decides to use a less offensive label such as "particularism." In this sense, Newbigin wisely evades the emotion-laden use of the terms, concentrating on the explication of his own position on theology of religions. His position is firmly based on his belief in the essential Christian dogmas: there is no salvation without confessing Jesus as Christ (exclusivistic, focusing on "no other name but Jesus"); no one but God knows who is to be saved (inclusivistic, being open-ended about salvation); the Trinitarian God revealed in the Bible and in creation will save all who believe in God as God is (pluralistic, being revealed to all, without exception).

Newbigin rejects the exclusivism that closes the heavenly gate of salvation to those who may or may not have the chance to hear the Gospel. Instead, he prefers "agnosticism" in the matter of "who is to be saved." He rejects the inclusivism that pretends to have information about "who is to be saved," including the conjecture that there are "anonymous Christians." Instead, Newbigin prefers to believe in "God's justice and His righteousness" on the last day. He rejects both John Hick and Paul Knitter's accounts of religious pluralism as these amount to a "fundamental pluralism" indistinguishable from nihilism:

> the kind of western thought which has described itself as "modern" is rapidly sinking into a kind of pluralism which is indistinguishable from nihilism—a pluralism which denies the possibility of making any universally justifiable truth-claims on any matter, whether religious or otherwise.[11]

Meanwhile, some religious pluralists, like Martin Forward and K. P. Aleaz, criticize Newbigin as an "exclusivist," influenced by the negative theology of religions developed by Hendrik Kraemer and Karl Barth. Forward introduces Newbigin, along with Visser 't Hooft, as one who "imbibed the cautious and negative theology of Karl Barth and Hendrik Kraemer toward the faith of other people, and insisted that only exclusive and introvert beliefs should be served to member churches."[12] The latter asserts that "Newbigin talks of dialogue, but as he was not willing to receive anything from other faiths, there was no dialogue; in what he meant by dialogue, it was a mere monologue. A preformulated understanding of Christ or Christian Gospel cannot be the criterion to judge other faiths."[13]

Newbigin is steadfast in his belief that God is the Trinitarian God, and that his God is fundamentally different from the many "pluralistic" ideas about God: the ultimate reality of Hick, the Divine Mystery of Panikkar, and the many Christs of Knitter.[14] Religious pluralists assert that all religions offer diverse ways to arrive at the same ultimate reality, regardless of how that reality is named. Yet, in the light of Newbigin's theology of religions, it is indeed impossible to believe in the "pluralist presupposition that the various religions are all talking about the same thing."[15] Conversely, the Christian faith must be rooted in belief in the Trinitarian God, revealed to us as the personal Godhead: God the Father, our Creator; God the Son, Jesus Christ; and God the Holy Spirit, the Comforter. In particular, Christian faith is inseparable from the dogma that the historic Jesus is the one and only savior: there is no other name on earth to save us from the power of sin, death, and Satan.

In an essay titled "The Centrality of Jesus for History" written as a chapter in *Incarnation and Myth*, Newbigin regards Jesus as the clue to the meaning of history, which can be grasped by faith alone. He believes that such general religious experiences as a sense of the transcendent, a feeling of absolute dependence, an awareness of absolute demand and final succor, or the mystical experience of the oneness of the Self with the All cannot be clues to understanding history.[16] Rather, his firm belief is that Jesus Christ is the clue to the meaning of history as a whole, and this meaning is to be grasped "not by induction from the generality of experience, but by a revelation in the form of happenings which are grasped by faith as the self-communication of the one whose purpose the story embodies."[17]

For this reason, in establishing dialogue with other religions, Newbigin is not tempted by the attractive attempt of religious pluralism to look at the Christian story from the perspective of a general religious experience. He argues, instead, that it is necessary to recognize that the Gospel of Jesus Christ is indeed a scandal to all non-Christians, for the Gospel is and remains incomprehensible from a perspective outside the Christian faith.[18] For Newbigin, "the general religious experience of [hu]mankind, if no event in history is allowed decisive place, does not and cannot furnish clues as to the meaning of history as a whole."[19] Rather, "the task of a Christian theologian is not to seek to place the story of Jesus within the general religious experience of [hu]mankind, but to place the myths of our contemporary culture in the light which streams from him when he is acknowledged as Lord."[20] As is evident from these words, Newbigin felt that any meaningful conversation with other religions required Christians to identify Jesus Christ as the definitive clue to the meaning of history.

Above all, Newbigin criticized John Hick's theory of the Copernican revolution in understanding religions. Newbigin notes that, "if the analogy of the Copernican revolution is to be applied to the relation of Christianity and the other religions without logical fallacy, then like must be compared with like," and since "God is not accessible to observation in the same sense in which the world religions are . . . we have no frame of reference within which we can compare 'God as he [*sic*] really is' with 'God as conceived in the world religions.'"[21] As a result, he rejects Hick's effort to interpret all religions, including Christianity, on the premise that the God they believe in is the same God, regardless of how each religion conceives God. Newbigin cannot accept the way Hick tries to construct a dialogue between Christianity and other religions, for he considers Hick wrong in using his own definition of God as the basis for seeking the unity of religions.

Newbigin argues that what Hick claims is the model for the unity of religions turns out to be a claim about Hick's own conception of God. By extension, what Hick propounds as the essence of religion is in fact his own religion.[22] Hick's concept of God cannot be accepted both by Christians and other religious peoples. "If the word 'God' really means 'Father, Son and Holy Spirit,' then Professor Hick's Copernican revolution will not be acceptable to people of other faiths. If it does not mean that, it will have to be rejected by Christians who, at this point, will join the atheists."[23]

In an article titled "Religious Pluralism and the Uniqueness of Jesus Christ," Newbigin criticizes Paul Knitter, Christopher Duraisingh, and others who advocate moving beyond a Christocentric position in favor of a theocentric or even soteriocentric position. Newbigin considers Knitter's and Duraisingh's proposals to be natural extensions of the movement initiated by Hick, who advocates moving from Jesus to God—a name that has almost as many meanings as there are human beings. In this case "God" is not God as revealed in Jesus or in the Qur'an or in any other specific religious tradition but God as *I* understand God. Concerning all of their efforts, Newbigin declares that "it is a move from the objective to the subjective." Although Hick speaks in several places of true religion as being turned from self-centeredness to reality-centeredness, Newbigin argues that this is in reality a move in the opposite direction, from objective reality to the self and its needs.[24]

Deeply troubled by the output of the "interfaith industry," Newbigin is extremely skeptical of the prospect of religious pluralism, which in his view is founded on the idea that "the universe so constructed that we can enjoy indubitable knowledge without the risks of personal commitment." He is convinced such an idea is an "illusion" that is "used to discredit the claims of a specific tradition of rationality such as is embodied in the Christian community."[25] Theologically, he does not believe we can arrive at the knowledge of God without the revelation of God: "The human mind cannot comprehend God, but we have no grounds for denying the possibility that God might make the divine known to human beings and that they might legitimately bear witness to what has been revealed to them."[26]

In a critical review of *The Myth of Christian Uniqueness* (1989), Newbigin does not accept the argument of the authors that they are on the point of crossing the Rubicon. He argues that there are three bridges to cross the Rubicon: the historical-cultural, theological-mythical, and ethical-practical, but these bridges do not hold religious pluralists like them, who "have been swept away in the powerful currents of modernity, out to that sea of subjectivity where there are no landmarks."[27] Concerning the historical-cultural bridge, religious pluralism equipped with "modern historical consciousness" that relativizes all truth claims can claim no epistemological privilege. As a result, it cannot escape from total relativism. Concerning the theological-mythical bridge, from the perspective of religious pluralism, he holds that "there are indeed no criteria by which truth in these matters can be assessed" and therefore "we are in a sea of pure subjectivity." He wonders why religious pluralism dismisses as imperialistic the idea that there might be one truth about God, and why it abandons the search for ultimate truth, so that what is left behind is only subjective experience. And concerning the ethical-practical bridge, he points out two problems of this bridge: first, "it is notorious that the demand for justice is precisely what fuels war, since, in the absence of a Judge, each of us is judge in our own cause"; and second, there is the problem of the "ethicopractical criterion," that is, "what ontological ground is there for the option for the poor?" And as to the proposal to move from a Christocentric view to the soteriocentric one, he thinks of it as a sort of reverse conversion, a shift from reality-centeredness to self-centeredness, not vice versa.[28]

In an article titled, "Christian Vedanta?," a review of *A Vision to Pursue* by Keith Ward (1992), Newbigin agrees with Ward's critique of fundamentalists who wrongly claim indubitable certainty with regard to the biblical testimony. Yet Newbigin accuses Ward of the same mistake in making his own dogmatic proposal, which he calls "convergent pluralism," according to which we must choose the best elements from every religion so that the religious traditions must and will grow together, and the religions will ultimately converge toward the realization of values. Newbigin is doubtful about the grounds for Ward's optimism about interreligious dialogue resulting in "convergent pluralism." Newbigin argues, "It is hard to see that there is any basis for Ward's optimism except the general ideology of evolution."[29] Newbigin thus rejects not only a religious pluralism in the style of Hick, in which all religions are equally valid ways to salvation, but also a pluralism in the style of Ward, in which all religions converge toward a common ground. He believes that we should accept neither as the proper way for Christians to engage in interreligious dialogue.

Newbigin stresses the importance of faith in the truth of the Gospel in his essay, "Certain Faith: What Kind of Certainty?" (1993). Pointing out that "a frequent cause of mutual alienation among Christians is the charge of too much certainty on the one hand and too little certainty on the other," he argues instead for "a kind of certainty which is confident and yet humble and teachable." And he argues that "Christian affirmation of the truth of the Gospel must not fall victim to a false concept of objectivity but must take the form of personal commitment to a faithful God."[30] By way of conclusion, he quotes the words of Dietrich Bonhoeffer: "Faith alone is certain. Everything but faith is subject to doubt. Jesus Christ alone is the certainty of faith."[31]

In his review of *No Other Gospel* by Carl E. Braaten (1992), Newbigin confirms he is in profound agreement with its central thesis, namely that "the kind of pluralism expounded in the writings of Hick, Knitter, et al., if accepted, must destroy the Church."[32] He clearly considers religious pluralism to be the enemy of the church, as it denies the uniqueness of Jesus as Christ as disclosed in the Gospel narratives. In his appreciation of Braaten's discussion of the relation of the Absolute to history, Newbigin avers that the pluralism of Hick and company is part of the wider phenomenon of relativism resulting from the pervasive influence of the Kantian affirmation that ultimate reality is unknowable and that we can know only the phenomena ordered according to the categories imposed by our minds.[33] But with regard to the central question of interreligious dialogue, he disagrees with Braaten, who is, like John Hick, primarily concerned with the question: "How can we be saved?" By contrast, Newbigin, like Barth and the Reformed tradition, does not want to place the question of salvation in the center, but rather the question: "How is this glorious God to be glorified?" Concurring with his position, I would agree that "the interreligious discussion is made very difficult if it is a discussion between those who are going to be saved and those who are going to be lost."[34]

NEWBIGIN'S AMBIVALENCE
TOWARD INTERRELIGIOUS DIALOGUES

On the whole Newbigin's writings reveal that he seems to have had a very negative or "ambivalent" view of other religions, specifically Hinduism in India. On the basis of his personal experience with Hindus, Newbigin, like Hendrik Kraemer, seems to have concluded that a "point of contact" is rare between the Christian faith and Hinduism, despite the fact he acknowledged the common grace of God in the natural order, including family, religions, and social, economic, and political structures.[35] In some of his writings, Newbigin tries to give Kraemer's discussion of "continuity and discontinuity" between the "Christian message" and the "non-Christian world" a sympathetic reading by contextualizing it, explaining that it should be understood from the perspective of the Tambaram meeting of the IMC, not from today's ecumenical movement. Just as Barth's infamous phrase, "religion is unbelief," should be understood from the perspective of the conflict between dialectical and liberal Protestantism at that time, and not between Christianity and other religions, so Kraemer's phrase should not be misinterpreted as if he were an anti-religious person. Because of what he learned from Kraemer's case, Newbigin did not highlight the idea of there being "no point of contact," thereby ceasing all interreligious dialogue, but instead he tried to describe the complex reality of religion, in which there are good things to learn and evil things to reject. The following quotes exemplify Newbigin's position:

> It would be wise to recognise an element of truth here: the sphere of religion is the battlefield par excellence of the demonic. New converts often surprise missionaries by the horror and fear with which they reject the forms of their old religion—forms which to the secularised westerner are interesting pieces of folklore and to the third-generation successors of the first converts may come to be prized as part of national culture. Religion—including the Christian religion—can be the sphere in which evil exhibits a power against which human reason and conscience are powerless. For religion is the sphere in which a man surrenders himself to something greater than himself.[36]

> I am bound to say that as I reflected on these long discussions on religious subjects with gracious and helpful Hindu friends, I became more and more sure that the "point of contact" for the Gospel is rather in the ordinary secular experiences of human life than in the sphere of religion. I had then read Karl Barth and did not know that "religion is unbelief" but I was certainly beginning to see that religion can be a way of protecting oneself from reality.[37]

Newbigin maintains an ambivalent position with respect to religions. On the one hand, he recognizes a "deep and often radiant sense of the presence of God" among non-Christians—which means we must learn to share in "our common patrimony as human beings made by the one God in his own image," to share in "one common world which is the gift to both of the one God"—and on the other hand, he recognizes the evil ideas and practices in religions, particularly among religious elite leaders, that prevent the Gospel from being heard in public.[38] Regarding this ambivalence, it seems that Jose Kuttianimattathil's description of Newbigin's theology of religions (in comparison to Kraemer) as "continuity without fulfillment and without salvific significance" is appropriate, for Newbigin argued simultaneously for the continuity between the Gospel and other religions (as part of God's creation) and for the inability of other religions to lead us to salvation.[39]

Despite his emphasis on Christian involvement in the public sphere on the premise that God's common grace is present in such places, his negative attitude toward other religions seems to have blocked him from going deeper into interreligious dialogue. In this sense, Robinson holds that—with respect to a typology of dialogue that distinguishes four kinds of dialogue: discursive, secular, interior, and existential—"N[ewbigin]'s understanding of religion in general and Hinduism in particular led to a willingness to enter dialogue in the first two of those senses (discursive and secular, albeit with conditions attached), but he displayed reluctance and even resistance to its other forms."[40] Robinson argues that Newbigin is far less interested in the more demanding forms of dialogue: interior and existential. "By 'interior' dialogue is meant the interior or inner and prior preparations of Christians and the Christian community for the 'external' encounter of actual dialogue with Hindus."[41] The usual definition of "existential" dialogue stresses "shared belief in a common search for truth and participation in a common religious experience." But Robinson argues that any such assumption is unacceptable to Newbigin, simply because of "a total and unconditional commitment to Jesus Christ as the one in whom all authority inheres."[42]

It is remarkable that Robinson found Newbigin's dialogue to be lacking with respect to interior and existential dialogue. But is it really necessary for Christians or Christian communities to adopt such approaches for interreligious engagement? It seems to me that Newbigin might have been worried again that they will be reduced to another kind of religious pluralism that he strongly rejected. Robinson appears to be unhappy that Newbigin was reluctant to continue his initial work of interreligious dialogues with Hindus in more interior or existential manner. Then he proposes some compelling explanations of why Newbigin did not continue to be intensively involved with interreligious dialogue. He suggests that there were both practical and theological reasons. Practically, he says, "As [Newbigin] became engrossed in (and at times came close to being overwhelmed by) ecclesiastical, mission, and ecumenical concerns within and beyond India, there was less time available for engagement with matters Hindu—even for someone of his energy and curiosity."[43] And theologically, he identified three considerations that shaped Newbigin's position toward Hindu-Christian encounter: his principled ambivalence toward the formal Hindu-Christian encounter in comparison with the engagement of many others, his reluctance to follow Indian colleagues in engaging with Hinduism in depth, and his negative discussion of the supposed Indian view of history.[44]

The practical rationale is certainly persuasive when we consider the historical context in India in the mid-1940s. Newbigin was deeply involved in the final stage of negotiations among the churches in South India leading to the founding of the historic reunited Church of South India. This became, in fact, a pivotal stimulus for the advancement of the ecumenical movement, ultimately resulting in the integration of the IMC and the WCC in 1961. During this period from the mid-1940s to the beginning of the 1960s, Newbigin wrestled with the problem of the unity of mission and church. Robinson rightly concludes that he was too busy to pursue deeper talks with other religious people. That could not be his priority at the time.

However, as I have argued in this chapter, the emergence of religious pluralism as a new force to threaten the Christian faith in Western Christianity gradually changed Newbigin's main concern from interreligious dialogue to religious pluralism. We need to see this shift in Newbigin's concern in connection with the fact that he began his work as a missionary in the context of Western post-Christendom, rather than as a missionary sent into the non-Christian heathen world of other religions. Newbigin's main problem with Western religious pluralism was that it has been far more dogmatic and exclusive in its practices than the Christian faith it has attacked on these grounds.

CAN WE REENGAGE IN
INTERRELIGIOUS DIALOGUES IN ASIA?

There has long been a need for more active interreligious dialogues in Asia, given that the influence of Hinduism, Buddhism, and Confucianism is still very strong in the ordinary lives of Asian people. It would be impossible to avoid any kind of dialogue with other religions in these religiously plural societies. For this reason, I believe that if Newbigin were sent to Asia as a missionary today, he would try to have more serious and profound interreligious dialogue than he did in the twentieth century.

Living in the early twenty-first century, our mission is to reengage in interreligious dialogue as a new adventure, just as it was Newbigin's mission to wrestle with the emergence of religious pluralism in the Western society. For this new mission, we must be prepared to sacrifice at least some aspects of the Westernized Christian faith handed down through Christendom in order to embrace the "translated message" of an Asianized Christian faith.[45] What will this Asianized Christian faith look like? In the chapter titled "Asian Perspectives on Twenty-First Century Pluralism," Allen Yeh argues that there should be more "self-theologizing" in Asian churches.[46] He insists that we should develop Asianized theologies that will translate the Gospel into Asian contexts. Until recently, however, we have known only a few forms of Asianized theology: Water Buffalo theology (Kosuke Koyama), *Minjung* theology (Korean liberation theology represented by Byung Moo Ahn), and *Mangoes or Bananas?* (Hwa Yung). Yeh wants to see many more Asian theologies produced out of the cultural encounters between the Christian faith and Asian religions or cultures. Yeh argues that the old Asian religions must be approached as "culture" rather than "religion," much as the

West regards Greco-Roman mythology. For this reason he insists that "Asian theology should be grounded in the pluralism of religious expressions."[47]

My own proposal, which differs slightly from Yeh, is that we first need to know more about the history of religions in Asia, including the history of the encounter between Christianity and other Asian religions. We will then discover that Asia has been religiously plural for a very long time and that Asians are not unfamiliar with the coexistence of and conflict between different religions. We will also hear many stories about interreligious dialogues long before the coming of Christianity. Second, we should examine the history of interreligious dialogue since the Christian faith was introduced into Asia and explore the reasons for conflict in these dialogues. Third, we should learn to translate the Christian message through the concepts of other religions without disgracing any religion involved in this dialogue. In this process, we should also learn to differentiate between what the Christian faith can share with other religions and what it cannot. Fourth, we should learn to share the social responsibilities with other religions in order to promote a just and fair civil society. Finally, I propose that we should not be afraid to embark on the adventure of engaging in interreligious dialogues, but rather we should consider it a way of Christian pilgrimage that promises many unexpected surprises ahead.

NOTES

This is a significantly revised version of an article originally published as Seong Sik Heo, "The Missional Implications of Lesslie Newbigin's Shift of Emphasis from Inter-religious Dialogues to Religious Pluralism Debates," *Korea Presbyterian Journal of Theology* 47, no. 3 (2015): 181–202.

1. J. E. Lesslie Newbigin, *Unfinished Agenda* (Grand Rapids, MI: Eerdmans, 1985), 57 58. In Kanchipuram, where Newbigin was a missionary between 1939 and 1946, he attended the interreligious study group at the local Math of the Ramakrishna Mission.

2. Bob Robinson, "Lesslie Newbigin and the Christian-Hindu Encounter: A Principled Ambivalence," *Studies in World Christianity* 8, no. 2 (2002): 296–315, here 296.

3. Robinson, 296.

4. Robinson, 296.

5. The consensus is that it was Alan Race who first introduced this typology in his book, Alan Race, *Christians and Religious Pluralism: Patterns in the Christian Theology of Religions* (Maryknoll, NY: Orbis Books, 1983). For a summary of the key points of the three types in a table, see Ida Glaser, *The Bible and Other Faiths: Christian Responsibility in a World of Religions* (Downers Grove, IL: IVP, 2005), 33.

6. Likewise uncomfortable with this taxonomy, Harold Netland points out some of its problems, commenting that "we should not think of these as three clear-cut categories so much as three points on a broader continuum of perspectives, with both continuities and discontinuities on various issues across the paradigms, depending upon the particular question under consideration. Within each paradigm there is considerable diversity on subsidiary issues, and we must recognize that, as the discussions become increasingly sophisticated and nuanced, it is often quite difficult to locate particular thinkers in terms of the three categories." Furthermore, he considers such categorization especially difficult when considering "a group of remarkable

twentieth-century missionary theologians such as Max Warren, Stephen Neill, Kenneth Cragg, and Lesslie Newbigin, who, while quite sympathetic to non-Christian religious traditions, nevertheless ably defended the supremacy of Jesus Christ and the imperative for Christian witness." Harold A. Netland, *Encountering Religious Pluralism: The Challenge to Christian Faith and Mission* (Downers Grove, IL: IVP Academic, 2001), 47.

7. In distinction from Newbigin, the evangelical scholar Richard Plantinga, completely dependent on this typology, states that "[t]he positions focus on the question of salvation, which is the principal question that Christian theologians have considered in thinking about the non-Christian religious traditions and peoples of the world. Who is saved? Who is not saved? How are people saved? While there are several key doctrines to be considered in the theology of religious pluralism—including the doctrines of God and creation—those most often appealed to in Christian theology have been the doctrines of Christ and redemption." Notably, he harshly criticizes "universalism" as a variant of pluralism, declaring that "its theological warrant has been judged at minimum ambiguous . . . at maximum heretical and clearly not in accordance with Christian orthodoxy." Richard J. Plantinga, *Christianity and Plurality: Classic and Contemporary Readings* (Oxford: Wiley-Blackwell, 1999), 5–6.

8. Paul F Knitter, *Introducing Theologies of Religions* (Maryknoll, NY: Orbis Books, 2002), 30–31.

9. J. E. Lesslie Newbigin, *The Gospel in a Pluralist Society* (Geneva: WCC, 1989), 182–83. Italics are mine.

10. Netland, *Encountering Religious Pluralism*, 46. See John Hick, et al., *More Than One Way? Four Views on Salvation in a Pluralistic World* (Grand Rapids, MI: Zondervan, 1996).

11. J. E. Lesslie Newbigin, "Religious Pluralism: A Missiological Approach," in *Theology of Religions: Christianity and Other Religions* (Roma: Pontifical Gregorian University, 1993), 227.

12. Martin Forward, *Inter Religious Dialogue, a Short Introduction* (Oxford: One World, 2012), 11.

13. K. P. Aleaz, "The Gospel according to Lesslie Newbigin: An Evaluation," *Asia Journal of Theology* 13, no. 1 (1999): 172–200, here 195.

14. In criticizing Panikkar's religious pluralism, Vanhoozer, referring to Bruce Demarest, argues that "Panikkar has exchanged a Western monism (of reason) for an Eastern one (of spirit)" and "what looks like pluralism may merely be a muddier monism, where everything is a mixture of everything else in a kind of metaphysical perichoresis." Kevin J. Vanhoozer, "Does the Trinity Belong in a Theology of Religions? On Angling in the Rubicon and the 'Identity' of God," in *The Trinity in a Pluralist Age: Theological Essays on Culture and Religion*, ed. Kevin J. Vanhoozer (Grand Rapids, MI: Eerdmans, 1997), 41–71, here 62–63.

15. Vanhoozer, 46. Vanhoozer criticizes pluralistic and universal theology of religions in four respects: (1) it is exclusivistic, meaning, "a number of critics argue that pluralism has by no means escaped an exclusive attitude, but merely transposed it from Christianity to modern Western liberalism"; (2) it is repressive; (3) it is interested in human welfare, not doctrine; and (4) it is bland. "Perhaps the blandness of a pluralistic theology of religion is its worst fault." Vanhoozer, 55–57.

16. J. E. Lesslie Newbigin, "The Centrality of Jesus for History," in *Incarnation and Myth: The Debate Continued*, ed. Michael Goulder (Grand Rapids, MI: Eerdmans, 1979), 197–210, here 202.

17. Newbigin, 205.

18. Newbigin, 209.

19. Newbigin, 210.

20. Newbigin, 210.

21. J. E. Lesslie Newbigin, *Christian Witness in a Plural Society* (London: British Council of Churches, 1977), 6.

22. Newbigin, 6.

23. Newbigin, 7.

24. J. E. Lesslie Newbigin, "Religious Pluralism and the Uniqueness of Jesus Christ," *International Bulletin of Missionary Research* 13, no. 2 (1989): 50–54, here 50–51.

25. Newbigin, 52–53.

26. Newbigin, 51.

27. J. E. Lesslie Newbigin, "Review of 'The Myth of Christian Uniqueness,' ed. by John Hick and Paul Knitter," *Ecumenical Review* 41, no. 3 (1989): 468–69.

28. Newbigin, 468–69.

29. J. E. Lesslie Newbigin, "A Christian Vedanta? Review of 'A Vision to Pursue,' by Keith Ward," *The Gospel and Our Culture (U.K.)* 12 (1992): 1–2.

30. J. E. Lesslie Newbigin, "Certain Faith: What Kind of Certainty?," *Tyndale Bulletin* 44, no. 2 (1993): 339–350, here 339.

31. Newbigin, 350. The citation is from Dietrich Bonhoeffer, *Ethics* (New York: Macmillan, 1965), 80.

32. J. E. Lesslie Newbigin, "Review of 'No Other Gospel: Christianity among the World Religions,' by Carl E. Braaten," *First Things* 24 (1992): 56–58, here 56.

33. Newbigin, 56.

34. Newbigin, 57.

35. See J. E. Lesslie Newbigin, "A Sermon Preached at the Thanksgiving Service for the Fiftieth Anniversary of the Tambaram Conference of the International Missionary Council," *International Review of Mission* 77 (1988): 325–31; J. E. Lesslie Newbigin, *The Open Secret: An Introduction to the Theology of Mission* (Grand Rapids, MI: Eerdmans, 1995), 169–73.

36. J. E. Lesslie Newbigin, "The Basis, Purpose and Manner of Inter-Faith Dialogue," *Scottish Journal of Theology* 30, no. 3 (1977): 253–70, here 257.

37. Newbigin, *Unfinished Agenda*, 58.

38. Newbigin, "Religious Pluralism and the Uniqueness of Jesus Christ," 51; Newbigin, "The Basis, Purpose and Manner of Inter-Faith Dialogue," 266–67.

39. Jose Kuttianimattathil, *Practice and Theology of Interreligious Dialogue: A Critical Study of the Indian Christian Attempts since Vatican II* (Bangalore: Kristu Jyoti Publications, 1995), 321–25.

40. See Eric J. Sharpe, "The Goals of Inter-Religious Dialogue," in *Truth and Dialogue in World Religions: Conflicting Truth-Claims*, ed. John Hick (Philadelphia, PA: The Westminster Press, 1974), 77–95. Here, he proposes four kinds of dialogue: discursive, human, secular, and interior. I think Robinson replaced "human" with existential dialogue, stressing the experiential aspect of dialogue. Quoted in Harold A. Netland, *Dissonant Voices: Religious Pluralism and the Question of Truth* (Leicester: Apollos, 1999), 285–90.

41. Robinson, "Lesslie Newbigin and the Christian-Hindu Encounter," 297.

42. Robinson, 298.

43. Robinson, 296.

44. Robinson, 296–304.

45. Lamin O. Sanneh, *Translating the Message: The Missionary Impact on Culture* (Maryknoll, NY: Orbis Books, 1989).

46. Allen Yeh, "Asian Perspectives on Twenty-First Century Pluralism," in *The Gospel and Pluralism Today: Reassessing Lesslie Newbigin in the 21st Century*, ed. Scott W. Sunquist and Amos Yong (Downers Grove, IL: IVP Academic, 2015), 215–232, here 220.

47. Yeh, 230.

BIBLIOGRAPHY

Aleaz, K. P. "The Gospel according to Lesslie Newbigin: An Evaluation." *Asia Journal of Theology* 13, no. 1 (1999): 172–200.

Bonhoeffer, Dietrich. *Ethics*. New York: Macmillan, 1965.

Forward, Martin. *Inter Religious Dialogue, a Short Introduction*. Oxford: One World, 2012.

Glaser, Ida. *The Bible and Other Faiths: Christian Responsibility in a World of Religions*. Downers Grove, IL: IVP, 2005.

Heo, Seong Sik. "The Missional Implications of Lesslie Newbigin's Shift of Emphasis from Inter-religious Dialogues to Religious Pluralism Debates." *Korea Presbyterian Journal of Theology* 47, no. 3 (2015): 181–202.

Hick, John, Clark H. Pinnock, Alister E. McGrath, R. Douglas Geivett, and W. Gary Phillips. *More Than One Way? Four Views on Salvation in a Pluralistic World.* Grand Rapids, MI: Zondervan, 1996.

Knitter, Paul F. *Introducing Theologies of Religions.* Maryknoll, NY: Orbis Books, 2002.

Kuttianimattathil, Jose. *Practice and Theology of Interreligious Dialogue: A Critical Study of the Indian Christian Attempts since Vatican II.* Bangalore: Kristu Jyoti Publications, 1995.

Netland, Harold A. *Dissonant Voices: Religious Pluralism and the Question of Truth.* Leicester: Apollos, 1999.

———. *Encountering Religious Pluralism: The Challenge to Christian Faith and Mission.* Downers Grove, IL: IVP Academic, 2001.

Newbigin, J. E. Lesslie. "The Basis, Purpose and Manner of Inter-Faith Dialogue." *Scottish Journal of Theology* 30, no. 3 (1977): 253–70.

———. "The Centrality of Jesus for History," in *Incarnation and Myth: The Debate Continued*, edited by Michael Goulder, 197–210. Grand Rapids, MI: Eerdmans, 1979.

———. "Certain Faith: What Kind of Certainty?" *Tyndale Bulletin* 44, no. 2 (1993): 339–50.

———. "A Christian Vedanta? Review of 'A Vision to Pursue,' by Keith Ward." *The Gospel and Our Culture (U.K.)* 12 (1992): 1–2.

———. *Christian Witness in a Plural Society.* London: British Council of Churches, 1977.

———. *The Gospel in a Pluralist Society.* Geneva: World Council of Churches, 1989.

———. *The Open Secret: An Introduction to the Theology of Mission.* Grand Rapids, MI: Eerdmans, 1995.

———. "Religious Pluralism: A Missiological Approach," in *Theology of Religions: Christianity and Other Religions*, 227–44. Roma: Pontifical Gregorian University, 1993.

———. "Religious Pluralism and the Uniqueness of Jesus Christ." *International Bulletin of Missionary Research* 13, no. 2 (1989): 50–54.

———. "Review of 'The Myth of Christian Uniqueness,' ed. by John Hick and Paul Knitter." *Ecumenical Review* 41, no. 3 (1989): 468–69.

———. "Review of 'No Other Gospel: Christianity among the World Religions,' by Carl E. Braaten." *First Things* 24 (1992): 56–58.

———. "A Sermon Preached at the Thanksgiving Service for the Fiftieth Anniversary of the Tambaram Conference of the International Missionary Council." *International Review of Mission* 77 (1988): 325–31.

———. *Unfinished Agenda.* Grand Rapids, MI: Eerdmans, 1985.

Plantinga, Richard J. *Christianity and Plurality: Classic and Contemporary Readings.* Oxford: Wiley-Blackwell, 1999.

Race, Alan. *Christians and Religious Pluralism: Patterns in the Christian Theology of Religions.* Maryknoll, NY: Orbis Books, 1983.

Robinson, Bob. "Lesslie Newbigin and the Christian-Hindu Encounter: A Principled Ambivalence." *Studies in World Christianity* 8, no. 2 (2002): 296–315.

Sanneh, Lamin O. *Translating the Message: The Missionary Impact on Culture.* Maryknoll, NY: Orbis Books, 1989.

Sharpe, Eric J. "The Goals of Inter-Religious Dialogue," in *Truth and Dialogue in World Religions: Conflicting Truth-Claims*, edited by John Hick, 77–95. Philadelphia: The Westminster Press, 1974.

Vanhoozer, Kevin J. "Does the Trinity Belong in a Theology of Religions? On Angling in the Rubicon and the 'Identity' of God," in *The Trinity in a Pluralist Age: Theological Essays on Culture and Religion*, edited by Kevin J. Vanhoozer, 41–71. Grand Rapids, MI: Eerdmans, 1997.

Yeh, Allen. "Asian Perspectives on Twenty-First Century Pluralism," in *The Gospel and Pluralism Today: Reassessing Lesslie Newbigin in the 21st Century*, edited by Scott W. Sunquist and Amos Yong, 215–32. Downers Grove, IL: IVP Academic, 2015.

Chapter Twelve

Converting Mission

Interfaith Engagement as Christian Witness

Deanna Ferree Womack

Preaching the Gospel and promoting neighborly peace are both essential forms of Christian witness, yet in Western Protestant communities, rigid divisions exist between those who prioritize the evangelization of non-Christians and those who emphasize interfaith dialogue. These lines of separation may be traced, in part, to old debates among leaders of the modern missionary movement, but the need to address such dichotomous thinking about the church's calling takes on new urgency in twenty-first-century America, where interreligious encounters have become a daily routine and public acts of religious bigotry are all too common. In response, this chapter approaches interfaith engagement as essential to the church's missionary nature.

Without such an understanding, interreligious neighborliness will remain a task for the few rather than a calling for all of Christ's followers. Leaders of interfaith movements will continue to view mission and evangelism as detrimental to peaceful coexistence, and zeal for conversion will bring others to treat non-Christians as rivals and enemies. The former view neglects the central Christian calling to share the Good News, while the latter mentality may lead to hostile rhetoric or even physical assaults against members of other faiths. To construct a bridge between these two opposing orientations, I turn to the work of Darrell L. Guder, Lesslie Newbigin, and John A. Mackay. Such theologians of mission uphold the church's evangelistic ministry as "being, doing, and saying the witness to the gospel" while also critiquing traditional modes of thought about Christian mission and Western Protestant culture.[1] Thus, I find their work nuanced and pliable enough to reach across the divide.

The driving question for this chapter—How do we reconcile a commitment to mission with our calling to live as loving neighbors alongside people of many faiths?—emerges from my context as an American minister and educator of seminary students, most of whom will serve in Protestant congregations in the United States. While I hope this inquiry will prove relevant for Christians elsewhere, I must leave to others the task of addressing the particular challenges for Catholic and Orthodox communities or for churches in a rapidly secularizing Europe and in African and Asian settings where Christians have lived among Muslims, Hindus, and Buddhists for centuries. The percentage of the American population that self-identifies with a tradition other than Christianity is rising but will remain low for the foreseeable future.[2] Regardless of the actual numbers, more Americans have become aware of this growing religious diversity through personal contact or media exposure, causing some to perceive such demographic shifts as a threat to their cultural values or faith convictions.[3] Considering the increase in attacks upon religious and ethnic minorities in the United States following the 2016 presidential election, American Protestants need more than ever to reflect on what it means to live as Christ's witnesses in a religiously plural society.[4]

While those who uphold acts of hate in the name of an Anglo-American Protestant heritage may be few, the tendency to make Protestant orientations, Western cultural affinities, or white normativity into an identity marker is a concern for the entire church. As Guder has argued, Christians must confront and repent from all such tendencies to ground our identities in something other than Christ:

> Our need for continuing conversion is linked directly with the reductionism of the gospel that has become pervasive in our traditions and churches. . . . Wherever Christian witness has effectively planted the church in a particular culture, the problem of cultural compromise has surfaced. Our faithful witness can only happen when we learn to see and repent of our conformities.[5]

The challenges that we face today are in many ways similar to those Guder had in mind when he published these words in the year 2000. A holistic understanding of the missionary nature of the church has taken hold among some scholars and church leaders. Yet tendencies for reductionism are certainly alive today: the neglect of incarnational witness, the perpetuation of forms of evangelism that separate salvation from the Kingdom of God, the failure to embrace the vocation of the whole church as "God's sent people."[6] Upholding such fundamental understandings of what it means to participate in the mission of God (*missio Dei*) is necessary work, but a general exploration of missional theology is not my purpose here.

I aim, rather, to aid the church's faithful witness in this post-9/11 and post-election era of American insecurity in which Islamophobia, anti-Semitism, and hate crimes against religious and ethnic minorities are on the rise. American Christians must take seriously the risk of becoming counter-witnesses to the Gospel of Jesus Christ when we practice or internalize such prejudices and when we fail to extend hands of fellowship to those who have been terrorized by intolerance. Without recognizing and responding to this reality, we cannot be the church for others. For guidance in this area, I look to two twentieth-century Protestant missionary thinkers who spent considerable time navigating religious and cultural differences, Lesslie Newbigin and John Mackay. We can learn much from their insights as well as from the limitations of their theological articulations. After considering Mackay's incarnational principle of cultural engagement and Newbigin's approach to the religions, I return to Guder's work on the conversion of the church as a means of reforming Christian orientations toward members of other faiths. The turn toward the marginalized religious other must become, I contend, a defining point for the church's witness in twenty-first-century America.

CULTURAL SENSITIVITY, CULTURAL CRITIQUE: THE WITNESS OF JOHN MACKAY

Interreligious engagement does not always involve cross-cultural encounter, but in Western Protestant history and in contemporary America, the two tend to go hand-in-hand. In the Middle East, for example, missionaries who developed an understanding of and affinity for Arab culture were more likely to speak with care and sensitivity about Middle Eastern Muslim or Christian communities.[7] Those who viewed Western civilization as innately superior tended to equate culture and religion as they condemned non-Western societies and traditions and proclaimed a particularly American or European brand of Protestantism. For many American Christians in predominantly English-speaking communities and racially homogenous congregations today, such blurring of the Gospel-culture distinction undermines the ability to understand and appreciate human diversity. Barriers to engagement inevitably arise when perceptions of another are grounded in one's own sense of cultural normativity. John Alexander Mackay (1889–1983) was acutely aware of this reality in the three global contexts in which he lived and served in ministry.

John Mackay's legacy as an ecumenist and international church leader stretches from his early theological formation in Scotland to his years of missionary work in Peru to his retirement in the United States after serving for more than two decades as president of Princeton Theological Seminary. His thought on the church, Christian unity, and mission endures in books and countless essays, lectures, and ecumenical documents he produced between the 1930s–1970s.[8] Until recently, however, Mackay's biography was available only in Spanish.[9] This indicates how revered he has been among Latin American Protestants,[10] as well as the general neglect of his thought today in the English-speaking world, outside of institutions like Princeton Seminary.[11] Mackay developed a cross-cultural proficiency that allowed him to be "at home" in British, American, and Latin American contexts, while his sense of living between worlds enabled him to view each setting through the critical lens of the Gospel. Such boundary-crossing sensitivity is worthy of emulation by Christians today in an inescapably globalized world. I will focus here on two of Mackay's approaches that I find particularly relevant for interfaith engagement across cultural differences: Mackay's articulation of incarnational witness and his advocacy for face-to-face dialogue.

The Incarnational Principle

Mackay's view of human diversity took on its deepest theological expression in the "incarnational principle," which he presented as the foundation for Christian witness. An early formulation of this idea emerged at the International Missionary Conference in Jerusalem in 1928, where Mackay argued that missionaries would only gain a hearing for the Gospel if, as foreigners in another culture, they closely identified with the community and demonstrated appreciation of "national thought, customs, and aspirations." Further, the missionary's message had to be "organic to need" and rooted in the outlook and circumstances of the people.[12] As Mackay refined his thoughts over the years, he moved beyond sympathy and understanding of language and customs to speak of missionaries becoming part of their host society.

In *Ecumenics: The Science of the Church Universal* (1964), Mackay argued that Christ's representatives must cease to be "mere outsiders in the life of a people, and become, not condescendingly, but joyously and emphatically, involved in their common life."[13] By identifying themselves so closely with the surrounding environment that they became one with the people and their needs, Mackay believed missionaries could make the evangelical word become indigenous flesh just as God became flesh in Christ. He later explained that incarnation signified something deeper than mere absorption into the human situation of a culture. In aiming to serve people, a concerned Christian "must also, on the analogy of the Lord's incarnation, become incarnate in their human persons."[14] To be for others, then, we must become so fully adopted into another's personhood that we become one with the neighbor whom Jesus called his followers to love.

This incarnational ideal excludes and repudiates any missionary practices that serve Western imperialism, exhibit racial patronization and nationalist superiority, or focus on evangelism without concern for community welfare.[15] In order to embody such incarnational witness in his global ministry, Mackay explained, he first had to "get the Scotchness out" through immersion in Hispanic culture. In reality, he did not lose his Scottish heritage but rather relativized it by developing an understanding of Spanish language, society, and history.[16] He took the same approach after relocating to the United States where, later in life, he reflected on his sense of incarnation into Latin American and North American culture and expressed his pain at the idolatries in both societies from the perspective of "a loyal naturalized American who owes to Hispanic culture and to friends of Spanish, Portuguese, and Latin American ancestry more than lips can tell or life repay."[17]

Dialoguing with Enemies

In Peru, Mackay's willingness to critique a culture he loved led him to denounce government corruption and identify commonalties between Peruvian revolutionaries' concern for the poor and the life of Christ.[18] In the United States, his openness to engage with individuals beyond the confines of a narrow Christianity caused some to view him as a modernist and a communist. When facing the prevailing fears of that period, Mackay's incarnational attention to human persons came to inform his advocacy for face-to-face dialogue in the arena of international politics.

Mackay accepted the appointment as president of Princeton Theological Seminary (1936–1959) in the wake of the fundamentalist-modernist controversy, in response to which he wrote, "The future of Christianity lies, I believe, with neither one band nor the other but with those who are resolved at whatever cost to seek the Truth."[19] It was this commitment to make his ultimate loyalty with God rather than with any human group or ideology that led Mackay to emphasize direct dialogue in political matters rather than polarization.

After a visit to Hong Kong in 1949, he described his stance on US relations with communist China as one of "incarnational sensitivity." He took seriously the mainland Chinese refugees in Hong Kong who petitioned for a "face-to-face encounter at the topmost level between representatives of the American government and the new Communist regime in China." Advocating this position back in the United States, however, he was immediately labeled as pro-communist.[20] Mackay explained:

> [F]or persons and groups fearful of any change in their country's social or political outlook, I had become an "unsafe" person, a Christian heretic. However, my position has remained unchanged. In the solution of issues that involve conflict or misunderstanding between persons or between nations, whoever they be, there is a timeless imperative. There can be no substitute for quiet, frank, face-to-face encounter. The incarnational approach applies to all human relationships. The foreign word must become indigenous flesh. An enemy must be met eye to eye, listened to ear to ear, spoken to mouth to mouth, in the light and spirit of the "Word become flesh."[21]

Mackay denied his support of communism but also challenged American tendencies for fanatical anti-communist crusades. His 1953 "Letter to Presbyterians," produced while touring the country as moderator of the Presbyterian General Assembly, stressed the need for absolute allegiance to Jesus Christ rather than to any particular nation, race, class, or culture. It indicated that instead of giving loyalty to Christ, some American Christians made national security their ultimate concern, and in relentlessly combating their communist enemies they ended up suppressing the truth. Embodying the incarnational openness that was key to Mackay's initiation into Hispanic culture, the message closed by advocating a foreign policy of face-to-face encounter with those who are perceived to be enemies.[22] Thus, Mackay's witness reminds us that Christ's command to love extends far beyond those whom we readily identify as neighbors.

Incarnational Dialogue Today

John Mackay left a rich legacy for the church to explore today, but it is important to recognize that he did not always live up to his own incarnational ideals. As Luis Rivera-Pagán has noted, Mackay tended to equate Spanish and Latin American cultures, and he demonstrated little sensitivity for popular Catholicism and the struggle of Latin American intellectuals "to forge their own cultural identity, to decolonize their spiritual consciousness" in opposition to Spanish hegemony.[23] Despite such limitations, Mackay's argument that the fullness of Christ transcends culture, nationality, ecclesiastical affiliation, and all practical forms of church life and worship is essential for Christian witness in a religiously plural society like the United States.[24] This will require confrontation with cultural norms and social trends, rather than accommodation. Toward this end, Mackay's guidance for the church remains relevant in a number of ways.

First, loyalty to Christ rather than to culture or nation means that Christians do not have a claim on American identity. This applies to the present-day conversations over the entry of Syrian Muslim refugees into the United States and the escalation of hate crimes against American Muslims and other religious minorities. Second, there are striking parallels between present-day American Islamophobia and the communist scare of the mid-twentieth century. As Mackay noted then, making national security our ultimate concern rather than our witness to the truth of the Gospel displaces the centrality of Christ in our self-understanding and in our relations with others. Further, the desire of some to return to a mythical white Protestant American heritage effectively replaces Christ with an idol, making a mockery of the Gospel and turning the church into a special interest group. While I am confident that most American Christians do not explicitly engage in such exclusivist rhetoric, the very fact that white supremacists have taken hold of Anglo-American

Protestant heritage as a symbol means that the church's witness has been compromised. [25]

Finally, Mackay's advocacy for incarnational dialogue in all human encounters should lead us toward interreligious engagement, particularly with American Muslims. Demonization of the other—whether of fellow citizens and neighbors or of entire communities in the Islamic world—neglects the humanity of the one seen as an enemy. This makes meaningful communication impossible and forecloses any chance of relationship. Incarnational sensitivity, however, requires humanization, communication, and personal relations, after the example of the One who became fully embodied in the human condition. Such openness to dialogue and willingness to become rooted in the outlook and circumstances of the "other" could move a long way toward reducing the fear that pervades many Christian and Muslim communities in America. For further guidance on Christian theological orientations toward other religious traditions, I turn now to the work of Lesslie Newbigin.

ASKING THE RIGHT QUESTION: THE WITNESS OF LESSLIE NEWBIGIN

While John Mackay has not received widespread attention from contemporary scholars, engagement with the work of British missionary and theologian of mission J. E. Lesslie Newbigin (1909–1998) has increased markedly in the years since his death. Adding to the books, biographies, and dissertations on diverse aspects of Newbigin's thought, Scott Sunquist and Amos Yong's recent volume demonstrates how relevant and versatile the former bishop of the Church of South India remains for the twenty-first century church. [26] In the religiously plural environment of South Asia, where he lived for more than thirty years, Newbigin gained insight on Christian relations with adherents to other faiths. After his return to England in the 1970s, he wrote about "the gospel and the religions" in *The Open Secret* and *The Gospel in a Pluralist Society* and reflected briefly on Islam in his final, co-authored book, *Faith and Power: Christianity and Islam in "Secular" Britain.* [27] His work as "the religious interlocutor" was, as Geoffrey Wainwright suggested, just one facet of Newbigin's ministry. [28] Yet this area of his thought has received relatively little attention, except from Indian theologians who revere Newbigin's legacy while also moving their own engagement with Hinduism in a different direction. [29]

Theologians and church leaders seeking a new model for mission to the West have taken up Newbigin's work on the challenge of secularism and pluralist relativism in Europe and the United States. Western Christian scholars with an interest in interfaith relations, on the other hand, have largely overlooked or dismissed Newbigin's writings. His rejection of John Hick's "soteriocentric" pluralism will remain a barrier for some advocates of interreligious harmony.[30] I believe, however, that his approach has something to offer to the growing number of Christian scholars, clergy, and laypersons who recognize the important distinctions between religious traditions and wish to root their commitment to dialogue in the particularities of their own faith. I also view Newbigin's thought as a bridge toward dialogue for mission-minded Christians in the United States who encounter religious diversity in their communities and have difficulty reconciling their theological convictions with a commitment to interfaith relations. Three areas of Newbigin's thought, in particular, might be adapted to our present need for interreligious understanding within the American public sphere. Newbigin offers instruction on: (1) identifying the proper goal of interfaith dialogue; (2) setting aside the question of salvation; (3) living out the Gospel as public truth.

First, to locate Newbigin at the "confessional end of the dialogue spectrum,"[31] as Hick does, is correct if this means that he believed the Christian's "personal commitment to Jesus as Lord and Saviour is not a matter for negotiation or compromise."[32] However, Hick's claim that Newbigin remained charitable toward people of other religions while maintaining an ultimate concern for their conversion is a reduction of Newbigin's nuanced approach to this subject.[33] His commitment to witnessing to the Gospel did not mean he was opposed to interfaith engagement or that he saw dialogue as a means of evangelizing. Conversion is not the goal of interfaith dialogue, Newbigin insisted, and neither is evangelism.[34] Dialogue, rather, should focus on what is taking place in the world and should aim toward cooperation with people of all faiths on projects in line with God's purpose in history.[35] To use such common endeavors to induce conversion would be contrary to the witness of the Gospel because followers of Christ do not possess the truth or have the power to convert. This point must be taken to heart in the West, Newbigin maintained, because such impositions of truth claims and dogma have "for so long been entangled with coercion, with political power, and so with denial of freedom. . . . When coercion of any kind is used in the Christian message, the message itself is corrupted."[36] Thus, like Mackay, Newbigin recognized the way missionaries capitalized on Western political hegemony, and he explicitly denounced such entanglements as contrary to the Gospel.

Second, Newbigin maintained, fixation on the question of salvation similarly prevents the Christian conversation partner from being a faithful witness to the Gospel. When it came to how Christians "regard the other commitments, faiths, worldviews to which the people around us and with whom we live and move adhere," he insisted that the question of salvation is the wrong question.[37] When we claim to know who is saved, we presume to play God. Indeed, Newbigin reminded us, even Christ refused to answer such queries.[38] This subject, we should note, is in a different category than the question of whether God works in the lives of non-Christians, to which Newbigin's response was decidedly affirmative.[39] Newbigin's approach was anchored, as Mackay's was, in his attention to the whole human person, and thus he remarked, "It is almost impossible for me to enter into simple, honest, open, and friendly communication with another person as long as I have at the back of my mind the feeling that I am one of the saved and he is one of the lost."[40] Further, such a question "abstracts the soul from the full reality of the human person as an actor and sufferer in the ongoing history of the world." The right question, then, to guide every Christian encounter is: "How shall God be glorified?"[41]

Third, this aim of the church to seek God's glory brings Christian witness into the public realm. We cannot fully worship God if the story of God's creative, redeeming work is kept as a private matter for the individual believer. It must be told and enacted in the world.[42] This was the center of Christian witness for Newbigin, explaining why he spoke of witnessing as the purpose of interfaith dialogue while rejecting questions of salvation, evangelism, and conversion. A Christian, simply put, is an obedient witness to Christ in every area of life, public or private, or she is not a Christian at all.[43] Likewise, the church that bears witness to Christ must always exist in dialogue with the world and must act publicly to seek the good of the society in which it dwells.[44] By implication, in a religiously diverse environment, Christians cannot hide the life in Christ that makes them who they are. We must, however, seek ways to testify to our faith in a manner that signifies our obedience to God and that recognizes the integrity of other children of God whose humanity we share.[45]

At this point I must address the limitations of Newbigin's thought before I consider the ways that he remains instructive for contemporary interfaith relations in America. Newbigin, like Mackay, was hampered by his own Anglo-Protestant predispositions, despite the years he spent immersed in the Indian context. Newbigin, in fact, recognized with humility the ways that he "failed in the sensitivity that is needed to understand another culture."[46] In later years, he was reluctant to vigorously engage the Hindu world, while he also gave insufficient attention to Indian Christian theologians' increasing concern for Christian-Hindu dialogue.[47] On a related note, I affirm Newbigin's claim that all religions are—or, rather, *can become*—areas of darkness and centers of human power rather than divine guidance. Yet in the current American climate of insecurity, I fear that Christians will take such statements out of context, overlooking the shadow sides of Christianity that Newbigin identifies and his expectation of seeing the light of God shining in every human being, regardless of religious affiliation.[48] A simplistic interpretation of Newbigin's view, therefore, might paralyze Christian work with non-Christian communities and uphold the Western Christian tendency to dehumanize and demonize the other rather than to hold ourselves equally accountable for the sins and human desires that compromise our religious practices.

Because such behaviors are entirely out of line with the spirit of Newbigin's theology, I find it troubling that when addressing Christianity and Islam in Britain, Newbigin's co-author of *Faith and Power*, Lamin Sanneh, divides Muslims into moderates and radical fundamentalists and condemns Christian groups for accommodating Muslim demands.[49] Newbigin himself gives little attention to Islam in the volume, focusing instead on Britain's secular ethos, which he and his fellow British Muslims find equally problematic. Yet if he had addressed Christian-Muslim relations explicitly, Newbigin surely would have upheld the need to set aside prejudgments and engage in "honest, open, and friendly communication" at the individual level.[50]

This emphasis on acts of love toward the other for the glory of God makes Newbigin instructive for American Christians, despite his critique of the freedoms of religion enshrined in the US Constitution.[51] In today's America, such legal establishments offer the strongest protection for Muslims and other religious minorities against an emerging pseudo-Protestant white nationalism. The public witness of the church in US society, however, could become an even more powerful force to counter such corruptions of the Gospel message. It is at this point that Newbigin's critique of religious neutrality resonates. In the American context—and perhaps in contrast to Newbigin's British setting—truth claims are frequently and publicly made on behalf of Christianity in many parts of the country. Yet those who speak the loudest often advance the most theologically and politically exclusivist visions for a Christian America.[52]

While such claims, as Mackay demonstrated, usually point to human authorities rather than to Christ, the silence of other Christians in the name of religious neutrality has also jeopardized the church's witness. As Newbigin maintained, when the church fails to defy the powers of evil in the world, "it becomes a countersign, and the more successful it is in increasing its membership, the more it becomes a sign against the sovereignty of God."[53] The proclamation of the Gospel as public truth therefore becomes a significant area of continuing conversion for followers of Christ who are committed to interfaith relations and for those with an interest in the missionary nature of the church.

CONCLUSION: A CONTINUING CONVERSION

In a multifaith society where religious differences have become the target of political rhetoric, American Christians today face a new challenge of reductionism or, in Darrell Guder's words, the tendency to "reduce the gospel, to bring it under control, to render it intellectually respectable, or to make it

serve another agenda than God's purposes."[54] Guder's analysis of the detrimental effects of reductionism upon missional practice resonates in a number
of ways with my discussion in this chapter of Mackay and Newbigin. First,
Guder is equally critical of Christians who avoid religion in "the conversations of polite and cultivated society" and of those who practice aggressive
evangelism. Both behaviors, he would agree, are countersigns to the Gospel.[55] Second, in the same spirit as Newbigin, Guder cautions against reducing mission to the question of individual salvation and making evangelism
into a set of strategies for bringing about conversion.[56] Mission, rather,
should be understood comprehensively as witness, an activity that is theocentric, Christocentric, pneumatological, historical, eschatological, ecclesiological, multicultural, and ecumenical.[57]

Third, when articulating the church's missional calling, Guder writes in
language strikingly reminiscent of Mackay:

> To witness to Christ incarnationally must always mean that we are moving
> between the fronts drawn by warring human parties, both inside and outside
> the church. Where others draw lines and assign people to camps, the mission
> community demonstrates that, in Christ, we can tear down walls and become
> friends, even brothers and sisters, of those who are completely different from
> us or even disagree profoundly with us.[58]

This approach to incarnational human relations applies directly to interfaith
encounters while also pointing to the way that Guder's work echoes Newbigin and Mackay's convictions about Christians' ultimate allegiance. When
Western Protestants assert our own way of understanding Christian faith, we
"enshrine one cultural articulation of the Gospel as the normative statement
for all cultures."[59] In defending our brand of Protestantism as absolute truth,
we displace Christ as the center of our identity. Instead, Euro-American
Protestantism itself becomes our identity marker.[60] It is for this reason that
the conversion and repentance of the church remains an ever-present necessity.[61] In his call for continuing conversion, Guder builds upon the legacy of
his two predecessors and provides a concept that is essential for making
interfaith engagement a key part of Christian witness in America today.

To move forward in interfaith relations, our conceptions and practices of
mission must undergo conversion. In approaching Americans of other religions, some committed Christians keep their own faith private for fear of
causing offense. Many others have reduced the Gospel to a culturally specific
truth that can be possessed and must be embraced by all. This narrow vision
is often accompanied by aggressive conversionary tactics, hostile denigration
of religious traditions, or the labeling of non-Christians as enemies to the
faith. In still other circles, the normative claims of Western Protestantism
have overcome the Gospel message entirely so that Anglo-Saxon Protestantism becomes a symbol of white supremacy, presented in the guise of Euro-

American nationalism. Soteriological questions are set aside, and people of color and religious minorities are rejected as a threat to white normativity. Although Protestantism in this schema is a cultural ideology rather than a theological tradition, such Euro-centric exclusivism feeds American Christian fears of religious others. For the sake of the Gospel, the church must distance itself completely from such perversions of Protestant identity. Further, as long as a sense of religious superiority remains operative among those who claim to follow Christ, a primary challenge for the twenty-first-century church will be to glorify God and witness to Christ through interfaith solidarity. Emulating Mackay, Newbigin, and Guder, we must offer friendship despite religious differences and witness to the redemptive work of God that cuts through the evils and corruptions of all hearts, especially our own.

NOTES

1. Darrell L. Guder, *Be My Witnesses: The Church's Mission, Message, and Messengers* (Grand Rapids, MI: Eerdmans, 1985). See also Darrell L. Guder, *The Continuing Conversion of the Church* (Grand Rapids, MI: Eerdmans, 2000), vii.

2. In 2014, 5.9 percent of Americans surveyed were members of non-Christian faiths. 70.6 percent self-identified as Christian and 46.5 percent as Protestant, making Protestants the largest single religious block. "America's Changing Religious Landscape," *Pew Research Center Report* (May 12, 2015): 3–4. Accessed January 6, 2017, http://www.pewforum.org/2015/05/12/americas-changing-religious-landscape.

3. As Diana Eck notes, the shift in the American religious landscape has been so gradual that for decades many Americans did not see the scope and dimensions of these changes. We are now coming to terms with the ways that immigration has changed our society. Diana L. Eck, *A New Religious America: How a "Christian Country" Has Become the World's Most Religiously Diverse Nation* (San Francisco, CA: HarperCollins, 2001), 1–2.

4. "Ten Days After: Harassment and Intimidation in the Aftermath of the Election," *Southern Poverty Law Center* (November 29, 2016), accessed 19 December, 2016, https://www.splcenter.org/20161129/ten-days-after-harassment-and-intimidation-aftermath-election.

5. Guder, *The Continuing Conversion of the Church*, 72.

6. Guder, *The Continuing Conversion of the Church*, ix–x.

7. One might point to the example of the American, Cornelius Van Dyck, in Syria and the British, Temple Gairdner, in Egypt, both of whom were respected and revered by the Muslims and Christians among whom they labored. See Uta Zeuge-Buberl, "'I Have Left My Heart in Syria': Cornelius Van Dyck and the American Syria Mission," *Cairo Journal of Theology* 2 (2015): 20–28; Deanna Ferree Womack, "The Authenticity and Authority of Islam: Rashid Rida's Response to Twentieth-Century Missionary Publications," *Social Sciences and Missions* 28 (2015): 89–115.

8. Mackay's publications include: Mackay, *The Other Spanish Christ: A Study in the Spiritual History of Spain and South America*; Mackay, *That Other America*; John A. Mackay, *God's Order: The Ephesian Letter and This Present Time* (New York: Macmillan, 1953); John A. Mackay, *Ecumenics: The Science of the Church Universal* (Englewood Cliffs, NJ: Prentice-Hall, 1964); John A. Mackay, *Christian Reality and Appearance* (Richmond, VA: John Knox Press, 1969).

9. Metzger, *The Hand and the Road*. The Spanish biography is: John H. Sinclair, *Juan A. Mackay: Un escocés con alma Latina* (Mexico: CPUSA, 1990).

10. The Spanish translation of Mackay's *The Other Spanish Christ:* is still popular among Latin American Protestants and has been published four times in México and Argentina and translated into Portuguese. See Luis N. Rivera-Pagán, "Myth, Utopia, and Faith: Theology and

Culture in Latin America," *The Princeton Seminary Bulletin* 21, no. 2 (2000): 142–60, here 143.

11. Darrell Guder taught courses at Princeton Seminary on Mackay's thought, and the school maintains a John A. Mackay Visiting Professorship in World Christianity. On Mackay's legacy at Princeton, see also James H. Moorhead, *Princeton Seminary in American Religion and Culture* (Grand Rapids, MI: Eerdmans, 2012), 370–421.

12. John A. Mackay, "The Evangelistic Duty of Christianity," in *The Christian Life and Message in Relation to Non-Christian Systems*, ed. Robert E. Speer (London: Oxford University Press, 1928), 393–96. In his later analogy of the "Balcony and the Road," Mackay expressed a similar view that the truth of human life is only accessible from a perspective on the road, where people gain a "first-hand experience of reality." John A. Mackay, *A Preface to Christian Theology* (New York: Macmillan, 1941), 44.

13. Mackay, *Ecumenics*, 175.

14. Mackay, *Christian Reality and Appearance*, 107.

15. Mackay, 176–77.

16. This he attempted first through a year of study at the University of Madrid after completing his degree at Princeton Theological Seminary in 1915. Metzger, *The Hand and the Road*, 81–85.

17. John A. Mackay, "Life's Chief Discoveries: Reminiscences of an Octogenarian," *Christianity Today* 14, no. 7 (1970): 3–5, here 5.

18. Mackay, *That Other America*, 131, 133. Mackay protected Peruvian opposition leader Haya de la Torre from government persecution.

19. Metzger, *The Hand and the Road*, 235, 238.

20. Mackay, "Life's Chief Discoveries: Reminiscences of an Octogenarian," 5.

21. Mackay, 5. Mackay visited Hong Kong as chairman of the International Missionary Council.

22. John A. Mackay, "A Letter to Presbyterians," *The Princeton Seminary Bulletin* 5, no. 3 (1984): 198–200. This publication is a reprint of Mackay's letter that was released in 1953 and published in the *New York Times*. The letter read, "While being patriotically loyal to the country within whose bounds it lives and works, the church does not derive its authority from the nation but from Jesus Christ," 199.

23. Rivera-Pagán, "Myth, Utopia, and Faith: Theology and Culture in Latin America," 143–44.

24. Mackay, *Ecumenics*, 95–96, 248–49.

25. One extreme example is "alt-right" leader Richard Spencer, who identifies WASP decline as the major problem plaguing our nation and who claims that white Americans and "Anglo-Saxon Protestants are the essential historic people" who are "that founding people, that indispensable people that really makes the country what it is." Al Letson, "A Frank Conversation with a White Nationalist," *The Center for Investigative Reporting* (November 10, 2016), accessed 22 December 2016, https://www.revealnews.org/episodes/a-frank-conversation-with -a-white-nationalist. See also Amy B. Wang, "White nationalist Richard Spencer's ex-classmates decry him—by raising money for refugees," *The Washington Post* (November 28, 2016), accessed 22 December 2016, https://www.washingtonpost.com/news/post-nation/wp/2016/11 /28/white-nationalist-richard-spencers-ex-classmates-decry-him-by-raising-money-for-refugee s/?utm_term=.39220e4a3f0a.

26. Scott W. Sunquist, and Amos Yong, eds. *The Gospel and Pluralism Today: Reassessing Lesslie Newbigin in the 21st Century* (Downers Grove, IL: IVP Academic, 2015).

27. Newbigin, *The Gospel in a Pluralist Society*, 171–83; Newbigin, *The Open Secret*, 160–89; J. E. Lesslie Newbigin, Lamin O. Sanneh, and Jenny Taylor, *Faith and Power: Islam and Christianity in Secular Britain* (London: SPCK, 1998).

28. Geoffrey Wainwright, *Lesslie Newbigin: A Theological Life* (Oxford: Oxford University Press, 2000), 204–36.

29. Deanna Ferree Womack, "Lesslie Newbigin's Indian Interlocutors: A Study in Theological Reception," *Princeton Theological Review* 18, no. 1 (2015): 45–61.

30. Wainwright, *Lesslie Newbigin*, 229. While teaching at Selly Oak Colleges, Newbigin encountered Hick, who was professor at the University of Birmingham. Wainwright, *Lesslie*

Newbigin, 220. For his critiques of Hick, see Newbigin, *The Open Secret*, 164–67; Newbigin, *The Gospel in a Pluralist Society*, 168–70.

31. John Hick, *God Has Many Names* (Philadelphia: Westminster Press, 1982), 118–19.

32. Newbigin, Sanneh, and Taylor, *Faith and Power*, 153.

33. Hick, *God Has Many Names*, 118–19.

34. Newbigin, *The Open Secret*, 182.

35. Newbigin, *The Gospel in a Pluralist Society*, 181.

36. Newbigin, 10. See also, Newbigin, Sanneh, and Taylor, *Faith and Power*, 153.

37. Newbigin, *The Gospel in a Pluralist Society*, 176.

38. Newbigin, *The Open Secret*, 173.

39. Newbigin, *The Gospel in a Pluralist Society*, 182.

40. Newbigin, *The Open Secret*, 173.

41. Newbigin, *The Gospel in a Pluralist Society*, 178–79.

42. Newbigin gave concerted attention to this subject in the early 1990s. See, Newbigin, *Truth to Tell*; Newbigin, "The Gospel as Public Truth," *The Gospel and Our Culture Movement Supplement* January (1992): 1–2; Newbigin, "The Gospel as Public Truth: Swanwick Opening Statement," National Consultation of the Gospel and Our Culture Network and the British and Foreign Bible Society, the Hayes, Swanwick, July 11–17, 1992.

43. Newbigin, *The Open Secret*, 182.

44. Newbigin, 180; Newbigin, Sanneh, and Taylor, *Faith and Power*, 163.

45. Newbigin, 183.

46. Newbigin, *Unfinished Agenda*, 251.

47. Robinson, "Lesslie Newbigin and the Christian-Hindu Encounter," 296–315, here 301.

48. Newbigin, *The Gospel in a Pluralist Society*, 173; Newbigin, *The Open Secret*, 181.

49. Lamin Sanneh, "Introduction to the new Edition," in Newbigin, Sanneh, and Taylor, *Faith and Power*, x.

50. Newbigin, *The Open Secret*, 173.

51. Newbigin, Sanneh, and Taylor, *Faith and Power*, 150.

52. Exclusivist theologies of religion are not innately dangerous in themselves and should not prevent individuals from embracing political pluralism. This often becomes the case, however, with devastating consequences for religious minorities. Miroslav Volf, *Allah: A Christian Response* (New York: HarperCollins, 2012), 221–28.

53. J. E. Lesslie Newbigin, "Cross-Currents in Ecumenical and Evangelical Understandings of Mission," *International Bulletin of Missionary Research* 6, no. 4 (1982): 146–51, here 148.

54. Guder, *The Continuing Conversion of the Church*, 102.

55. Guder, 118.

56. Guder, 114–19, 120–41.

57. Guder, 61–62.

58. Guder, 169.

59. Guder, 100–101.

60. This dislocation of Protestant identity parallels the phenomenon Volf described of religion becoming understood as a marker of identity and thus creating barriers between members of different religious traditions. Volf, *Allah*, 188–90, 241, 245.

61. Guder, *The Continuing Conversion of the Church*, 141.

BIBLIOGRAPHY

Eck, Diana L. *A New Religious America: How a "Christian Country" Has Become the World's Most Religiously Diverse Nation.* San Francisco, CA: HarperCollins, 2001.

Guder, Darrell L. *Be My Witnesses: The Church's Mission, Message, and Messengers.* Grand Rapids, MI: Eerdmans, 1985.

———. *The Continuing Conversion of the Church.* Grand Rapids, MI: Eerdmans, 2000.

Hick, John. *God Has Many Names.* Philadelphia: Westminster Press, 1982.

Mackay, John A. *Christian Reality and Appearance.* Richmond, VA: John Knox Press, 1969.

———. *Ecumenics: The Science of the Church Universal*. Englewood Cliffs, NJ: Prentice-Hall, 1964.

———. "The Evangelistic Duty of Christianity," in *The Christian Life and Message in Relation to Non-Christian Systems*, edited by Robert E. Speer, 393–96. London: Oxford University Press, 1928.

———. *God's Order: The Ephesian Letter and This Present Time*. New York: Macmillan, 1953.

———. "A Letter to Presbyterians." *The Princeton Seminary Bulletin* 5, no. 3 (1984): 198–200.

———. "Life's Chief Discoveries: Reminiscences of an Octogenarian." *Christianity Today* 14, no. 7 (1970): 3–5.

———. *The Other Spanish Christ: A Study in the Spiritual History of Spain and South America*. New York: Macmillan, 1932.

———. *A Preface to Christian Theology*. New York: Macmillan, 1941.

———. *That Other America*. New York: Friendship Press, 1935.

Metzger, John Mackay. *The Hand and the Road: The Life and Times of John A. Mackay*. Louisville, KY: Westminster John Knox Press, 2010.

Moorhead, James H. *Princeton Seminary in American Religion and Culture*. Grand Rapids, MI: Eerdmans, 2012.

Newbigin, J. E. Lesslie. "Cross-Currents in Ecumenical and Evangelical Understandings of Mission." *International Bulletin of Missionary Research* 6, no. 4 (1982): 146–51.

———. "The Gospel as Public Truth." *The Gospel and Our Culture Movement Supplement* (1992): 1–2.

———. *The Gospel in a Pluralist Society*. Geneva: World Council of Churches, 1989.

———. *The Open Secret: An Introduction to the Theology of Mission*. Grand Rapids, MI: Eerdmans, 1995.

———. *Truth to Tell: The Gospel as Public Truth*. Grand Rapids, MI: Eerdmans, 1991.

———. *Unfinished Agenda*. Grand Rapids, MI: Eerdmans, 1985.

Newbigin, J. E. Lesslie, Lamin O. Sanneh, and Jenny Taylor. *Faith and Power: Islam and Christianity in Secular Britain*. London: SPCK, 1998.

Rivera-Pagán, Luis N. "Myth, Utopia, and Faith: Theology and Culture in Latin America." *The Princeton Seminary Bulletin* 21, no. 2 (2000): 142–60.

Robinson, Bob. "Lesslie Newbigin and the Christian-Hindu Encounter: A Principled Ambivalence." *Studies in World Christianity* 8, no. 2 (2002): 296–315.

Sinclair, John H. *Juan A. Mackay: Un escocés con alma Latina*. Mexico: CPUSA, 1990.

Sunquist, Scott W., and Amos Yong, eds. *The Gospel and Pluralism Today: Reassessing Lesslie Newbigin in the 21st Century*. Downers Grove, IL: IVP Academic, 2015.

Volf, Miroslav. *Allah: A Christian Response*. New York: HarperCollins, 2012.

Wainwright, Geoffrey. *Lesslie Newbigin: A Theological Life*. Oxford: Oxford University Press, 2000.

Womack, Deanna Ferree. "The Authenticity and Authority of Islam: Rashid Rida's Response to Twentieth-Century Missionary Publications." *Social Sciences and Missions* 28 (2015): 89–115.

———. "Lesslie Newbigin's Indian Interlocutors: A Study in Theological Reception." *Princeton Theological Review* 18, no. 1 (2015): 45–61.

Zeuge-Buberl, Uta. "'I Have Left My Heart in Syria': Cornelius Van Dyck and the American Syria Mission." *Cairo Journal of Theology* 2 (2015): 20–28.

Chapter Thirteen

Christian Mission and Globalization

Current Trends and Future Challenges

Henning Wrogemann

Christianity is present today in almost every single country on earth. It also continues to be very active in its missionary endeavors.[1] Yet, though the number of missionaries from European and North American countries has diminished considerably, globally, new missionary enterprises have come into being in contexts like Africa, Asia, and Latin America.[2] It is estimated that there are currently about thirty thousand people serving in Indian mission ventures.[3] The number of Protestant missionaries from Brazil alone numbers five thousand persons serving in more than one hundred mission agencies. Today, missionaries are being sent from anywhere to anywhere. For instance, transnational Pentecostal churches from Latin America have established congregations in southern Africa, and large West African Pente-costal churches have founded daughter congregations in several countries around the globe.[4] We may conclude that a *quantitative increase* of mission efforts is taking place, along with a great deal of *diversification* and *unpredictable directions of movement*. Mission agencies are often globally inter-linked, with significant use of media like radio, television and the internet. As a result, they are both *drivers* of globalization and *products* of globalization.

CURRENT CHALLENGES
DIRECTED TO A THEOLOGY OF MISSION

As encouraging as the missionary trends in some regions of the world are, elsewhere the situation is very troubling. As far as the Islamic world in North

Africa, the Near East, and the area stretching from Iran to Pakistan is concerned, it is very clear that no reforms have yet been carried out in terms of the issue of apostasy, that is, the renunciation of Islam.[5] In many countries it is just about impossible publicly to proclaim the Gospel. In a number of societies, pressure is increasingly being exerted on religious minorities. Calls were made for so-called anti-conversion laws in several Indian states and in Sri Lanka, with the subsequent partial enactment of such laws. European countries continue to experience a strong secularization trend.[6] Here, church membership is declining in practically all countries—an observation that applies also to Muslim communities. Strong secularization trends are also making themselves felt in places like Australia and New Zealand. By contrast, the Latin American continent is experiencing a process of Protestantization. Even though the Roman Catholic Church has pursued new initiatives in a number of countries, Protestant (especially Pentecostal) churches are experiencing significant growth through transfer in membership.

Christian mission is challenged by its being an event of intercultural boundary-crossing and interreligious relationships; Christian mission is carried out in contexts marked by poverty, insufficient medical care, HIV/AIDS, water scarcity, violence, corruption, bad governance, environmental pollution, urbanization, automation, media revolutions, rapid societal change, secularization, increasing fundamentalism, and gender violence.[7]

In the face of such a plethora of challenges, is it even possible to formulate a *single* definitive theology of mission? Should there not be many theologies of mission that vary according to continent, country, culture, and context? In what follows, I affirm the need for an *adaptable theology of mission* today, a theology of mission that enables Christians worldwide to engage in constructive discussions as to how Christian mission can and should be defined and carried out. This will be presented under the heading of *mission as oikumenical doxology.*

A plurality of missions and motives for mission exists today. Is the primary goal of mission to plant churches, to give witness in the field of social ethics, to achieve numerical growth, to propagate a Social Gospel, or to engage in power encounters? The following begins at a different point: *Christian mission is grounded in the praise of God, in which human beings tangibly experience the power of God. Mission aims at enabling the creatures to praise God as redeemed creatures, and to participate in the glorification of God.* At issue is a kind of groundswell of *doxological impact* that affects *the entire ecumenical scope, pervading the household of the whole creation—or "oikos."* Instead of the word "ecumenical," I prefer the term "*oikumenical*" because it better accords with the Greek root. This is about an *oikumenical* plurality in which the praise of God finds expression in physical incarnations.[8]

MISSION AS *OIKUMENICAL* DOXOLOGY: BASIS

The New Testament includes various images to portray Christian mission, including energetic images such as the *flow* of power, the *shining* of splendor, and the *emission* of fragrance: Paul speaks of himself as "the aroma of Christ" among people (2 Cor. 2:15–16). Flowing, shining, and emitting go beyond a state of being; they are broad in scope, they overcome limitations, and they cover wide expanses, and this implies that we are dealing with *the crossing of boundaries and thus with missionary activity*. Mission takes place as the reflection of the splendor radiating from the face of Christ. 2 Corinthians states: "Now the Lord is the Spirit, and where the Lord's Spirit is, there is freedom. As all of us reflect the glory of the Lord with unveiled faces, we are becoming more like him with ever-increasing glory by the Lord's Spirit" (2 Cor. 3:17–18). The Christian life, the exposure to and the emanation of the splendor of God, is also an aesthetic event.[9]

Here we have a confluence of three aspects that are of great significance as far as their mutual interrelatedness and interdependency is concerned, namely the aspects of the *testimony of one's life*, the *glory of God*, and the *increase of human thanksgiving* (2 Cor. 3:9).[10] The service of Christians to other people and creatures is not an end in itself, but is rather aimed toward a doxological horizon. A little further on it reads: "For it is all for your sake, so that as grace extends to more and more people it may increase thanksgiving, to the glory of God" (2 Cor. 4:15). At issue is the increase of the praise of God by the mouths of God's creatures who have *experienced* liberation, redemption, or reconciliation. *But it is precisely because these same creatures have begun to experience healing that the glorification of God cannot be separated from ethical actions.* Just like the two focal points of an ellipse, both aspects belong together.

One might misunderstand this doxological understanding of mission by assuming that this reference to the glorification of God denudes a Christian's prophetic commission, leading to an insufficient emphasis on the *political dimension*. Others might take the glorification of God to mean a *certain form* of the praise of God, which would lead to a *limitation of the plurality of worship forms*. For this reason, mission is here defined as oikumenical doxology—the dimension of the entire inhabited world (oikoumene) and the dimension of the praise of God (doxology) modify and define each other. By encompassing more and more people and thus radiating out into the inhabited world, the glorification of God shows itself to be a *crossing of boundaries* and thus a missionary event. By integrating the inhabited world into the praise of God, Christian mission shows itself to be a *holistic* event.

THE DOXOLOGICAL DIMENSION:
MISSION AS THE GLORIFICATION OF GOD

The following describes the doxological dimension under the aspects of prophetic criticism, power, physicality, and name. Prophetic criticism refers to the *political implications* of the praise of God, power to the *anthropological implications* of the praise of God, physicality to the *aesthetic implications,* and the name to the significance of the praise of God for *identity.*

The Praise of God as Prophetic Criticism: Political Implications

We misunderstand mission as the oikumenical praise of God when we fail to interpret it in terms of its prophetic power. The *Magnificat* (Luke 1:47–55) cites a liturgical text that follows the traditional pattern of Old Testament motifs, praising God as the mighty one who exalts those of humble estate and brings down the mighty from their thrones (Luke 1:52). That means: the "Son of the Most High" will be born into a world full of social and political conflict, and he is extolled proleptically in Mary's song: "This hymn of thanksgiving focuses on the themes of *humiliation and exaltation, of poverty and wealth, of the power of God and the bringing down of the mighty of this world, of the glory of God and of his mercy.*"[11]

   This song of praise sets the glory and justice of God over against the mighty of this world. It is no coincidence that Luke associates this praise of God with the mission of the one bearing the Spirit, namely Jesus.[12] Using the words of Isaiah 61:1–2, Jesus confesses in Luke 4:18 the God who cares for the poor, the captives, and the blind. The task of his messianic mission as the one bearing the Spirit is to make this *reality of the Kingdom of God*—the Kingdom of *this* God—manifest and tangibly experienced in his presence, and, in so doing, to elicit faith that God is present in him, that is, in Jesus Christ. This shows that the glorification of God brought about by the praise of God does not only pay tribute to a reality, but also brings it about emblematically, for *as a prophetic criticism in a liturgical form*, this praise of God *orients the hearer against the delusion of power in this world*: the true balance of power is evident in him, providing a strong counter to attempts at intimidation by the rulers of this world.

   The praise of God simultaneously has *political implications* for it challenges the powers that be that exist in real life. The glorification in the praise of God serves as a constant reminder that Christians are called to reflect this assertion in their own lives. It is not for nothing that Luke's Gospel characterizes discipleship with the call to forgo the ownership of property.[13] Doxological-prophetic criticism is political for the triune God is the power which relativizes all the powers and all the mighty of this world:

- *Bad governance and corruption*: Many countries of the world are ruled by despots who oppress people by means of tyranny and corruption. It is easy to recognize the relevance of the praise of God as a criticism of the powers that be.
- *Poverty and privation*: For the very reason that God desires to hear praise coming from the mouths of his redeemed creatures, mission means addressing issues of poverty and privation.
- *Superabundant, affluent societies*: God is the Lord of all people, nations, and societies, and for rich industrial societies the praise of God implies prophetic criticism and the imperative to share the superabundance with other people and not to acquiesce all things to market forces.

The Praise of God as a Source of Power: Theological-Anthropological Implications

The praise of God makes prophetic criticism possible by invoking God as the true power. It enables Christians to look away from themselves, since it focuses on the honor and action of the God who as the powerful one and as the Lord puts all possible human actions and designs in their place. The praise of God protects against burnout and resignation. 2 Corinthians states: "For to be sure, he was crucified in weakness, yet he lives by God's power. Likewise, we are weak in him, yet we will live with him by God's power, (which will also reveal its potency) in you" (2 Cor. 13:4).[14] With respect to the power of God, Paul is speaking here not so much of miracles or wonders, but rather expressly of the resurrection of Jesus by God. This is where he sees the power of God at work. This means that God saves in two ways: first, by relieving the weakness and suffering of people in this world, and second, because he is able to save them from sin, corruption, and death. *It is not legitimate to propose on the basis of Paul's statements a third alternative to earthly well-being and eternal salvation—despite the obvious differences between the two.*

According to Paul, the apostolic authority consists of his boasting not in his strengths, but in his weaknesses (2 Cor. 11:30; 12:9b). In this instance, weakness is not the goal. It is merely the *location* in which Christ's power may be experienced to an appreciable extent. Paul's admission that he is reliant on the power of Christ shows him to be an apostle. Mission from a doxological perspective locates the glorification of God in one's own consciousness and in acceptance of one's own weakness, on the one hand, and, on the other, in the willingness to accept the weakness of other people, and to share and to witness to the power of Christ within this weakness. This witness takes place when one *speaks up for others*, *serves* people in need, and *confesses one's hope* in the power of God which is able to bring about new life even in failure and death. Christians lead a missionary life as they draw on this power. What does that mean?

- *Oppression, persecution, and discrimination*: Wherever Christians are oppressed, persecuted, or discriminated against, the praise of God means the power to remain strong in the face of the pressure. Even martyrdom cannot be ruled out. In several countries in this world, mission means to persevere and proclaim the God of love.
- *Secularization and burnout*: In especially Western societies, the church continues to decline. In these contexts, though many Christians remain active, they watch the number of members shrink year after year. Many pastors and coworkers suffer from burnout. Only the praise of God can help, for it provides the salutary reminder that the future of the church is in God's hands.
- *The struggle for life and justice*: In all countries, Christians are faced with the many different challenges of poverty, violence, HIV/AIDS, or the destruction of the environment. According to my experience, it is the power of faith and hope that sustains people and which motivates their missionary efforts.

The Praise of God as a Communal-Physical Experience: Aesthetic Implications

In the Sermon on the Mount, Jesus Christ applies the image of the *city on a hill* to the community of people who want to follow him. Christians *are to let their light shine* as a city on the hill, but this is a *collective image*. Christian mission is not to be undertaken by a number of individuals, but by a community. Because the congregation is illuminated by the glory of Christ, according to the Sermon on the Mount, the following holds true: "In the same way, you are to serve as a light for the people. They are to see what you do, and so to find their way to God and to praise your Father in heaven" (Matt. 5:16, own translation). Here, too, the praise of God is the goal of the actions of God, of his salutary actions that are intended to help his creatures become open to praising him. In this sense, a doxological theology of mission serves as a corrective to tendencies to individualize Christian mission. The focus falls not only on the "inward person," the "soul," and the "life to come," but on the praise of God, which connects and interlinks this life and the life to come. The praise of God already begins in this world, even in weakness, brokenness, and failure, and it will continue in the world of God that is to come.

Many people enter the Christian faith through *experiencing fellowship with the Christian community*, that is, not in the first instance by means of intentional proclamation, but *through incidental, everyday occurrences*, not through verbal activities, but *through atmospheres that communicate*. Mission from the perspective of the praise of God helps us recognize that mission is more than strategy, organization, or technique, more than intentional actions, more holistic than the exclusive proclamation of the Word, and perceptible in other ways as well. How then can Christians find the courage and enhance their creativity so as to create new worship forms or to place new emphases within the old forms, and so experience again anew the joy of worship and from other forms of spiritual life? How can the proclamation be simplified (without being trivialized) so as to make it intelligible to people who have not been socialized into the Christian life? How and by whom can people be invited to take part in events or activities without such invitations coming across as awkward? Mission as a joint, that is, communal, witness of faith is especially important for the following contexts:

- *Urbanization and individualization*: In a few years' time, more than fifty percent of the world's population will live in cities with more than a million inhabitants. For many people, urbanization means individualization and increasing loneliness. In this regard, Christian community is able to welcome people into a new social world.
- *The experience-driven culture and mediality*: Many people today are searching for special experiences and this includes the area of faith. There is good reason why it is Pentecostal churches with their emphasis on experience have great appeal to people worldwide. What forms might this take in terms of worship services, prayers, and everyday life? When it comes to helping congregations become more missional, it is important to have a doxological understanding of mission for this addresses our social and material environments, and how the faith may be experienced through the medium of human communality.

The Praise of God as a Testimony of Names: Implications for Identity Formation

Names are not just a form of nomenclature. They also always convey something of the persons to whom they belong. The New Testament's theology of names finds its highest expression in Peter's famous confession: "Salvation is found in no one else, for there is no other name under heaven given to humankind by which we must be saved" (Acts 4:12). The adage that *names open doors* is especially true when it comes to the name of Jesus. According to John 16:24, the name of Jesus is the key to the heart of God. A number of New Testament passages argue that through Christ we have obtained "access to the Father." The Holy Spirit took part in the glorification of the name of Jesus. "But the Advocate, the Holy Spirit, whom the Father will send in my name, will teach you all things and will remind you of everything I have said to you" (John 14:26). *This glorification of the name is to continue by means of the prayers, life witness, and good deeds of the believers.*

Reference to the name of Jesus Christ evokes a range of sensibilities: *Memories* are invoked, *trust* is expressed, *hope* is kindled, *authority and power* are acknowledged. And it is expected that the divine demonstrations of power in his name will continue. But how can this name be made known today? We may list the following hurdles:

- *The danger of anonymization*: The danger of anonymization exists in many European societies. In Germany, for instance, only the state employs more people than the Christian social welfare [diaconal] institutions. Hospitals, welfare centers, nursing homes, homes for the handicapped, and the like may call themselves "Christian." However, the name of Christ does not often feature in the daily course of affairs. Many people have no idea what *diaconia* means, or that the institution in question is a Christian one.
- *The danger of the magical use of the name*: Pentecostal churches often invoke the name of Jesus in prayers for healing and in exorcisms. It is not uncommon, however, for this invocation of Jesus's name to resemble the invocations used in magical practices. In these cases, the name of Jesus is used as a kind of magic word.
- *Media-driven societies and recognizability*: The question is how to use the name of Jesus Christ appropriately, for it summarizes the story of God's interaction with human beings. In the context of media-driven societies worldwide, what is at issue is the recognizability of the name of Jesus Christ—this is about the distinctive emblem of Christianity.

THE OIKUMENICAL DIMENSION:
THE ECUMENICAL SCOPE OF MISSION

We define mission here as oikumenical doxology. The *doxological* dimension comprises the aspects of prophetic criticism, power, communal-physical experience, and the name of Jesus Christ. We will now proceed by describing the *oikumenical dimension* under the aspects of solidarity, plurality, cooperation, and ecology: solidarity refers to the *ethical implications* of the praise of God; plurality refers to the *cultural implications*; cooperation addresses the *implications of partnership*; and ecology addresses the *implications* of the praise of God in terms of *the theology of creation*.

Oikumenism in Terms of Solidarity: Ethical Implications

The glorification of God is not a self-contained event, and the impact of oikumenism is not the result of some mindless performance. Rather, these phenomena are mutually interdependent. That is why "material things" like taking the offering during worship services should be understood as Christians training themselves in a kind of *spiritual "letting go,"* as an antidote to avarice and egocentricity, and as expression of solidarity with those in need, with outcasts, and with strangers. The collections raised by the Macedonian churches discussed in 2 Corinthians 8 are a good example of Christian support for one another and for others, in general. According to this text, wealth is to be understood as *an expression of the abundance available in the time of salvation.* But, the wealth in question is the wealth of God's grace, which has given rise in the Macedonian churches to an "abundance of joy" and "a wealth of generosity on their part" (2 Cor. 8:2).

In light of this theological framework, it is legitimate to speak of a circulatory system in the flow of missionary abilities: Christians have been enriched by the grace of God, they have been liberated and enabled to give thanks, to give selflessly, and to perform all kinds of works of mercy: "You will be enriched in every way to be generous in every way, which through us will produce thanksgiving to God. For the ministry of this service is not only supplying the needs of the saints but is also overflowing in many thanksgivings to God" (2 Cor. 9:11–12). This implies that as the *"needs of the saints"* are supplied, so the praise of God by the mouths of redeemed creatures increases. These two aspects are inseparably joined. It is no accident that in the Greek, the expression "ministry of service" is rendered as "the ministry of the liturgy (in Greek: *leitourgia*)."[15] Hence, raising a collection is not just a charitable action, but also a *liturgical one.*

The gratitude toward God and the extolling of his deeds, as the *obedience of faith* of the Macedonian churches demonstrates, allows us to recognize not only the *location* of God's salvific action, but also the *name* by which it is effected. And it is precisely this quality that constitutes the missionary dynamic of the whole thing: the gratitude to God and the extolling of his deeds have a referential function.

- *Mission as a charitable event*: There is a missionary dynamic in effect in global Christianity in the sense that people who have received help talk about it and in so doing refer others to those who supply charitable help in the name of God.
- *Mission as healing action*: The praise of God is also increased by means of prayers for healing and by healing services. Mission history demonstrates that healing services have often resulted in missionary outcomes and impacted many people.

Oikumenism as Plurality: Cultural Implications

The aim of the divine mission is salvation for the entire world. By making this possible and by bringing it about, God glorifies Godself. God glorifies Godself through the praise arising from the mouth of the redeemed creation, which may be expressed by the mouths of infants (Ps. 8:3) just as well as by the trees of the field clapping their hands (Isa. 55:12); this is anticipated by the image of the pilgrimage of the nations to Mount Zion (Isa. 2:2–5; Mic. 4:1–5) and transcends all boundaries of age, sex, and milieu (Joel 3:1–5). In other words, the radiating praise of God is imbued with a missionary power, with an ability to cross boundaries, since it implies the transcending of ethnic, cultural, social, and other boundaries. According to Philippians 2:5–11, the goal of Jesus's mission is that his act of salvation is to have an ongoing effect among peoples and creatures, with the result that by the plurality of tongues, that is, in an oikumenical scope, the entire household of God's creation is to be filled ever more with vocalized praises. Many tongues, that is, the various languages, cultures, dances, and songs of the nations, will apply all their creativity to sing the praises of God. The plurality of creation reflects God's creative power. The mutual glorification sounds the chords not only of the plurality of the *gifts of creation*, but also of the plurality of the *gifts of the Holy Spirit*.

- *The recognition of cultural polyphony*: This praise transcends boundaries; it recognizes plurality as a gift and spreads out to encompass the world in its entirety. But this also highlights the challenges facing Christians worldwide. The question is whether they are prepared: first, to acknowledge other forms of praise given to God, which seem foreign to them; second, to grow in their own understanding of these other forms; and third, to value or at least to tolerate them.
- *Recognition and trial*: Christians experience the cultural and confessional plurality of the glorification of God not only as an *abundance*, but frequently also as a *trial*. There is an ongoing debate about which forms of glorification are appropriate. What about the sometimes aggressive prayers for healing by Pentecostal Christians? What about the charismatic hymns of praise that seem so sickly sweet to the ears of conservative Protestant Christians? What of the developing rites that seem so strange from a European perspective, such as the rites of purification used in African Initiated Churches?
- *Plurality and unity*: When is a worship service truly a worship service in the full sense of the term? Is this sacrament of the Eucharist definitive, instituted by priests standing in the apostolic succession (Roman Catholic) or at least in the historic succession (Anglican)? What media are permissible? Must a church be empty, as is common in Reformed churches? Are

incense, singing, candles, and icons expendable, or are they even distractions from the "real thing"? Are worship services always to be held according to the rigid liturgical prescriptions of tradition, as is commonly held by Orthodox churches with their *divine liturgy*? Are the gifts of the Spirit necessary as a reference to the true faith? Which kinds of conversion sermons are permitted, and which type of political engagement is still appropriate?

- *Unity and mission*: Mission as oikumenical doxology points to the immense significance of these questions. As credible witnesses, churches and mission agencies must seek to cultivate ecumenical contacts. The purpose is not to establish organizational unity, nor to achieve unity in confession, nor even necessarily to enable cooperation; rather, the purpose is to maintain contact with other Christians.

Oikumenism as Cooperation: The Implications of Partnership

The above examples already raise the issue of cooperation and partnership between Christians of different cultural backgrounds. One often hears reports of missionary initiatives by Christians of one country, such as Canada, causing tensions in a different cultural context, such as Sri Lanka, because the foreign missionaries did not establish contact with the local Christians. Inappropriate cultural or religious behavior can severely compromise the relationships between local Christians and their neighbors who belong to different religions. Ecumenical partnership is not just significant because Christians are supposed to have a mutual appreciation for one another as foreign siblings. The significance is deeper than this: according to the New Testament witness, the praise of God is to sound forth in cultural plurality. Nor is ecumenical partnership only Christians acting in solidarity with each other. It serves the greater purpose of avoiding all harm and violence to others— regardless which religion or worldview they may hold.

- *Partnership and society*: If the aim is to increase the praise of God coming from the mouths of healed, liberated, or reconciled creatures, then this includes seeking "the welfare of the city" (Jer 29:7) in all things. From this perspective, those engaged in missionary initiatives may not simply attempt to attain their own goals with no regard to the context; rather, for sound reasons dictated by the theology of mission, they are called to establish contact with local Christians.
- *Partnership and respect*: It is a mark of respect for other churches when mission agencies establish ties with resident Christians. Often, unconsidered mission initiatives have done great harm to local Christians, such as when a mission drive by foreign Christians results in the persecution of local Christians.

Oikumenism as Creatureliness: Ecological Implications

Let us approach the issue of mission and creatureliness from the perspective of the Old Testament. Claus Westermann distinguishes between beauty as *being* and beauty as *occurring*.[16] Beauty as being refers to works of art. Beauty as occurring means something very different according to Westermann. This type of beauty may apply in the case of an enjoyable festive celebration, of an unexpected smile, of impressions gathered through the experience of nature. Beauty as occurring has a "functional character"; it does not exist for its own sake. Rather, beauty is a matter of *being for the benefit* of the creatures. The occurrence of beauty is an expression of abundant blessings and possesses a referential character. Beauty includes human beings and creatures, and in this sense applies to the whole of creation.

This is the broad *oikumenical* scope that constitutes the end point toward which such occurrences take place. Wherever possible, all being is to be incorporated into this process. Beyond that, beauty as occurring takes place in a *doxological context*, which for its part also embraces within itself the tendency to transcend itself, to go beyond itself, to radiate outwards.

- *Mission and creation*: All of creation is to take part in the praise of God; or, better yet: all of creation is to be transformed by the salvation of God and in that way come to serve as a sounding board for the praise of God.
- *Mission and ecological issues*: What does this mean in the face of extensive environmental pollution by international mining companies, for instance, which contaminate the environment in Latin American countries, putting out heavy metals, which poison human beings, animals, and plants in the process? What does this mean in the face of the extensive land grabbing taking place in African countries, in the face of the ongoing deforestation of jungles, and in the face of the many examples of irresponsible behavior by human beings toward their environment?
- *Mission and Christ as the mediator of creation*: From a doxological perspective, these challenges pertain to Christian mission, not in the sense of a diffuse spirituality of creation, but rather in the sense of glorifying the name of God in accordance with the way God revealed Godself in Jesus Christ, who was simultaneously the mediator of creation, the son of God, and a creature, according to the Christian understanding.

CONCLUSION

In consequence, a relevant theology of mission faces the task of having to offer a high degree of adaptability to and integrability into many contexts and challenges. I have attempted to accomplish this by presenting mission from the viewpoint of oikumenical doxology: The goal of mission is to make it possible for more and more redeemed people to sing praises to and thus contribute to the glorification of God. This is about the name of Jesus Christ, in which salvation is given, both in terms of its political and ethical dimensions, both as far as issues of spiritual power and of salvation and healing are concerned, both in terms of corporal experiences of community and in the proclaimed Word, both in terms of cultural plurality and ecumenical breadth, both with an appreciation of partnership and in the pursuit of the social well-being of all. This is about mission in the holistic sense which aims at the glorification of God in the name of Christ Jesus.

NOTES

1. Michael Jaffarian, "Are There More Non-Western Missionaries than Western Missionaries?," *International Bulletin of Missionary Research* 28, no. 3 (2004): 131–32.

2. Oswaldo Prado, "A New Way of Sending Missionaries: Lessons from Brazil," *Missiology* 33, no. 1 (2005): 48–60. See also Laura Heikes, "Una perspectiva diferente: Latin Americans and the Global Mission Movement," *Missiology* 31, no. 1 (2003): 69–85.

3. Frampton F. Fox, "Why Do They Do It? Lessons on Missionary Mobilization and Motivation from Indian Indigenous Missionaries," *International Review of Mission* 96 (2007): 114–27.

4. Paul Freston, "The Universal Church of the Kingdom of God: A Brazilian Church Finds Success in Southern Africa," *Journal of Religion in Africa* 35, no. 1 (2005): 33–65.

5. Abdullah Saeed and Hassan Saeed, *Freedom of Religion, Apostasy and Islam* (Burlington, VT: Ashgate, 2012).

6. Henning Wrogemann, "Mission as Oikumenical Doxology—Secularized Europe and the Quest for a New Paradigm of Mission: Empirical Data and Missiological Reflections," *Missionalia* 42, no. 1–2 (2014): 55–71.

7. For an overview of current mission theologies worldwide, see Henning Wrogemann, *Intercultural Theology 2: Theologies of Mission* (Downers Grove, IL: IVP Academic, 2018).

8. In what follows, I can only provide a brief outline of what I have discussed in detail elsewhere: Henning Wrogemann, *Den Glanz widerspiegeln: Über den Sinn der christlichen Mission, ihren Kraftquellen und Ausdrucksgestalten* (Berlin: LIT, 2012).

9. See Eph. 1:17; Heb. 1:3; 1 Pet. 4:14.

10. See James R. Harrison, "The Brothers as the 'Glory of Christ' (2 Cor 8:23): Paul's *Doxa* Terminology in Its Ancient Benefaction Context," *Novum Testamentum* 52, no. 2 (2010): 156–88; Jesper Tang Nielsen, "The Narrative Structures of Glory and Glorification in the Fourth Gospel," *New Testament Studies* 56, no. 3 (2010): 343–66.

11. Ulrich Berges and Rudolf Hoppe, *Arm und Reich* (Würzburg: Echter, 2009), 80.

12. Berges and Hoppe, 82.

13. Berges and Hoppe, 92.

14. Adapted from the NIV to follow the translation proposed in Ulrich Heckel, *Schwachheit und Gnade: Trost im Leiden bei Paulus und in der Seelsorgepraxis heute* (Stuttgart: Quell, 1997).

15. Erich Grässer, *Der zweite Brief an die Korinther* (Gütersloh: Gütersloher Verlagshaus, 2002), 2:62–63.

16. Claus Westermann, "Das Schöne im Alten Testament," in Herbert Donner et al., eds., *Beiträge zur alttestamentlichen Theologie: Festschrift für Walther Zimmerli zum 70. Geburtstag* (Göttingen: Vandenhoeck & Ruprecht, 1977), 479–97. See also Claus Westermann, "Biblische Ästhethik," *Zeichen der Zeit* 8 (1950): 277–89.

BIBLIOGRAPHY

Berges, Ulrich, and Rudolf Hoppe. *Arm und Reich*. Würzburg: Echter, 2009.

Fox, Frampton F. "Why Do They Do It? Lessons on Missionary Mobilization and Motivation from Indian Indigenous Missionaries." *International Review of Mission* 96 (2007): 114–27.

Freston, Paul. "The Universal Church of the Kingdom of God: A Brazilian Church Finds Success in Southern Africa." *Journal of Religion in Africa* 35, no. 1 (2005): 33–65.

Harrison, James R. "The Brothers as the 'Glory of Christ' (2 Cor 8:23) Paul's *Doxa* Terminology in Its Ancient Benefaction Context." *Novum Testamentum* 52, no. 2 (2010): 156–88.

Heikes, Laura. "Una perspectiva diferente: Latin Americans and the Global Mission Movement." *Missiology* 31, no. 1 (2003): 69–85.

Jaffarian, Michael. "Are There More Non-Western Missionaries than Western Missionaries?" *International Bulletin of Missionary Research* 28, no. 3 (2004): 131–32.

Nielsen, Jesper Tang. "The Narrative Structures of Glory and Glorification in the Fourth Gospel." *New Testament Studies* 56, no. 3 (2010): 343–66.

Prado, Oswaldo. "A New Way of Sending Missionaries: Lessons from Brazil." *Missiology* 33, no. 1 (2005): 48–60.

Saeed, Abdullah and Hassan Saeed. *Freedom of Religion, Apostasy and Islam*. Burlington, VT: Ashgate, 2012.

Westermann, Claus. "Biblische Ästhethik." *Zeichen der Zeit* 8 (1950): 277–89.

Wrogemann, Henning. *Den Glanz widerspiegeln: Über den Sinn der christlichen Mission, ihren Kraftquellen und Ausdrucksgestalten*. Berlin: LIT, 2012.

———. *Intercultural Theology 2: Theologies of Mission*. Downers Grove, IL: IVP Academic, 2018.

———. "Mission as Oikumenical Doxology—Secularized Europe and the Quest for a New Paradigm of Mission: Empirical Data and Missiological Reflections." *Missionalia* 42, no. 1–2 (2014): 55–71.

Chapter Fourteen

Can These Dry Bones Live Again? The Priority of Renewal

Wilbert R. Shenk

One measure of a movement's impact is the range of publications, consultations, and conversations it generates. By that standard the "Gospel and Our Culture Network" (GOCN) initiative, has been of considerable significance. It has contributed to an extensive publishing industry, ranging from the scholarly to the popular, devoted to changing the way North American Christians understand the cultural context they find themselves in today and challenging them to embrace their *missional* responsibility. Academic programs devoted to this new field are now on offer from many seminaries. Consultants are working with denominations and congregations to turn the tide from stagnation and decline to growth. A vision expressed through new vocabulary has developed around this concern for a fresh engagement of the Gospel with the peoples of historical Christendom. Essential to this quest is a vital and witnessing church.

In recent decades a new generation of scholarship has challenged the traditional Christendom assumption that mission was an extra-ecclesial activity. Although missions were not approved by the established church, such activity might be organized and administered by a voluntary society or agency.[1] In the twentieth century this attitude changed and many denominations incorporated their related mission society into their denominational structures, but this was done on pragmatic rather than theological grounds.[2]

Today we acknowledge mission to be God's initiative disclosed to us in the sending of God the Son into the world in the power of God the Spirit. Jesus Christ instituted the church to continue his mission to an unbelieving world that all people might hear the good news. The efforts we undertake in response to God's call to join in the *missio Dei* ought to draw people to God.

213

Mission must always be understood comprehensively as both local and global. But since the rise of the modern mission movement in the seventeenth century in Europe and North America, the focus has been on continents and peoples beyond the West. Letting go of entrenched patterns of thought and action is not at all easy. Speaking about mission to the West is still not welcomed by many. In spite of ample evidence to the contrary, people continue to cling defensively to the myth that Western culture remains a Christian culture. Others remain satisfied with the status quo.

This is not the occasion to attempt a thorough review of the effectiveness of this initiative to develop a missiology that addresses modern and postmodern culture. That would require a careful empirical study. My aim here is to draw attention to a dimension that appears to have been largely overlooked. These reflections and queries were stimulated by Darrell L. Guder's challenging book, *The Continuing Conversion of the Church*.[3] In that work Guder shows how the extensive institutionalization of Christian activity since the seventeenth century has narrowed and reduced our understanding of the Gospel and the Christian mission. As a consequence, we have been left with fragments rather than the whole. Special interest groups and programs have been formed around these fragments. While all of these activities may be legitimate, the tendency has been to treat each one as an end in itself. In critical ways the North American church has become a mirror image of its historical-cultural environment where specialization and independence are prized. The work in self-criticism and reconstruction begun by GOCN and others a quarter century ago must be ongoing. My purpose here is to identify a salient issue that seems to have gone largely unremarked and raise questions that call for response.

MANIFESTO

A convenient point of departure is Lesslie Newbigin's manifesto, *The Other Side of 1984*,[4] which was a catalyst for setting a new missiological agenda in the West. Newbigin reported having been challenged to face up to the spiritual crisis of historical Christendom by Indonesian church leader T. B. Simatupang who remarked at a conference in 1973: "The Number One question is, Can the West be converted?"[5] A decade after retiring to Great Britain, Newbigin offered a compelling analysis of the main issues pressing on the churches in Europe and North America. The church of Christendom was in decline, whether measured numerically or in terms of morale. Many churches were hollowed out. Christians were uncertain about the Gospel and hesitant to witness to their faith. Simatupang's question continued to nag at us.

In his 1952 Kerr Lectures, delivered in Glasgow and published as *The Household of God*,[6] and speaking from the perspective of a cross-cultural missionary, Newbigin pointedly summarized the operative ecclesiology that Western missionaries had been transplanting in other countries for several centuries: It is "a replica of our own, . . . a fundamentally settled body existing for the sake of its own members rather than . . . the sign and instrument of a supernatural and universal salvation."[7] This is a patently static and introverted ecclesiology. Although Newbigin did not address ecclesiology again in a sustained way, the church continually played a fundamental role in his thought.[8] After returning to Great Britain he focused on the cultural and epistemological barriers the Christians faced in their witness to modern/postmodern culture.

From the 1980s on, Newbigin argued that the West itself was a vast and challenging mission field for it was unlike any that missionaries had ever faced.[9] Millions of Western people had had some kind of experience with Christianity and rejected it. Indeed, the rejection rate was accelerating as people continued to abandon the church. He insisted that the local church was the key to effective mission on this new frontier. He itinerated widely across Europe and visited North America several times speaking, writing many articles, and several books on this challenge. Until his death in January, 1998, Newbigin worked to put mission to the people living in modern and postmodern culture on the conscience of churches in the West.

ORGANIZING A RESPONSE

In Great Britain a six-year initiative was launched in 1986 as the Gospel and Our Culture Programme (GOCP), directed by Newbigin, with the goal of mobilizing Christian lay leaders, academics, and leaders in church and society for a revitalized Christian witness.[10] Subsequently, projects were organized in North America and New Zealand around similar goals but adapted to the national contexts.

The Gospel and Our Culture Network (GOCN) was formed in North America in 1990 to awaken interest and cultivate support for mission to this continent. George R. Hunsberger served as GOCN coordinator. A newsletter was instituted, annual consultations were held, and a publishing project was launched under the rubric "The Gospel and Our Culture Series." These various initiatives stimulated an outpouring of articles, pamphlets, and books. The GOCN's driving concern was to provide resources that would help North American Christians think in fresh ways about the Christian mission in their communities. The premier volume published in the series has been *Missional Church: A Vision for the Sending of the Church in North America*.[11] This was a team-written volume for which Darrell L. Guder served as editor. This book has been widely used.

Reviewing the volumes in this series, along with other books in the field of "missional church" studies, one observes terms such as "renewal" and "revival," long-time staples of North American church and cultural history, are conspicuously absent.[12] Nothing suggests that this has been a conscious or deliberate omission. This may mean that leaders in this initiative assumed that the fundamental challenge at this juncture was to redirect the energies of the local church to its own community, while giving lower priority to global missions. The literature associated with this movement of the past twenty-five years has focused on re-conceptualizing, motivating, restructuring, and mobilizing the church in North America for ministry to its own culture.

This project marked a decisive departure from the popular missiology of the past two centuries. But it was never intended that this should signal a retreat from global Christian witness. Indeed, many of the leaders promoting "mission to modern and postmodern culture" had long been active as cross-cultural missionaries and missionary agency leaders. It was agreed that the definition of *mission* associated with the modern mission movement was truncated and on biblical, theological, and missiological grounds it had to be jettisoned and replaced by an understanding based on the *missio Dei.* Geography, as Jesus instructed the disciples, is quite incidental. His disciples are always located in the "mission field" (cf. Matt. 9:35—10:15; Luke 10:1–12; John 4:35). The challenge to them is to "see" the mission at hand. Before his ascension Jesus clarified the mandate, which hereafter was to encompass all peoples.

A considerable body of new scripture and theological studies in the past two generations has shown convincingly that the *missio Dei* is integral to the whole of scripture.[13] The fundamental problem has not been that mission was detached from the church; rather this critical anomaly arose from the fact that for more than one thousand five hundred years the church has been cut off from its fundamental purpose as servant of the *missio Dei.* From the fifth century the institutional church became increasingly focused inward. The laity was treated as a passive body with no active role. Whenever the church is functionally severed from its constitutive purpose, it will exist, as it were, like a seriously ill patient on "life support" with little prospect for recovery.

RETRIEVING THEOLOGY OF RENEWAL

Every human system is subject to historical forces that, if left unchecked, can bring it to an end. This is inherent in the life-cycle of all institutions. The church is no exception. Institutions that resist adapting to their changing environments are typically short-lived. Only those that address institutional renewal and adapt to their changing cultural environment survive. This applies equally to the local congregation, an educational institution, or a business enterprise. The point can be illustrated from the history of organized Protestant missionary activity that began in the seventeenth century as missionary societies. Only a handful of these agencies still existed in the twentieth century. The survivors now bore names with little resemblance to the original ones. In the twenty-first century, agencies that have been willing to form multi-lateral and international partnerships and networks have the best prospects of surviving.

While Christian organizations and agencies have survived by redefining their programmatic purpose, restructuring, and innovating new programs, this can be done without a deep renewal of commitment to witness to the reign of God. Indeed, in modern culture such restructuring is typically justified in terms of making the agency attractive to younger supporters, achieving greater operating efficiency, and encouraging program innovation. This rationale can be applied equally to a commercial, governmental, or secular service agency. It is quite possible to convince ourselves that renewed and intensified activism is the primary goal. But activism per se has no salvific power. If our service does not point beyond ourselves to the Suffering Servant Messiah, we have given only a half loaf in Christian witness. The scriptures constitute an essential sourcebook on the critical importance of continuing renewal for the people of God.

Across two millennia of Christian history we observe that renewal has consistently begun on the margins of society. The center controls institutional power and guards its position. The church of Christendom is the outstanding historical example of this dynamic, by virtue of having survived so long. Repeatedly, the church hierarchy has worked to fend off renewal impulses, sensing that these forces threatened to disrupt the status quo and, thus, posing a challenge to ecclesiastical leadership. Church leaders were typically risk-averse and renewal could be messy and divisive. Of course, that is the inevitable outcome when the "new creation" breaks in and displaces the "old" (2 Cor. 5:17). The thesis of this chapter is that the *Continuing Conversion of the Church* that Darrell Guder calls for hinges on a deep conversion to God's mission as the foundation on which new structures and practices can be developed. Such transformation will only be experienced through life-changing encounter with the Word that leads to repentance and covenant renewal.

ISRAEL AND COVENANT RENEWAL

A leitmotif running through the Old Testament is the struggle of the Israelites to live in faithfulness to their covenant with Yahweh. Chosen by Yahweh for a special role in salvation history, they were to be a set-apart people. Their way of life was to be a continuous testimony to "the nations." The Old Testament is framed by the continuous interplay between the Israelites' covenant faithfulness and unfaithfulness: Israel's apostasies, Yahweh's judgment, and the essential role of the prophets who implore the people to "return." This literature is vivid and poignant as Yahweh's messengers plead with the people—reminding them of Yahweh's compassion, patience, and yearning that "the people called by my name" turn around—in repentance and renewal of their covenant with Yahweh.

The land Yahweh promised to Abraham and his descendants was to be held in trust as stewards exercising their covenant responsibility (Lev. 25:26). Unfaithfulness inevitably resulted in judgment, often taking the form of exile. Eventually, a prophet would appear with a fresh word from Yahweh: repent and recommit to covenant faithfulness. The condition for liberation from miserable enslavement was renunciation of idolatrous worship and reconciliation with Yahweh. Their return to the land was always contingent on repentance and covenant renewal.

Herbert Butterfield pointed out that what set the Hebrews apart from other people was their "historiography rather than their history."[14] A nation's history is typically told—often through the biography of a great leader—to glory in that nation's heroic struggle to defend itself and advance the interests of its people. By contrast, the criterion by which Israel's history was recounted and evaluated was the people's faithfulness to Yahweh's purpose for them: "a covenant to the people, a light to the nations" (Isa. 42:6b). An important part of Israel's history takes the form of prophetic critique. The singular focus of the prophets' proclamation is Israel's rebellious behavior. We hear Isaiah, Jeremiah, and Ezekiel passionately preaching against their people's faithlessness, ranging from anemic nominalism to callous unbelief that left the Israelites vulnerable to the idolatrous practices of their neighbors. Each time the Israelites turned their backs on their covenant with Yahweh, they lost their moral compass.

The condition for Israel's restoration to the land was radical change, that is, *conversion*. Jeremiah prophesied that the day was coming when Yahweh would "make a new covenant with the house of Israel and the house of Judah" (Jer. 31:31). A renewed covenant required a deep transformation that changed the fundamental disposition from self-centeredness to Yahweh-centeredness. This would happen because Yahweh promised to "put my law within them . . . I will write it on their hearts" (Jer. 31:33b). If they were to live in obedience to Yahweh's will, their basic orientation had to be changed.

In 597 BCE, Nebuchadnezzar's army invaded the land of Israel and drove them into exile in Babylon. While in exile, the prophet Ezekiel was instructed to remind the people of the reason they were being punished: "I had concern for my holy name, which the house of Israel had profaned among the nations to which they came" (Ezek. 36:21). Yahweh was determined to "sanctify my great name"—which Yahweh's people had dishonored among the nations—so that the nations "shall know that I am the Lord." This would be accomplished *"when through you I display my holiness before their eyes"* (Ezek. 36:23, emphasis added). In the background is the Abrahamic covenant and Yahweh's promise that "I will make you a blessing [so that] . . . in you all the families of the earth shall be blessed" (Gen. 12:2c, 3c). The prophet Ezekiel was about to be given a vision of what Yahweh had in mind for the people then held captive in Babylon.

In this vision Ezekiel finds himself in a valley littered with piles of sun-bleached bones. This is a picture of utter desolation. It is impressed on Ezekiel that he cannot "fix" the problem. Its scale and depth are beyond human solution. Ezekiel is challenged to have faith that through an act of *re-creation* Yahweh can assuredly restore these dry bones to life. The prophet's role is to be Yahweh's herald to the people, announcing that Yahweh is about to act. He is instructed to prophesy to the bones "you shall live" (Ezek. 37:6c). Then he calls the four winds to breathe life into the bones, causing the dead to come alive, "a vast multitude" filling the valley. Yahweh assures Ezekiel that the spiritually dead Israelites will be resurrected and enabled to return to their land. Israel will know that Yahweh has acted on their behalf. Indeed, they can only return to the land because they have renewed their covenant with Yahweh and are now a *recreated* people restored to covenant relationship.

With one voice, as it were, Isaiah and Ezekiel declare that Israel's covenant responsibility is not only to Yahweh. The Abrahamic covenant binds them to Yahweh *and the nations*: "you will be a blessing . . . in you all the families of the earth shall be blessed" (Gen. 12:2c, 3c; cf. Isa. 42:6b–7; Ezek. 36:20b–23). The people of Israel were elected to be servants of the *missio Dei*. This is the prototype for the people of the New Covenant.

THE NEW COVENANT

The prophets of Israel repeatedly assured the people that a new age lay ahead. The messiah would emerge and lead God's people into this messianic age. The prophets proclaimed that this would be an age in which God's righteousness/justice would prevail and people would experience God's shalom in its fullness. The new order would triumph over the evil and injustice of the present order. As his crucifixion and resurrection approached, Jesus told the disciples that this event marked the inauguration of this new covenant (Matt. 26:27–28; Mark 14:24; Luke 22:20). Yet the apostles assured the first believers that the experience of the people of Israel was of continuing relevance to them. Paul wrote to the Christians at Corinth: "These things happened to them to serve as an example, and they are written down to instruct us" (1 Cor. 10:11). He impressed on the young Christian community that in Jesus Christ the covenant has been amended and renewed, but there

was an essential continuity. The Christian community must guard its commitment to this covenant that is celebrated in the Eucharist in a continuous
process of renewal and growth in obedience (1 Cor. 11:25).

CRITERION OF FAITH: NEW CREATION

The nascent Christian movement faced all the questions that confront any
new group trying to clarify and establish its identity. Acts gives a running
account of the issues that arose from the first days of the church and continued into the following decades. Acts 15 records a pivotal moment. It seemed
clear to the core leadership of the fledging church that they were a Jewish
sect. But the Apostle Paul saw what was at stake with great clarity: the
Gospel is about the "new creation." To the Corinthians he wrote, "If anyone
is in Christ, there is a new creation" (2 Cor. 5:17a). In the Epistle to the
Galatians he spelled out this criterion on which the New Covenant rested
(Gal. 2:15–16, 19b–20; 3:1–14, 29). Paul rejected the Judaizers' argument
because it would have foreclosed on the new thing God was doing. This
would have simply ratified the status quo. Paul had had an encounter with
Jesus Christ on the road to Damascus and he could never go back. He was
now a Christ-follower. *Renewal* required starting from the correct premise:
God had done something unprecedented in Jesus Christ. It is nothing less
than the *new creation.* This is the criterion of faith that we must now affirm.
This criterion would be tested in various ways by the church over the course
of history. Other criteria have been proposed and adopted—to the detriment
of the church. The "new creation" is the sole source of the Christian faith,
and renewal means re-engaging with what God has done for us in Jesus
Christ.

WARNING

In contrast to the Old Testament that recounts events that unfolded over
many generations, the New Testament is compressed into a much briefer
time period. The Synoptic Gospels report the coming of the Messiah, as
foretold by the prophets. Through his life and ministry Jesus the Messiah
established the promised New Covenant. The New Testament narrates the
founding of the church and the struggles involved in making the transition
from a Jewish sect to a fellowship based on the redemptive work of Jesus
Christ on behalf of all people. A decisive development that followed from
this was the launching of the Christian mission to the Gentile world.

The New Testament confronts the reader with the continual struggle between the Kingdom of God and the powers of the Evil One. On the eve of the
launch of his public ministry, Jesus encountered and was tempted by the

Devil (Matt 4:1–11). Jesus's ministry involved confronting and dispelling evil powers that held people in bondage. Similarly, the apostles were tested by political and religious powers that were hostile to followers of the Way. Especially in the Apostle Paul's epistles, the theme of "the powers" is important (Rom. 8:38–39; 1 Cor. 2:8, 15:24–26; Eph. 1:20–21, 2:1–2, 3:10, 6:12; Col. 1:16, 2:1). But persecution provided no shield against unfaithfulness and spiritual decline. New Testament writers urged the young churches not to ignore the Old Testament prophets' warnings to the people of Israel about their unfaithfulness. Neither will Christians be spared if they rebel and disobey God's will (1 Cor. 10:1–22; Heb. 3–4, Jude).

It is noteworthy that in the final book of the New Testament canon, John's Revelation, the first three chapters are addressed to the *seven* churches, representative of all churches. These chapters offer no grounds for self-satisfaction. In John's vision the majority of churches are not in spiritual health: some are characterized by nominality, in others false teaching is tolerated, certain churches ignore sin among their members, some churches are spiritually dead while in others commitment is lukewarm. In response, John's Revelation is an impassioned plea that the churches honestly confess their lack of passion for the Gospel and earnestly seek renewal and recommit themselves to covenant faithfulness.

Like all human institutions, the church cannot escape the effects of "institutionalization": patterns and routines become entrenched, spontaneity is discouraged, cliques form within the congregation and strangers feel unwelcome, there is little enthusiasm for sharing the Gospel, and spirituality becomes a mere formality. All institutions are time-bound and reflect the historical moment and culture in which they are established. Unless an institution undergoes renewal, it will be short-lived. It is significant that this is acknowledged already within the New Testament.

RENEWAL IN THE EARLY CHURCH

Over the following centuries the Christian movement grew in numbers and spread geographically. Inevitably these scattered churches faced situations not shared by other churches. One such local movement that cast a long shadow was the controversial Montanist prophetic movement that emerged in Phrygia around 170 CE. Tensions developed between leading bishops and teachers as to how to respond to issues raised by such movements. But, increasingly, leaders tried to avoid contentious issues by maintaining the status quo. W. A. Visser 't Hooft observes that compared with the New Testament church, the church of the second and third centuries showed little, if any, awareness of the need for continuing renewal by the Holy Spirit.[15]

The issue that dominated this generation was heresy. This was to have long-term consequences.

Increasingly, church leaders were preoccupied with guarding against deviant beliefs. Vincent of Lérins (d. ca. 445 CE), a contemporary of Augustine, in his *Commonitorium* proposed a three-fold basis for deciding doctrinal issues: antiquity, universality, and content.[16] This formulation was to have an enduring influence by privileging "tradition . . . [in] the development of Christian doctrine."[17] By giving the greatest weight to antiquity, the church must always align its decisions with the earliest bishops and teachers and innovation and adaptation to culture were rejected. This was tantamount to annulling the Jerusalem Council's ruling (Acts 15). Vincent explicitly condemned "newness." He urged "that in the Catholic Church 'all possible care should be taken' to 'hold that faith which has been believed everywhere, always, and by all.'"[18] Visser 't Hooft comments cryptically: "The burden of the New Testament message would seem to be the opposite, namely, that in the life of the Church the old must constantly be transformed by the new."[19] Thus, the apostolic criterion formulated by the Apostle Paul, "the new creation," was set aside. The *kerygma,* which cannot be bound by culture and time, was eclipsed by the privileging of tradition.

The Vincentian Criterion was influential in shaping the official position of the Roman Catholic Church, making tradition a powerful and enduring influence throughout Christendom. Renewal impulses that surfaced from time to time and challenged this criterion were met by suppression or by siphoning such initiatives off into monastic orders. In this way the deep covenant renewal the church needed was suppressed by asserting the claim that the church was truly safeguarded only by holding firmly to the past. The Church qua church developed a fortress mentality that would remain deeply averse to renewal. The masses of lay people were largely cut off from renewing influences.

SIXTEENTH-CENTURY REFORMATION
AND ITS AFTERMATH

The sixteenth century was marked by a series of waves of reform.[20] All the leading reformers, both Protestant and Roman Catholic, were motivated by a fresh encounter with the Word of God that resulted in personal renewal, awakened concern for the laypeople, and stirred commitment to ecclesial reform. Reformation history is consistently told from this viewpoint. What has been largely overlooked is how short-lived this reforming impulse was.

Reformers quickly became defenders of what they had established. What began as streams of renewal were soon attenuated by the powerful counter-force of Christendom's traditionalism. Once the major Protestant churches were organized, they began to fall back on the default position of historical Christendom. T. F. Torrance offered this trenchant summary: "the descendants of these Reformation churches have themselves tended to erect a rigid tradition, stabilizing the forms of the Reformation period, and forgetting that the Holy Ghost moves on, and that the Church can only fulfill its mission on earth when it allows itself to be broken on the anvil of the Word and re-formed again and again."[21]

By the 1590s, thoughtful observers were disturbed by the sterile scholastic sermons pastors and priests were preaching to the largely illiterate masses of people. Spiritual famine was widespread in the land. English Puritans who espoused a form of Pietism and pastors such as Johann Arndt (1556–1621) saw the situation for what it was: a spiritual desert. Taking their stand against the establishment viewpoint, these advocates of renewal began addressing the needs of the people through their preaching, teaching, and writing. In 1606, Arndt published *True Christianity* to "lead believers in Christ out of dead belief to fruitful faith."[22] Arndt's book had wide and prolonged influence. A young German pastor, Philipp Jakob Spener (1635–1705), was deeply influenced by Arndt's message of renewal. In 1675, Spener wrote a preface for a new edition of Arndt's sermons that stirred great interest. It was soon published separately as *Pia Desideria*, which became a significant resource for the emerging Pietist movement.

Pietism and the subsequent Evangelical Revivals in the following centuries, all bear witness to the enduring influence of the Vincentian Criterion on the erstwhile Reformers. The churches, both Protestant and Roman Catholic, continued to hold at arm's length the various forms of revival and reform. Lay Christians in German parishes who had experienced spiritual quickening—what Spener called "new birth"—formed Pietist cells where they studied the Bible and encouraged one another in discipleship. In the eighteenth-century, Anglican priests George Whitefield and the Wesley brothers, John and Charles, dared to transgress ecclesiastical law by "preaching in unconsecrated places"—that is, in public squares and the countryside where large crowds could gather. The impact of Pietism and the evangelical revivals awakened personal devotion and encouraged Christian activism—including evangelism, social justice, philanthropy, foreign missions, and the anti-slavery movement.

Yet the Protestant churches refused to formally recognize any of these developments as legitimate. Christian activists were forced to pursue new forms of ministry beyond the church. These revived Protestants turned to the voluntary society as the vehicle for carrying out their witness in word and in deed. Roman Catholics, of course, had long ago looked to the monastic and missionary orders to provide an outlet for intensified piety. Tragically, the spiritual vitality engendered by reform and revival was held at arms' length by the established churches. By the twentieth century some of the mutual antagonism had dissipated; parachurch agencies were increasingly taken for granted.[23] But the underlying issue has never been adequately addressed. The long-established churches have been reluctant to embrace renewal as a permanent priority for the church.

VARIETIES OF REVIVAL AND RENEWAL

When one turns to the vast literature on the history and practice of "revival," it is apparent that the focus was on "reviving" nominal Christians and evangelizing the general population.[24] This is understandable in light of the historical context. The people to be evangelized comprised the population of the "Christian West." But the established churches were jealous to maintain control over their territory and people. By default, "revival" was left to the parachurch agencies. Many people maintained a dual identity: they remained loyal to the church, but they also regularly participated in revival meetings, prayer circles, and supported publications produced for the edification of participants. This "split" has had long-lasting influence.

In his survey of how renewal has been understood across church history, W. A. Visser 't Hooft identified six views, which may be summarized briefly.[25] The first view is that the church is not subject to renewal and the idea per se must be rejected. This "originalist" theory holds that the church is by its very nature perfect and cannot be improved. A second view accepts renewal that takes the form of allowing the full flowering of what was present from the beginning. In nineteenth-century Catholicism this was promoted as "doctrinal development" symbolized by Vatican Council 1 (1870) that promulgated the doctrine of papal infallibility. The third concept emerged in the nineteenth century as a part of the wider modernist cultural movement. Proponents of modernist ideas urged that the churches be brought into line with the intellectual and cultural movements of that time. This eclipsed eschatology, without which the church cannot survive. A fourth option, adopted by some Protestants, posited a radically futurist eschatology that offers no resources for engaging with the world, except as individuals trying to remain "unstained by the world" (James 1:27). The fifth approach is the opposite of the preceding one: this is a call to establish a "pure" church here and now. Historians cite the second-century Montanists as the first, of a long series, of such sectarian movements that arose in protest against the growing worldliness of the church of their time. These movements have been energized by an apocalyptic eschatology combined with a vision of a purified church. We will consider the sixth vision of renewal in the next section.

REFOUNDING THE CHURCH

The Old Testament makes clear that just as the Abrahamic covenant was initiated by God, the renewing of the People of God throughout the Old Testament was always at God's initiative. God called prophets to announce divine judgment and grace. They pled with the people to remember God's faithfulness, which stood in sharp contrast with their own faithlessness. The prophets did not propose a grand scheme or plan for renewal. They proclaimed God's word to the people: repent and return to renewed covenant relationship. Worship and serve the God of Exodus and liberation. Everything depended on reestablishing this fundamental relationship.

Gerald A. Arbuckle coined the term "refounding" in his study of renewal in the Roman Catholic Church.[26] John XXIII convened Vatican Council 2 (1962–1965) to address issues facing the church that the traditional system was incapable of resolving. There was no lack of historical examples that showed where the Vatican had blundered in decisions handed down in the past. For example, in 1633 the church declared the astronomer Galileo a heretic for views that did not align with traditional church teaching. In 1742, after protracted study, the Vatican condemned Matteo Ricci's pioneering approach to a contextual evangelization in China. Attempts to contextualize the Christian message and ecclesial forms in diverse cultures were ruled impermissible. This stricture continued to complicate and frustrate the work of missionaries in many cultures and languages around the world. Traditionalists who controlled the Vatican simply refused to make concessions to cultural and linguistic barriers. It was difficult to understand how the church could remain credible if it continually turned a blind eye to cultural and historical change and reacted mechanically to these deeply human concerns.

Many people were heartened by the readiness signaled by the Second Vatican Council to engage with contemporary people in their cultures. Predictably, not everyone was ready to accept such fundamental change as was called for in the Council documents. Almost immediately following the Council, powerful and entrenched traditionalists began taking steps to restore traditional positions on a range of questions, practices, and interpretations. Arbuckle characterizes the post-Vatican II period as a time of chaos. From a Renewalist viewpoint this is a necessary prelude to change: "It is from chaos God creates and recreates. So our situation does not call for restoration. . . . The solution cannot be found in going back, but in refounding."[27] This is the opposite of attempting to turn back and restore the past. *Refounding* involves starting over through fresh engagement with the Gospel and discerning God's call to mission in the light of the Word. We cannot go back and resume ministry as it was in the past; maintaining the status quo means remaining tied to the past. But the Holy Spirit gives vision for ministry in the future.

Thus far, the discussion of refounding has been based on the Roman Catholic experience. But there are important parallels within Protestantism. Earlier we noted T. F. Torrance's observation that Protestants have by no means avoided reifying certain forms and patterns that become barriers to contextual ecclesial responsiveness. One of the most powerful of these "structures" among Protestants is the way Enlightenment values have been adopted and made absolute in all areas of life.[28] Nothing makes the point clearer than the role of the "autonomous self" in Protestantism, starting with the insistence that every person is entitled to interpret the scriptures for themselves.[29] This limits capacity for self-criticism and encourages a "live-and-let-live" attitude that undermines true *koinonia* that we claim characterizes the body of Christ. The Apostle Paul's criterion of faith—"new creation"—surely calls into question the self-centeredness promoted by modernity. Renewal can only take place when we start from the proper premise.

CONCLUSION

Ezekiel faced a bleak situation when he tried to rally the Israelites who were captive in Babylon. They had lost their way and no longer remembered their covenant. But Yahweh did not forget the people but rather intervened to renew them. As Ezekiel's prophecy makes clear, the renewal of the Israelites was directly related to God's mission.

One of the most compelling observations we can make from what the Gospels record about the life and ministry of Jesus Christ is that as he came to the end of his earthly ministry he gave a mandate to his disciples. They were now to spread to the nations the "good news" they had heard, experienced, and witnessed firsthand. This follows the basic structure of the Abrahamic covenant, but it boldly dramatizes that the *missio Dei* has moved to a new stage. The "new covenant in my blood" that Jesus enacted with his disciples was not focused on their "personal salvation." Rather this was the action by which Jesus was inducting the disciples into his mission to the world, accompanied and empowered by the Holy Spirit.

The body of Christ is most vital when it is engaged in the *missio Dei.* Whenever the church becomes preoccupied with itself, it becomes something other than the living body of Christ. From the beginning the church's purpose was to be sign, foretaste, and instrument of the advancing reign of God. In helping others find new life in Christ the church itself is renewed. Without participation in God's mission, the church cannot live. It has become the "dry bones" Ezekiel saw in his vision. But the prophet's vision included a second stage: a resurrected, renewed, and witnessing people. Genuine renewal will issue in mission. Mission without renewal risks becoming mere activism.

NOTES

1. A considerable body of historical studies has been devoted to this question, especially in Great Britain and Europe where state churches dominated. See Max Warren, *The Idea of the Missionary Society* (London: CMS, 1943); Max Warren, "Why Missionary Societies and Not Missionary Churches?," in *History's Lessons for Tomorrow's Mission* (Geneva: World Student Christian Federation, 1960), 149–56.

2. The classic study of the impact of modern bureaucracy on a denomination is Paul M. Harrison, *Authority and Power in the Free Church Tradition: A Social Case Study of the American Baptist Convention* (Princeton, NJ: Princeton University Press, 1963). Important insights are found in the seven-volume Presbyterian study, Milton J. Coalter, John M. Mulder, and Louis B. Weeks, eds. *The Presbyterian Presence: The Twentieth-Century Experience* (Louisville, KY: Westminster/John Knox, 1990). See especially: *The Presbyterian Predicament* (1990), *The Diversity of Discipleship* (1991), and *The Organizational Revolution* (1992). Based on Presbyterian data, the observations and insights are widely applicable.

3. Grand Rapids, MI: Eerdmans, 2000.

4. Geneva: WCC Publications, 1983.

5. J. E. Lesslie Newbigin, "Can the West be Converted?," *International Bulletin of Missionary Research* 11, no. 1 (1987): 2–7.

6. New York: Friendship Press, 1954.

7. Newbigin, *The Household of God*, 166.

8. An especially provocative presentation is, "The Congregation as Hermeneutic of the Gospel," *The Gospel in a Pluralist Society* (Grand Rapids, MI: Eerdmans, 1989), ch. 18. For a critical interaction with Newbigin's thesis of "the congregation as hermeneutic" see, Flett, "What Does It Mean for a Congregation to Be a Hermeneutic?," 195–213. Also, in the same volume, Veli-Matti Kärkkäinen and Michael Karim, "Community and Witness in Transition," especially pp. 81–99.

9. A remark by Sydney Evans, Dean of Salisbury, in a sermon to the General Synod of the Church of England in 1982, spurred Philip Morgan, secretary of the British Council of Churches, to call for fundamental rethinking of the church's responsibility in a time of cultural crisis. Recounted briefly in, J. E. Lesslie Newbigin, *Unfinished Agenda: An Updated Autobiography* (Edinburgh: Saint Andrew Press, 1993), 251–52.

10. Newbigin, 245–56. Newbigin traces the convergence of several streams of activity from the mid-1970s that influenced formation of this initiative.

11. Grand Rapids, MI: Eerdmans, 1998. Eerdmans has published all the volumes in this series.

12. A notable exception: William R. Burrows, "Witness to the Gospel and Refounding the Church," in *Confident Witness—Changing World: Rediscovering the Gospel in North America*, ed. Craig Van Gelder (Grand Rapids, MI: Eerdmans, 1999), 189–202. On the history and theology of renewal see, Howard A. Snyder, *Signs of the Spirit: How God Reshapes the Church* (Grand Rapids, MI: Zondervan, 1989). Recently, work has been done around a A. F. C. Wallace's concept of "revitalization." The Center for the Study of World Christian Revitalization Movements, Asbury Seminary, supports research into these movements. See, Proceedings of Consultation II, in J. Steven O'Malley, ed. *Interpretive Trends in Christian Revitalization for the Early Twenty First Century* (Lexington, KY: Emeth Press, 2011). William J. Abraham, in his *The Logic of Renewal* (Grand Rapids, MI: Eerdmans, 2003), deploys a series of fourteen mini-case studies of well-known and diverse Christian leaders of the past generation to explore the varieties of renewal of Christian life, thought, and action since 1950.

13. See, for example, John G. Flett, *The Witness of God: The Trinity, Missio Dei, Karl Barth and the Nature of Christian Community* (Grand Rapids, MI: Eerdmans, 2010); Wright, *The Mission of God: Unlocking the Bible's Grand Narrative*.

14. Herbert Butterfield, *Christianity and History* (London: G. Bell and Sons, 1949), 73.

15. W. A. Visser 't Hooft, *Renewal of the Church* (London: SCM, 1955), 61, 62.

16. Hooft, 63.

17. H. G. J. Beck, "Vincent of Lérins, St.," in *The New Catholic Encyclopedia*, ed. Thomas Carson (New York: Thomson/Gale, 2003), 14:523–24.

18. K. S. Latourette, *A History of Christianity* (New York: Harper and Brothers, 1953), 182.

19. Hooft, *Renewal of the Church*, 64.

20. Latourette, *A History of Christianity*. See, ch. 31, "The Great Awakenings of the Sixteenth and Seventeenth Centuries: Inclusive Generalizations."

21. T. F. Torrance, "History and Reformation," *Scottish Journal of Theology* 4, no. 3 (1951): 279–90, here 290.

22. David Tripp, "Arndt, Johann (1556–1621)," in *Encyclopedia of Protestantism*, ed. Hans J. Hillerbrand (Routledge, 2003), 102–3.

23. In a widely influential article, Ralph Winter argued on pragmatic grounds that "modalities" and "sodalities" are the two structures needed to facilitate the task of world evangelization; see, Ralph D. Winter, "Two Structures of God's Redemptive Mission," *Missiology* 2, no. 1 (1974): 121–39. Lesslie Newbigin critiqued Winter's thesis on theological grounds in the 1978 CMS Annual Sermon, published as J. E. Lesslie Newbigin, "Context and Conversion," *International Review of Mission* 68, no. 3 (1979): 301–12, see especially, 305–7.

24. See especially chapters 3–5 in Snyder, *Signs of the Spirit: How God Reshapes the Church*.

25. See chapter 5 in Hooft, *Renewal of the Church*.

26. Gerald A. Arbuckle, *Refounding the Church: Dissent for Leadership* (Maryknoll, NY: Orbis Books, 1993).

27. See Arbuckle, citing John M. Lozano, "Review," *New Theology Review* 3, no. 2 (1990): 81.

28. See Burrows, "Witness to the Gospel and Refounding the Church," 193.

29. Stanley Hauerwas asserted: "No task is more important than for the Church to take the Bible out of the hands of individual Christians in North America. . . . They read the Bible not as Christians, not as a people set apart, but as democratic citizens who think their 'common sense' is sufficient for 'understanding' the Scripture." Stanley Hauerwas, *Unleashing the Scripture: Freeing the Bible from Captivity to America* (Nashville, TN: Abingdon Press, 1993), 15. Hauerwas cites Kierkegaard, who in the early 1800s made a similar observation in Søren Kierkegaard, *Journal,* trans. Alexander Dru (New York: Harper and Row, 1958), 150.

BIBLIOGRAPHY

Arbuckle, Gerald A. *Refounding the Church: Dissent for Leadership*. Maryknoll, NY: Orbis Books, 1993.

Beck, H. G. J. "Vincent of Lérins, St.," in *The New Catholic Encyclopedia*, edited by Thomas Carson, 14: 523–24. New York: Thomson/Gale, 2003.

Burrows, William R. "Witness to the Gospel and Refounding the Church," in *Confident Witness—Changing World: Rediscovering the Gospel in North America*, edited by Craig Van Gelder. Grand Rapids, MI: Eerdmans, 1999.

Butterfield, Herbert. *Christianity and History*. London: G. Bell and Sons, 1949.

Coalter, Milton J., John M. Mulder, and Louis B. Weeks, eds. *The Presbyterian Presence: The Twentieth-Century Experience*. Louisville, KY: Westminster/John Knox, 1990.

Flett, John G. "What Does It Mean for a Congregation to Be a Hermeneutic?," in *The Gospel and Pluralism Today: Reassessing Lesslie Newbigin in the 21st Century*, edited by Scott W. Sunquist and Amos Yong, 195–214. Downers Grove, IL: IVP Academic, 2015.

———. *The Witness of God: The Trinity, Missio Dei, Karl Barth and the Nature of Christian Community*. Grand Rapids, MI: Eerdmans, 2010.

Harrison, Paul M. *Authority and Power in the Free Church Tradition: A Social Case Study of the American Baptist Convention*. Princeton, NJ: Princeton University Press, 1963.

Hauerwas, Stanley. *Unleashing the Scripture: Freeing the Bible from Captivity to America*. Nashville, TN: Abingdon Press, 1993.

Hooft, W. A. Visser 't. *Renewal of the Church*. London: SCM, 1955.

Kierkegaard, Søren. *Journal*. Translated by Alexander Dru. New York: Harper and Row, 1958.

Latourette, K. S. *A History of Christianity*. New York: Harper and Brothers, 1953.

Lozano, John M. "Review." *New Theology Review* 3, no. 2 (1990): 81.

Newbigin, J. E. Lesslie. "Can the West be Converted?" *International Bulletin of Missionary Research* 11, no. 1 (1987): 2–7.

———. "Context and Conversion." *International Review of Mission* 68, no. 3 (1979): 301–12.

———. *Unfinished Agenda: An Updated Autobiography*. Edinburgh: Saint Andrew Press, 1993.

O'Malley, J. Steven, ed. *Interpretative Trends in Christian Revitalization for the Early Twenty First Century*. Lexington, KY: Emeth Press, 2011.

Snyder, Howard A. *Signs of the Spirit: How God Reshapes the Church*. Grand Rapids, MI: Zondervan, 1989.

Torrance, T. F. "History and Reformation." *Scottish Journal of Theology* 4, no. 3 (1951): 279–90.

Tripp, David. "Arndt, Johann (1556–1621)," in *Encyclopedia of Protestantism*, edited by Hans J. Hillerbrand, 102–3. Routledge, 2003.

Warren, Max. *The Idea of the Missionary Society*. London: CMS, 1943.

———. "Why Missionary Societies and Not Missionary Churches?," in *History's Lessons for Tomorrow's Mission*, 149–56. Geneva: World's Student Christian Federation, 1960.

Winter, Ralph D. "Two Structures of God's Redemptive Mission." *Missiology* 2, no. 1 (1974): 121–39.

Wright, Christopher J. H. *The Mission of God: Unlocking the Bible's Grand Narrative*. Downers Grove, IL: IVP, 2006.

Select Bibliography of Darrell L. Guder's Writings

BOOKS

"The History of Belles-Lettres at Princeton: The Development and Secularization of Curriculum at an Originally Christian American College, with Special Reference to the Curriculum of English Language and Letters," diss., University of Hamburg, 1965.

Be My Witnesses: The Church's Mission, Message, and Messengers. Grand Rapids, MI: Eerdmans, 1985.

As editor: *Missional Church: A Vision for the Sending of the Church in North America.* Grand Rapids, MI: Eerdmans, 1998.

With Robert Benedetto and Donald K. McKim. *Historical Dictionary of Reformed Churches.* Lanham, MD and London: The Scarecrow Press, 1999.

The Incarnation and the Church's Witness. Harrisburg, PA: Trinity Press International, 1999.

The Continuing Conversion of the Church Grand Rapids, MI: Eerdmans, 2000.

Unlikely Ambassadors: Clay Jar Christians in God's Service. A Bible Study for the 214th General Assembly of the Presbyterian Church (U.S.A.). Louisville, KY: Office of the General Assembly, 2002.

Called to Witness: Doing Missional Theology. Grand Rapids, MI: Eerdmans, 2015.

ACADEMIC TRANSLATION

Thielicke, Helmut. "The Resurrection Kerygma," in *The Easter Message Today: Three Essays by Leonhard Goppelt, Helmut Thielicke, and Hans-Rudolph Müller-Schwefe*, 59–116. London: Nelson, 1964.

Lochman, Jan Milic. "The Doctrine of Justification in a Society of Achievers." *Reformed World* 35, no. 5 (1979): 205–14.

Weber, Otto. *Foundations of Dogmatics*, 2 vols. Grand Rapids, MI: Eerdmans, 1981–1983.

Jüngel, Eberhard. *God as the Mystery of the World: On the Foundation of the Theology of the Crucified One in the Dispute between Theism and Atheism.* Grand Rapids, MI: Eerdmans, 1983.

With Judith Guder: Barth, Karl. *The Theology of the Reformed Confessions.* Louisville, KY: Westminster/John Knox, 2002.

Edited and annotated with Judith Guder: Busch, Eberhard. *The Great Passion*, translated by Geoffrey Bromiley. Grand Rapids, MI: Eerdmans, 2004.
With Judith Guder: Busch, Eberhard. *The Barmen Theses Then and Now: The 2004 Warfield Lectures at Princeton Theological Seminary*. Eerdmans, 2010.
English editor: Barth, Karl. *Barth in Conversation: Volume 1, 1959–1962*, edited by Eberhard Busch. Louisville, KY: Westminster John Knox Press, 2017.
English editor: Barth, Karl. *Barth in Conversation: Volume 2, 1963*, edited by Eberhard Busch. Louisville, KY: Westminster John Knox Press, 2018.

CHAPTERS AND ARTICLES

"Who Is Man and What is Love?" *Eternity* 15, no. 10 (1964): 23–25.
"The Merger of the Reformed Families: Is It Significant for Missions?" *World Vision Magazine* 15, no. 10 (1971): 10–12.
"Die Jesus People begegnen der Kirche." *Evangelische Kommentare* 5, no. 1 (1972): 24–26.
"Freude über die geistliche Einheit der Gemeinde Jesu." *Evangelisches Allianzblatt* 5 (1973): 71–75, 78.
"Erprobung des Modellenentwurfs 'Abgelehnt werden—angenommen werden,'" in *Thematischer Kindergottesdienst in Der Erprobung*, edited by F. W. Bargheer, and H. B. Kaufmann, 38–80. Münster/Westfalen: Comenius-Institut, 1974.
"Volkskirche und Freiwilligskeitskriche: Gedanken eines amerikanischen Presbyterianers." *Arbeit und Besinnung: Zeitschrift für die Evangelische Landeskirche in Württemberg* 28, no. 13 (1984): 25–27.
"The Youth Minister as Theologian: The Incongruous Necessity." *Reformed Review* 39, no. 3 (1986): 215–21.
"Forward" to Charles Van Engen's *You Are My Witnesses: Drawing from Your Spiritual Journey to Evangelize Your Neighbors*. New York: Reformed Church in America, 1992.
"Evangelism and the Debate over Church Growth." *Union Seminary Review* 48, no. 2 (1994): 145–55.
"Incarnation and the Church's Evangelistic Mission." *International Review of Mission* 83, no. 330 (1994): 417–28.
"The Integrity of Apostolic Ministry: 1 Thessalonians 2:1–13." *Reo: A Journal of Theology and Ministry* 1 (1995): 12–19.
"Locating a Reformed Theology of Evangelism in a Pluralistic World," in *How Shall We Witness? Faithful Evangelism in a Reformed Tradition*, edited by Milton J. Coalter, and Virgil Cruz, 165–86. Louisville, KY: Westminster John Knox Press, 1995.
With Sherron Kay George. "Salvador as an Ecumenical Classroom: A Missiological Course within the Salvador Conference." *International Review of Mission* 86 (1997): 145–51.
"The Missional Center of Reformed Worship." *Reformed Liturgy and Worship* 32, no. 2 (1998): 100–4.
"Missional Church: From Sending to Being Sent," "Missional Structures: The Particular Community," and "Missional Connectedness: The Community of Communities in Mission," in *Missional Church: A Vision for the Sending of the Church in North America*, edited by Darrell L. Guder, 1–17, 221–47, 248–68. Grand Rapids, MI: Eerdmans, 1998.
"Missional Theology for a Missionary Church." *Journal for Preachers* 22, no. 1 (1998): 3–11.
"Evangelism and Justice: From False Dichotomies to Gospel Faithfulness." *Church and Society* 92, no. 2 (2001): 14–20.
"Growing Evangelizing Churches," in *Teaching Mission in a Global Context*, edited by Patricia Lloyd-Sidle, and Bonnie Sue Lewis, 134–47. Louisville, KY: Geneva Press, 2001.
"The Context of the Church's Discussion of Human Sexuality," in *More Than a Single Issue: Theological Considerations Concerning the Ordination of Practicing Homosexuals*, edited by Murray Rae, and Graham Redding, 105–21. Hindmarsh, South Australia: ATF Press, 2002.
"Pentecost and Missionary Preaching in North America." *Journal for Preachers* 25, no. 4 (2002): 19–25.

"From Mission and Theology to Missional Theology." *The Princeton Seminary Bulletin* 24, no. 1 (2003): 36–54.

"Pattern 2, Biblical Formation and Discipleship," and "Pattern 7, Pointing toward the Reign of God," in Barrett, Lois Y., et al., eds. *Treasure in Clay Jars: Patterns in Missional Faithfulness*, 59–73, 126–38. Grand Rapids, MI: Eerdmans, 2004.

"Chosen Vessels: The Dedication of the Moffett Korea Collection." *The Princeton Seminary Bulletin* 26, no. 2 (2005): 212–14.

"The Church as Missional Community," in *Community of the Word: Toward an Evangelical Ecclesiology*, edited by Mark Husbands and Daniel J. Treier, 114–28. Downers Grove, IL: IVP Academic, 2005.

"Global Mission and the Challenge of Theological Catholicity." *Theology Today* 62, no. 1 (2005): 1–8.

"Worthy Living: Work and Witness from the Perspective of Missional Church Theology." *Word and World* 25, no. 4 (2005): 424–32.

"Missional Theology for a Missionary Church." *Journal for Preachers* 22, no. 1 (2006): 3–11.

"The Challenges of Evangelization in America: Theological Ambiguities," in *Antioch Agenda: Essays on the Restorative Church in Honor of Orlando E. Costas*, edited by Daniel Jeyaraj, Robert W. Pazmino, and Rodney L. Petersen, 163–75. New Delhi: ISPCK, 2007.

"Walking Worthily: Missional Leadership after Christendom." *The Princeton Seminary Bulletin* 28, no. 3 (2007): 251–91.

"Christlicher Studentenweltbund," "Ehrenamt/ehrenamtlich, 2. Bedeutung in Nordamerika," "Evangelisation: Nordamerika," "Klerus/Klerus und Laien: 2. Ökumene, 1. Nordamerika," "Laien, V. In den Kirchen Nordamerikas," "Ökumenischer Rat der Kirchen, 1. Geschichte und Programme," "Protestantismus, 1. Kirchengeschichtlich, 2. Weltweit," and "Reformierte Kirchen, II. Reformierte Kirchen der Gegenwart, 3. Verbreitung, a) in Europa und Nordamerika," in *Religion in Geschichte und Gegenwart*, 4th ed. Tübingen: J. C. B. Mohr, 1998–2007.

"Practical Theology in the Service of the Missional Church," in *Theology in the Service of the Church: Essays in Honor of Joseph D. Small 3rd*, edited by Charles A. Wiley, Sheldon W. Sorge, Barry A. Ensign-George, and Chip Andrus, 13–22. Louisville, KY: Geneva Press, 2008.

"The Christological Formation of Missional Practice," in *Jesus Christ Today: Studies of Christology in Various Contexts. Proceedings of the Académie Internationale des Sciences Religieuses, Oxford 25–29 August 2006 and Princeton 25–30 August 2007*, edited by Stuart G. Hall, 317–35. Berlin: De Gruyter, 2009.

"Missio Dei: Integrating Theological Formation for Apostolic Vocation: Presidential Address." *Missiology* 37, no. 1 (2009): 63–74.

"Theological Significance of the Lord's Day for the Formation of the Missional Church," in *Sunday, Sabbath, and the Weekend: Managing Time in a Global Culture*, edited by Edward O'Flaherty, Rodney L. Petersen, and Timothy A. Norton, 105–17. Eerdmans: Grand Rapids, MI, 2010.

"'The Christians' Callings in the World': Pastoral Formation for Missional Vocation." *New Theology Review* 24, no. 4 (2011): 6–16.

"Mission Possible: Barths Missionsekklesiologie als Integration zwischen Kirchenlehre und -praxis." *Zeitschrift für Dialektische Theologie* 29, no. 1 (2013): 35–57.

"John Mackay's Missional Vision." *Theology Today* 71, no. 3 (2014): 292–99.

"A Multicultural and Translational Approach," and "Response by Darrell L. Guder," in *The Mission of the Church: Five Views in Conversation*, edited by Craig Ott, 21–40, 131–138. Grand Rapids, MI: Baker Academic, 2016.

Index

About the Contributors

Stephen Bevans is a priest in the Roman Catholic missionary Society of the Divine Word. He is Louis J. Luzbetak, SVD Professor of Mission and Culture, emeritus, at Catholic Theological Union, Chicago.

James Brownson is the James and Jean Cook Professor of New Testament at Western Theological Seminary, where he has taught since 1989. He teaches in a variety of areas, with a central focus on the Gospels and interpretation of the New Testament.

Eberhard Busch is professor emeritus of systematic theology at the University of Göttingen. His most recent text, *Meine Zeit mit Karl Barth*, is a published version of his journals written when he worked as Karl Barth's assistant.

David W. Congdon is acquisitions editor at the University Press of Kansas and adjunct instructor at the University of Dubuque Theological Seminary, He earned his PhD at Princeton Theological Seminary, and his dissertation, on the committee for which Darrell Guder served as a member, was published as *The Mission of Demythologizing: Rudolf Bultmann's Dialectical Theology* (2015).

Benjamin T. Conner is professor of practical theology and director of the Graduate Certificate in Disability and Ministry at Western Theological Seminary in Holland, Michigan. His PhD was conducted under the supervision of Darrell Guder and was published as *Practicing Witness: A Missional Vision of Christian Practices* (Eerdmans, 2011).

Samuel Escobar, from Perú, is professor emeritus of Palmer Theological Seminary, and presently teaches at the Facultad de Teología UEBE in Alcobendas, Madrid, Spain.

John G. Flett is associate professor of missiology and intercultural theology at Pilgrim Theological College, Melbourne. His PhD was conducted under the supervision of Darrell Guder and was published as *The Witness of God* (Eerdmans, 2010).

Seong Sik Heo is visiting professor at SoongEui Women's College, minister at SoongEui Moffett Memorial Church, and lecturer in missiology at Presbyterian University and Theological Seminary in Seoul, Korea. He wrote his doctoral dissertation on Lesslie Newbigin under Darrell Guder.

George R. Hunsberger is the professor emeritus of missiology at Western Theological Seminary in Holland, Michigan, where he taught from 1989 to 2014. He was the founding coordinator of the Gospel and Our Culture Network in North America (1987–2010).

Christine Lienemann-Perrin is professor emeritus of missiology and ecumenical studies at the Faculty of Theology, University of Basel.

Richard J. Mouw joined the faculty at Fuller Theological Seminary in 1985, after teaching philosophy for seventeen years at Calvin College. He became Fuller's provost in 1989, and then began a twenty-year presidency in 1993.

Wilbert R. Shenk is senior professor of contemporary culture and mission history at Fuller Graduate School of Intercultural Studies, Pasadena, California.

Deanna Ferree Womack is assistant professor of history of religions and multifaith relations at Emory University's Candler School of Theology and director of the Leadership and Multifaith Program (LAMP), a collaboration between Candler and Georgia Tech. Womack earned her PhD at Princeton Theological Seminary.

Henning Wrogemann holds the chair for science of religion and intercultural theology at the Kirchliche Hochschule Wuppertal/Bethel, Germany. Wrogemann is chairman of the *Deutsche Gesellschaft für Missionswissenschaft*, and heads the Institute of Intercultural Theology and Interreligious Studies (www.iitis.de).